THE BEST
SPIRITUAL
WRITING
1999

THE BEST
SPIRITUAL
WRITING
1999

EDITED BY
PHILIP ZALESKI

INTRODUCED BY
KATHLEEN NORRIS

HarperSanFrancisco
A Division of HarperCollinsPublishers

Page 339 constitutes a continuation of this copyright page.

Grateful acknowledgment is made for permission to reprint lines from Jane Hirshfield's translation of Mechtild of Magdeburg in Jane Hirshfield, *Women in Praise of the Sacred* (HarperCollins, 1994). Copyright © 1994 by Jane Hirshfield. Reprinted by permission of HarperCollins Publishers.

HarperCollins books may be purchased for educational, business, or sales promotional use. For information please write: Special Markets Department, HarperCollins Publishers, 10 East 53rd Street, New York, NY 10022.

HarperCollins Web Site: http://www.harpercollins.com

HarperCollins®, 📖®, and HarperSanFrancisco™ are trademarks of HarperCollins Publishers Inc.

FIRST EDITION

Library of Congress Cataloging Card Number 98–12368

ISSN: 1525–5980

ISBN 0–06–251805–4 (pbk.)

99 00 01 02 03 ❖RRD(H) 10 9 8 7 6 5 4 3 2 1

Contents

PHILIP ZALESKI

Preface

Late summer 1662, rented rooms on rue de Francs-Bourgeois, Paris: a servant sorting the clothes of his deceased master discovers a curious thickening in a well-worn doublet. Something has been sewn into the fabric. A coin? A letter of credit? A note sealed by lover's lips? The servant cuts the stitches, and out tumbles a treasure rarer than kisses or gold: a scrap of paper wrapped in waxy parchment bearing, in a fine, scrabbled hand, one of the fairest fruits of that literary genre that we call "spiritual writing." The key passage runs:

> The year of grace 1654
> Monday 23 November. Feast of St. Clement
> Pope and martyr, and others in the martyrology.
> Eve of St. Chrysogonous martyr, and of others.
> From about half-past ten in the evening until half-past midnight
>
> FIRE
>
> God of Abraham, God of Isaac, God of Jacob,
>   not of philosophers and savants
>   Certitude. Certitude. Joy. Feeling. Joy. Peace.
> God of Jesus Christ. . . .
>   Grandeur of the human soul
> Just Father, the world has not known you but I have known you.
>   Joy Joy Joy and tears of Joy

As students of literary arcana have already guessed, the doublet belonged to Blaise Pascal (1623–1662), Catholic philosopher, master of French prose, mathematician and scientist of genius, inventor of the syringe, the digital calculator, and the hydraulic press, founder of probability theory and of the world's first municipal bus system, and—to the eternal gratitude of all seekers of truth—incessant scribbler of aphorisms, conundrums, and reflections on the mysteries of God and creation.

Pascal's jottings, now familiar as the *Pensées,* hold an honored place in the history of thought for their brilliant exploration of faith and doubt. But Pascal's "Night of Fire" testament, known to historians as the "Memorial," exerts a special attraction for those who love writing that deals in the enigmas of the soul. First and foremost, it is a masterful recounting of a mystical encounter with God, so intimate that Pascal never breathed a word of it to another human being—if not for that diligent servant, we would not be aware of it at all—and so compelling in its tenderness and terse intensity that it has brought consolation to thousands since its unveiling. Second, it stands as a watershed in the history of spiritual writing. The genre has a long pedigree, dating back at least to Plato's dialogues and the Indian Vedas. But modern spiritual writing, with its characteristic note of struggle against a culture steeped in skepticism, came into being only in the mid-sixteenth century, at the dawn of what some have dubbed the Age of Reason. "The heart," counters Pascal, "has its reasons of which reason knows nothing." He was one of the first to realize the direction in which Enlightenment thought would soon be hurtling, and he fought against it with all his might. This combat rings throughout the "Memorial," as Pascal explicitly turns his back on the "philosophers and savants" with whom he has mixed so comfortably in his youth in order to embrace the decidedly countercultural God of Genesis, Exodus, and the Gospels.

The "Memorial," or at least its hiding hole in Pascal's doublet, also provides an essential clue to what we mean by "spiritual writing." This issue seems to be of great interest just now. When I am asked about the Best Spiritual Writing series, the most frequently posed questions are, "What is spiritual writing?" "How does it differ from religious writing?" and "What are the marks of good spiritual writing?" It seems that some definitions are called for.

Now, to assay a definition of spirituality can be a dangerous enterprise: one risks losing one's bearings, if not one's soul. "I had rather feel compunction than understand the definition of it," observes Thomas à Kempis in *The Imitation of Christ*. Of course Thomas is right; a realized virtue is worth any degree of intellectual understanding. Yet definitions are indispensable, for they order and regulate existence; they turn chaos into cosmos. It could be said that bringing definition to the inchoate inner life is one of the great tasks faced by every human being.

Here Pascal points the way. His "Memorial" is great spiritual prose because it deals directly with the movements of the soul. It reminds us that spirituality is more than psychology, philosophy, politics, or physics; it is the secret life that animates these realms and all else that falls within human experience. The term *spirituality* derives from *spirare,* Latin for "to breathe" or "to blow" (as the wind). In the Bible, the Spirit is the wind, the breath of God, which "moved upon the face of the waters" and which "bloweth where it listeth, and thou hearest the sound thereof, but canst not tell whence it cometh, and whither it goeth: so is every one that is born of the Spirit." Like breath, the spirit is intimate and essential; like the wind, it is unpredictable, a vector of force. For human beings, to breathe, to live in the spirit, is to deal in words. Among the Amassalik Eskimo, anthropologist Sam Gill reports, the same word means "to breathe" and "to make poetry." A Netsalik Eskimo comments that "all my being is song, and I sing as I draw breath. . . . It is just as necessary for me to sing as it is to breathe." Spiritual writing, then, is a fundamental human act—the way in which the soul walks erect.

We can learn more about the definition of spirituality and its implications for writers by seeing how the word is employed in ordinary speech and writing. In *Psychology of Religion* (1997), David M. Wulff offers a list, culled from recent periodicals, of 129 nouns modified by the adjective *spiritual*. Some examples, picked at random: hunger, hope, vacuum, journey, values, director, beliefs, elite, gnosis, inflation, tyranny. Wulff lumps his lexicon into six types, in a valiant attempt at intelligible classification, but the overall impression remains that almost any word can be modified by *spiritual*. That is, just about everything has its inner aspect. Spiritual writing takes anything as its subject—and then bores straight to the heart. In the past several months, I've read essays on the spiritual dimensions of baseball, batik, and bees. This year's collection touches, inter alia, on music, military service, painting, television, housecleaning, hospitals, wardrobes. If one knows how to look, all these activities tell us something about truth, beauty, and goodness; about heaven and earth; about how to live the good life.

There's something else about Wulff's list worth noting: almost all of the words modified by *spiritual* can also be modified by *religious*. We have no trouble speaking of religious hunger, religious hope, religious malpractice, and so on. In our secular culture, some people draw a stark opposition between spirituality and religion, saying "I'm spiritual" and then hastening to add "but not religious." Wulff's list suggests, however, that the two realms are closely allied. Spirituality is, if you will, the inner lining of religion. Spirituality is Pascal's parchment sewn to the inner lining of his doublet, pressed to his heart. Yet the Night of Fire, with its transfiguring revelations, did not descend willy-nilly upon a man unprepared to receive it. Pascal readied the ground with a life of prayer and worship, confession and communion. He spent thirty years laying the kindling for his Night of Fire.

Nor is this an uncommon story. Almost all great spiritual writers—past masters like Augustine, Rumi, and Bashō, as well as modern practitioners like Suzuki, Heschel, and Merton—worked within a religious tradition. There is a reason for this. The best writing comes from robust cultures; thus the literary glories of Attic Greece or Elizabethan England. Great spiritual writing is no different; it requires a rich culture to work within or react against. Where, in the modern world, do we find such a culture? In rare cases, secularism rises to the occasion: Camus comes easily to mind. But by and large, today as yesterday, religion remains the cultural womb in which the best spiritual writing is conceived, nourished, and brought to term. In our skeptical epoch, each of the great religious traditions functions as a quasi-autonomous counterculture, with its own vocabulary, symbol systems, hierarchy of values, history, and art. Thus every religion is an all-embracing way in which spiritual writing finds its proper place and the spiritual writer finds a home. Indeed, such literature holds a vital place in almost every great religion, for the pen helps to define and mature the tradition. Writing becomes a rung on the ladder linking heaven and earth.

I don't mean to suggest that spiritual writing is limited to religious themes. There exist vital streams within the genre that cannot easily be classified as religious—nature writing being perhaps the most obvious example. Moreover, religion itself is a vast and diffuse enterprise that seeps into all areas of life. Everything is fuel for the religious imagination, including many ostensibly worldly subjects. And then, who would constrict the future of the genre? In particular, it remains to be seen whether the New Age, which can be called a religion only in the loosest terms, will develop a viable culture—a philosophy, a theology, an aesthetic—to support its literature and plastic arts; if so, this may be one of the more interesting developments of the new century.

What, then, are the marks of good spiritual writing? The answer requires that we first strip away an adjective: good spiritual writing is, always, good writing. It must please the literary palate. As for the effect of adding that vexing modifier, here again Pascal will be our guide. The "Memorial" shows us that great spiritual literature is the result of absorbing, filtering, and refining the wisdom of the past in the light of one's own lived experience. To be a spiritual writer, then, the sage counsel seems to be: Know yourself and know the world. Reflect, contemplate, pray. Learn the subtleties of your own soul, the ideal laboratory for acquiring wisdom. Study history. Immerse yourself in those traditions that harbor the treasuries of the world's best religious writing. Sit at the feet of the great spiritual masters and the great spiritual writers (and remember that they are not the same). With this prescription in mind, I have no doubt that more and more writers will be able to exclaim, along with Pascal, "Joy Joy Joy and tears of Joy."

As always, submissions are encouraged for subsequent volumes of *Best Spiritual Writing*. Please send writings to Philip Zaleski, 138 Elm Street, Smith College, Northampton, MA 01063. The best way for a periodical to submit material is to add the Best Spiritual Writing series, at the above address, to its complimentary subscription list.

Many people helped in the production of this volume. Heartfelt thanks go to John Loudon, Karen Levine, and the entire crew at Harper San Francisco; to Kim Witherspoon, Gideon Weil, and Josh Greenhut of Witherspoon Associates; to Kathleen Norris; to Andrew Delisle and all others who contributed in ways large and small; and, as always, to Carol, John, and Andy, who put even the great enterprise of spiritual writing into proper perspective.

KATHLEEN NORRIS

Introduction

A cursory look at the "inspiration" or "spirituality" section of any bookstore will reveal that writing on spiritual themes constitutes an embarrassment of riches. Evelyn Underhill's groundbreaking studies of mysticism are reaching a new generation of readers, while American classics of spiritual practice such as Richard Foster's *Celebration of Discipline* are being reissued. The fiftieth anniversary of Thomas Merton's groundbreaking autobiography, *The Seven Storey Mountain,* has occasioned a fresh outpouring of Merton studies as well as books reflecting a new appreciation of Christian monastic spirituality. The works of the prolific Buddhist monk Thich Nhat Hanh might fill a shelf, if stores could keep them in stock. The spiritualities of the world's major religious traditions—Hinduism, Buddhism, Judaism, Christianity, Islam—are being addressed, not in the dry tones of comparative religions textbooks, but in engaging personal narratives. Diana Eck's *Encountering God,* which tells the story of a Protestant's engagement with Hinduism, is but one example of a book that, while it might help to make a religious faith comprehensible to the general reader, also reflects the fact that "spiritual seeking" within or without one's religious heritage has become a hallmark of our age, a contemporary variation on the ancient theme of pilgrimage.

Like many members of the baby boom generation, I chose as a young adult to describe myself as "spiritual" but not "religious." In assuming a defensive posture with regard to anything that might be deemed "organized religion" (to some extent a healthy and even necessary stance in a maturing adolescent), I made the mistake of ignoring the spiritual riches of my ancestral religion. But in my thirties, I began to take another look, expanding my reading to include what I had previously ignored. And I learned that the Christian religion, which I had stereotyped as rigid and monolithic, has always incorporated a variety of spiritualities. Contrary to what I had assumed—and what a typically spotty instruction in the faith had allowed me to assume—I learned that diversity, and not uniformity, is one of the religion's major strengths. A root strength, as it were, exemplified in four canonical Gospels, individual in tone, which provide widely differing accounts of the life and ministry of Jesus Christ.

From the great biblical scholar Raymond Brown, in his book entitled *The Churches the Apostles Left Behind,* I learned that each of the fledgling congregations addressed in the New Testament epistles—the churches at Rome, at Antioch, at Corinth, for example—reflected a radically different approach to scripture and Christian life. And in studying the texts and traditions of the Christian religious orders, I also found a healthy variety. The Benedictines offer 1500-plus years of experience in fostering human community by paying close attention to the practice of communal liturgy, conceived holistically as a daily round of praying, eating, working, and playing together; Dominicans seek to rescue both preaching and teaching from academic sterility, employing both reason and faith in holy service to others; the Jesuits foster a deep respect for learning and the processes of disciplined prayer; Franciscan spirituality can help us learn to live more simply among the other creatures of this earth.

At its Greek root, the word *ecumenical* means "the whole world," and it seems that in recent years, the understanding of spirituality has become more fully ecumenical. It is only in our time, for example, that a series of books from a Roman Catholic publisher entitled "The Classics of Western Spirituality" could contain texts from the Sufi, Safed, Muslim, and Native American religious traditions along with the works of Christian theologians and mystics. As human society becomes more secular, in the sense that it is market driven, its values dictated by strictly financial concerns, human beings themselves seem more driven to seek spiritual wisdom wherever it may be found. The Buddhist and Christian monasteries of the United States find that their retreat houses are booked solid for a year in advance, often by people who profess no religious faith but deeply appreciate the quality of hospitality and quiet offered in a monastic setting. These guests may or may not participate in traditional worship with the monks, but like the monks, they conceive of worship as including an hour spent in solitude, in silent meditation, walking in a woods or along the shores of a lake.

The ecumenical spirit of our age has opened the way for writers to explore and describe their experience of faith in ways that transcend labels. For many readers, I suspect that the quality of the narrative matters far more than whether a writer is a practitioner of a traditional religion, a New Ager, or professes no belief whatsoever. Readers of the distinguished poet Mary Oliver, for example, may not know or care what (if any) religion she practices. Her writing stands on its own as an inspiration to anyone who has ever sought spiritual solace in nature or who needs a bracing reminder of how an ordinary walk in the woods or along a beach can turn into something holy. But this book is happy evidence that spirituality is so ecumenical, so profoundly steeped in common experience, that such illumination may also be found in less likely places, even the most dismal environments that human beings can create. In Philip Levine's "After Leviticus," it is the doorway of a metal hut, one of seventeen identical buildings housing workers at an automobile factory. Even there, he insists, one finds real life going on, suffused with spiritual gladness. Levine's woman, exhausted after a week of assembling automobile chassis, stands at her doorway experiencing the stars above as "God's / breath, a magical gift carried / all the dark way from Him to you on the wind / no one can see." All she can do is stand before her humble home, which the world knows as "number seven Mud Lane taking / into her blood one gasp after another / of the holy air: the numbers say it all." The poet seems to be reminding us that all of us live in the humble "Mud Lane" of our bodies, mere earthly matter, and yet we also aspire to find meaning in our lives and the world around us.

The work of such poets epitomizes the very best of the art of spiritual writing, in that it does not tell us how to pray or seek to convert us to a point of view. Like a deer sipping from a stream or the weary factory worker standing alone beneath the night sky, these poems simply are. And being themselves, they offer a view of the world that is spiritually alive, taking into account that which is not productive, efficient, or economical, but which remains stubbornly invisible, as essential as it is ephemeral, as mysterious as it is common. What ancient wisdom literature speaks of as being beyond price.

Spiritual writing is so broad a category today that it includes not only such luminous poetry but also the best-selling *Chicken Soup* series of inspirational prose, whose brief reflections provide daily nourishment to many harried people who are too distracted, busy, or just plain weary to concentrate on reading a book from cover to cover. For good and ill, the topic of spirituality has become highly marketable. At its best, spiritual writing acts subversively, its quiet tones alerting us to the perpetual noise of our advertising-driven culture, its simple pleasures exposing the folly of our insistence that more and bigger are always better. At its worst, spirituality becomes just another consumable in the quest for a more fulfilled life. A gym membership, masseuse, and personal trainer to take care of the body, weekend retreats, gurus, and shelves weighed down with how-to books for the soul.

The increased popularity of spiritual writing makes it vulnerable to exploitation, and all too often powerful words such as *spiritual, sacred,* and *holy* become mere buzzwords, ciphers into which we are free to pour any meaning we desire. They may be used to lull the spirit in the interest of feeding that all-American desire for instant results. Or they may be employed to repackage the well-worn messages of the self-help industry. The man who made a fortune writing *How to Be Your Own Best Friend,* for example, has now produced a volume entitled *Your Sacred Self.*

Titles such as *How to Get What You Want and Want What You Have: A Practical and* Spiritual *Guide to Personal Success* (emphasis mine) offer evidence that much of the "spiritual" and "inspirational" writing available today does not content itself with sharing the commonalities of the human religious impulse but seeks to elevate our ordinary narcissistic impulses into a religion. A friend told me that she recently heard an address by a popular self-help author who defined meditation as focusing on your plans for the day and thanking God for making them happen. This is not the sort of "spirituality" the reader will find in this volume. It does strike me as a contemporary version of the optimistic pragmatism that once was served by Norman Vincent Peale and Dale Carnegie and now finds expression in books that speak with radiant ease about controlling the world around you while channeling your goddess, your warrior, your inner child, your personal angel, your shaman, the Indian chief you were in a former life—in short, your wondrously enlightened, so very special self.

I like to think that this book is for the rest of us, the hoi polloi
of the spirit, as it were, who realize that they are not terribly special, not in control of the universe. Burdened by the cares of
everyday life, they feel themselves in matters of the soul to be relatively unenlightened, uncertain, and unsuccessful at realizing
their potential for holiness. The poet William Stafford once said
that successful people cannot write poems, as the poet has to kneel
down for them, humbly exploring life at ground level. Or, in the
case of writer Louise Rafkin, at the level of the toilet bowl. Her reflections on the Japanese commune Ittoen, which practices bathroom cleaning as a path to self-knowledge, is one of the
unexpected pleasures of this volume. And it brought to mind a
story from Anne Lamott's *Operating Instructions:* as the frazzled
single mother of a newborn, Lamott learned much about the
value of her church community when a man from the congregation, her pastor's husband, came with bucket and mop in hand to
clean her bathroom.

The best spiritual writing, it seems to me, is like good poetry in
that it is not about success or failure but allows us to find value in
what seems meaningless or dull, or even filthy. It does not offer
answers but hints at possibilities for transcendence. It does not
transport us magically to a realm of light "above" the ordinary, beyond the capacities of more common people, but instead offers us
insight into living through the contradictory and often painful
processes of life and death that are at work in us all. It is no accident that many of the writers in this anthology—Burton-
Christie, Cochran, Tompkins, van de Wetering—so openly address
their own fears, spiritual rigidity, and naïveté. This is the baggage
of the spiritual journey, and it forms the essence of spiritual writing that is good nourishment for its readers.

But spiritual writing is a kind of paradox, perhaps even a con-
tradiction in terms. Experiences that people describe as mystical or

religious are immediate and intense, while writing requires distance and discipline. Spiritual insights are deeply personal, and often experienced in solitude, while writing, as a form of communication, inevitably entails reaching out to others. The depth of spiritual experience is entirely democratic, available to the intelligent and the mentally handicapped, the rich and the poor alike. Any person is capable of loving life and grieving its loss with a fiery intensity; any person might suddenly be struck dumb by the wonder of God's being made manifest in the world. I suspect that most spiritual experience is carried silently, in the heart. It is pondered and savored in secret, the way in which the woman in Philip Levine's poem recognizes that, at 2 A.M. at the end of a hard winter, a long week of work, the light from slag heaps that allows her to avoid stepping into the muddy ruts of her streets is a kind of grace. The poet seems to nudge her gently, reminding her that "You're not drunk either. You're actually filled / with the same joy that comes to a great artist / who's just completed a seminal work."

But spiritual writing is an attempt to describe this experience to another in such a way that a stranger can experience it in their own terms. An art like any other, it generally requires the practice of a skill over years of apprenticeship. Unlike the experience itself, which is a gift that may pass in a minute, the writing of it takes time. It requires deliberation and revising and hard work, after which the writer submits the text to an editor and begins all over again. The poems and essays in this book epitomize the process.

Larry Woiwode's "A Fifty-Year Walk," for example, recounts an experience that anyone might have had, recalling, some fifty years later, desultory walks in a woods taken in one's adolescence, after the death of a parent. Such memories do loom, suddenly, revealing a new significance in one's life. But few people would have developed the ability to render so explicitly that old experience so that a reader might see and smell the rotting "hedge apples [that] lay in the sand like limes so bloated that the pebbling of their peels resembled worms locked in molten swirls," or understand how in a forest grove the boy "never felt the sense of the absence of my mother that I felt everywhere else."

This is the essence of good spiritual writing; the hard stuff of the world come together with the deepest desires of the soul. A profound sense of absence may be the taproot of all desire; theologian Barbara Brown Taylor finds it "underrated" in our culture. "[Absence] is not nothing," she reminds us, but "something: a heightened awareness, a sharpened appetite, a finer perception." Her words serve as a definition of spiritual experience and of writing about that experience. Although she is speaking specifically about the absence of Christ as the core relationship in the Christian religion, Buddhists might also find great treasure in meditating upon absence as a kind of presence, the significant "No One" of Virginia Hamilton Adair's poem "Zazen."

The individual voice is strong in Woiwode's brief essay, as it must be in order to portray so vividly an individual's experience. Individuality is one of the hallmarks of good spiritual writing and is amply evident in this volume. But it is important for the reader to recognize that the writer's voice does not arise out of a vacuum, but out of a specific time, place, and culture. At its best, spiritual writing connects the reader with other seekers, in other times and places. Woiwode's reflections, for example, do not short-circuit in narcissistic ramblings about what those woods meant to him or even how hard his mother's death was on him. Instead they branch, much like a tree, out of deep roots in a religious tradition and address a universal experience, the death of a loved one. Theologically, the essay might be seen as a contemporary flowering of the mystical communion with nature that is common to all religious traditions, as recognizable in the sayings of the Buddha as in the writings of a medieval theologian such as Hildegard of Bingen, who, like Woiwode, discovered in nature the "communications of Christ."

Literature is itself a communication, and Woiwode summons up a kind of manifesto for the spiritual writer, even though others would use terms other than *God* to represent the glory and fullness of holiness:

> *Carefully and with the greatest accuracy I may write a description of my favorite six-foot patch of nature or, if my spirit is feeling expansive, my favorite ten acres, and if anyone who reads it afterward doesn't sense in the description some hidden attributes of God that we are told exist but try to deny because they do not fit with the rationalism that enlightened thinking (rather than the language of God) has brought to us, then our description is a failure in His face.*

The poet Howard Nemerov, in an essay entitled "Poetry and Meaning," describes poetry as "language as it ought to be, language as it was in the few hours between Adam's naming the creation and his fall." He adds, "The whole art of poetry consists in getting back to that paradisial condition of the understanding, the condition that says simply, 'yes' and 'I see' and 'it is so.'" When we read a great poem, or an essay such as Woiwode's, such "amens" are our likely response, akin to an act of prayer. But we are not worshiping the author or making an idol of his or her work. We are simply responding to how well the writer has, in words and yet silently, given back to us a sense of rightness, of the holiness of creation, including human life.

The writers who endure, be they ancient pagans, medieval mystics, or more-or-less secular contemporaries, tend to see nature, and life itself—the normal act of becoming a father, perhaps, or mothering a child who in turn mothers you—as holy speech, the language of God. The spirit of their writing reflects how God has spoken to them, and if they have listened well, and responded with care in their work, their readers may well say "yes, I see" and walk away with a new appreciation of their own life's work. These writers have transformed what might seem the merely personal stuff of their lives into writing that becomes truly personal, in that it connects in profound ways with the experience of others.

The language that these writers employ has little in common with what is ironically stereotyped as "spiritual" language: the vague, abstract, and arcane jargon of the pseudosciences. As a twentieth-century prophet of language, and inventor of a word—*doublespeak*—that has become all too useful in our time, George Orwell was early in detecting the entry of airy, meaningless verbiage into the religious realm. In his essay "Politics and the English Language," he contrasted the jargon of politics, business management, and psychology with the soulful language of the King James Version, Ecclesiastes 9:11: "I saw under the sun, that the race is not to the swift, nor the battle to the strong, nor yet bread to the wise, nor yet riches to those of understanding, nor yet favour to those of skill; but time and chance happeneth to them all." Orwell's little spoof, which is as contemporary as New (Age) Speak and the "Dilbert" comic strip, reads: "Objective considerations of contemporary phenomena compel the conclusion that success and failure in competitive activities exhibits no tendency to be commensurate with innate capacity, but that a considerable element of the unpredictable must invariably be taken into account."

Unfortunately, it is possible to find pretentious spiritual writing that is as dense and impenetrable as Orwell's bit of play. It tends to make me feel—and I suspect is designed to make me feel—like a lower life form. Words such as *integrative, hegemonic, facilitating, associative,* and even *enlightenment* have become so overworked in the spiritual realm as to have lost any meaning they once had, driving writer Mark Matousek, in an interview in *Common Boundary,* to comment that he had grown so tired of "sacred lingo," he had resolved to "rejoin the plain-speaking human race."

The best spiritual writing is hospitable to the reader; it offers an open door. Its language is approachable, accessible to the many and not just the few. While it may aim for the stars, it is firmly grounded in the material of ordinary experience. Its language does not float just out of reach, in the vague ether of wish fulfillment, but is salted with the grit of the real world. And in that sense, it is profoundly humble. As Louis Simpson states in his essay, "A God in Darkness," even when writing about matters of the spirit, his credo is to "continue to write as I have, about real events, in language that can be understood." And the true writer knows that even this effort will never do justice to the mystery of life, for, as the great twelfth-century poet and mystic Mechtild of Magdeburg has written:

> Of all that God has shown me
> I can speak just the smallest word,
> Not more than a honeybee
> Takes on his foot
> From an overspilling jar.

VIRGINIA HAMILTON ADAIR

Zazen

from The New Yorker

When I first floundered in
no one knew me

not even myself
staggering under a Saratoga trunk
crammed with humiliations
bottled like urine samples
nailkegs of anger
carbons of abusive letters
chemistry quizzes with F's
even the horse I never had
and two casseroles left over
from the dime-a-dip supper.

No one remarked that
I had brought too much.

I was wearing three fur hats
donated by opulent cousins
my feet encased in cement
ever since the failure
of the patio project
and my mouth full of barbs
as an old trout.

No one praised my appearance.

The trunk fell off my back
disgorging its unusual contents
at my stone feet
which also came off.
The fur hats tumbled like a
motheaten avalanche
burying a small monk.

No one noticed.

My sweat began to dry
I folded myself into one piece

No One

Max and Mottele
from Pakn Treger

Lives are distorted, or occasionally salvaged, by questions of identity, and people are sometimes consumed by who they are or, even worse, who someone else is. Yet this is a struggle I've never felt in my own bones. Identity is someone else's problem; I've always known who we are. In this compact body that barely seems to fulfill the requirements of one, there are in fact two: Max and Mottele.

You could think of us as the American and the Jew, or the modernist and the traditionalist, or the nonbeliever and the believer, but none of these categories wholly fits either of us. Mottele, who knows almost nothing about the real America of politics and economics, is uncritically in love with Yankee ways, while Max, who does understand America, is a European socialist.

Of course, Mottele isn't really a citizen. He's the son of immigrants. He grew up among Yiddish-speaking parents and grandparents in a place called Michigan, which he thinks is a province of Lithuania. With his mother's milk and his grandmother's Sanka coffee he took in the shtetl. The things he knows about happened before 1920—many of them closer to 1920 B.C.E. Thanks to his grandmother's favorite book, *Tsena Urena,* the women's Bible commentary, he's as comfortable with Abraham and Moses as Max is with Bill Clinton and Shimon Peres. Mottele believes that his ancestors keep tabs on him, even after their death. And, as if that's not enough, God checks the record every year between Rosh Hashanah and Yom Kippur and has been known to make unannounced appearances. This constant checking keeps Mottele close to the fold, but within his limits he likes to have a good time. America is made for him: it's a gigantic amusement park filled with good-natured clowns in every shop and office.

Max, however, knows better. Max discarded the shtetl. He realized at an early age that by speaking English and reading books he could please his Gentile teachers. He knew these pleasant women were Gentiles by their failure to talk about cholera or pogroms or Hitler. They passed out gold stars and, later, scholarships. Max understood a good deal when he saw one. To impress his teachers he memorized the Gettysburg Address. He practiced every night at bedtime as his grandmother marveled at how well he said the *Shema Yisroel* in English. He read so many books that his grandmother was afraid he would ruin his eyes and never get a good job, and she was right. After more than twenty years in school he became merely a teacher.

While Max immersed himself in Shakespeare, Milton, and Christian humanism, Mottele stayed away—more than that, he disappeared. In the seminars and classrooms Mottele was a forgotten remnant, a Yiddish Puff, the Magic Dragon. Then, with formal education behind him and his head filled with the glories of English literature, Max began to write stories. He wanted them to sound like the stories he read in the anthologies. He hoped for British characters who would experience epiphanies, those obscure but luminous moments that reveal the human condition. But all of his people turned out to be Americans, and none of them even knew what an epiphany was. They were good-natured folks, clowns in every shop and office.

Mottele had not disappeared. He had been there all along, busy taking notes on the raw material, mostly Max. When Max started up with women and memorized "To His Coy Mistress" to impress them, Mottele almost died laughing. When Max lectured on Christian humanism, Mottele took quiet revenge for the Crusades. And when Max started writing stories, Mottele squeezed in his characters, the kinds of Americans he loved to laugh at: ballplayers, truth seekers, entrepreneurs, and vegetarians. Max, of course, did the serious work of being an American. Mottele stayed in the background unless Max carried seriousness too far.

"You live in the Garden of Eden," Mottele said. "Everything around you is funny, and you don't know it because you spend all your time in the library."

"The life of the mind exists in the library," Max said. "My Garden of Eden is the card catalogue."

"Then why are you always looking around at the girls?" Mottele said. "Be honest about it. Let's go to a mall—there you can read a book *and* look at girls . . . as well as at shoes and dry goods."

"I can't write in a mall," Max said. "I need a quiet place to work."

"That's why there's a Christian Science Reading Room," Mottele said. "Meet me there in two months and I'll give you a book of stories."

After Mottele delivered the stories as promised, Max gave him a freer hand, and over the years they've collaborated so well that no outsiders recognize the differences between them. Yet the differences are all over their stories. They squabble like the president and Congress, and, like them, they pretend to do so for the common good. For example, Mottele noticed that Max was getting a little too full of himself. His picture was in the paper, people paid him to read aloud to them, and he got free tickets to ball games. So Mottele wrote a story about a fellow just like Max, a sportsloving lightweight who thought he was a big shot ready to enter the arena of letters. Mottele set the story in a boxing ring, where

Max had to prove himself against a real heavyweight, Norman Mailer. Max danced around in the story, threw a few jabs and metaphors, but when he landed his best shot, Mailer took it in the midsection without even noticing the punch or Max. The lightweight disappeared, engulfed by Mailer.

"I did you a favor," Mottele said. "Now you can see where ambition will lead you."

To return the favor, Max wrote a story about Mottele's favorite couple: a boy and his mother. He made the boy resemble Mottele. "You like boxing so much," Max said, "try this." The boy, almost middle aged, had had enough of Mom. One day he punched her and went off to Saudi Arabia to find a good job.

It took Mottele a long time to recover from that fictional blow. "Nobody hits a mother," he said. "You're worse than a lightweight, you're avant-garde." After that punch the mother said she wanted no part of any of their stories, so Mottele wrote a whole book about his grandmother.

Still, none of their internal bickering caused any problems, because the commotion took place in literature, one of the quietest neighborhoods in America. And even within that neighborhood Max and Mottele spent most of their time in the real boondocks, the short story.

Then they moved briefly to a much more expensive neighborhood, the movies, and there they encountered for the first time questions about Who They Were. Max will explain:

I wrote a book called Roommates. *The main characters were a grandfather, Yerachmiel, and his grandson, Max. They spoke Yiddish. Yerachmiel prayed three times a day. He wore a yarmulke on his head, a tsitsis under his shirt. It was not hard to guess his tribal identity—or mine. About a year later a movie came out, also called* Roommates. *The film, like my book, featured a grandfather and a grandson, and their religion and ethnicity is also easy to identify. They're Polish Catholics.*

Max and Mottele, that solid couple, seemed to have split down the middle: one wrote the book, the other the movie. Many people noticed this split and didn't like it. Max received angry mail from Jews. One letter he can quote in its entirety. "So," wrote a Brooklyn rabbi who'd read an excerpt in *Reader's Digest,* "if you weren't ashamed for the magazine, why were you ashamed for the movies?"

Max tried to explain. "There is no shame," he wrote, "in imagining what it's like to be someone else. That's what I do for a living. The world is full of writers writing about characters like themselves—lawyers writing about lawyers, alcoholics about alcoholics, Jews about Jews. There is no danger that this will come to an end. Our likenesses will always be among us. The writer's job is to make you believe a character is real, not Jewish. This is called 'verisimilitude,' and it evokes empathy, the attempt to put yourself into someone else's skin. Hath not a Gentile skin, Rabbi?

"This is what writing is all about, and in order to do it the writer must be free to imagine anything, even a non-Jewish version of himself and his grandfather. If you need examples of great freedom of imagination, may I suggest that you check the Midrash.

"As far as causing you confusion, for that I do apologize. I assume that you went to the movie expecting it to be the same as the book since the title was the same. I can tell you that you're not the first to be fooled by a movie title. About twenty years ago a Hadassah chapter in New Jersey bought out an entire showing of a movie called *Tora! Tora! Tora!* a World War II epic. They didn't pay attention to spelling, so instead of Rashi and Rambam they got Guadalcanal and Iwo Jima. The lesson, Rabbi: Buyer beware."

Mottele read Max's reply to the rabbi and tore it up. He wrote his own reply:

"Dear Rabbi,

"Business is business. The movie people wanted goyim. They thought that would sell more tickets. The movies are about millions, not about who counts for a *minyan*. If they had left us alone we could have made a nice Jewish picture."

Max tore up that reply and was about to do the same to the rabbi's letter when Mottele stayed his hand and held the sheet of paper up to the writer's face.

"Look who you're writing to about freedom and imagination. Instead of preaching to him about empathy, use a little yourself. Does this look like congregational stationery? Are there names of rich people down the left-hand side of the page? Don't mistake this rabbi for the kind you know, men who play golf and give speeches and have closets full of suits. This man probably lives in a few miserable rooms on Avenue J and supports his five or six children by working nights for a caterer. While people stuff themselves at weddings and bat mitzvahs, he's in the kitchen making sure there are no bugs in the broccoli or the cauliflower. And don't flatter yourself. He didn't read *Roommates*—he said *Reader's Digest,* didn't he?

"His boss, the caterer, a rich nonbeliever, probably tossed him a smeared magazine and said, 'Rabbi, here's something you'll like.' He did like it, and a few weeks later when he saw the movie poster with the picture of Peter Falk, he took a chance.

"This is a man who had never gone to a movie before. The closest he'd come to excess was a video of street dancing on Simchat Torah. Because he liked your characters so much, he went to a movie house and risked sitting next to a woman. Don't lecture to him about empathy and freedom. In Crown Heights those words don't mean anything. Send him a refund for the movie ticket and throw in an autographed book. And be sure to sign your name in Yiddish."

Max refused. They fought to a standstill, and the rabbi, still awaiting an answer, has probably been taken in by *Tora! Tora! Tora!* on video.

In their second movie adventure, Max and Mottele stayed away from Jews. They wrote a film called *The Air Up There,* which featured a college coach and his would-be recruit, a six-foot-nine African youth. No rabbis complained, but a New York sportswriter skewered Max. The sportswriter said that a white man shouldn't have written the film. And he took literally a line from the press kit that quoted Max, a five-foot-four, white writer, as saying he liked to imagine himself as a six-foot-nine, black power forward. "If you want to imagine black heroes," the sportswriter said, "forget basketball, write about real heroes."

"Mazel tov," Mottele said. "You got what you always wanted. You made it to the sports page."

Max threw the paper down with disgust. "Who does he think he is giving me directions about what I'm allowed to write? Didn't Shakespeare imagine Othello, and Mark Twain Jim? Didn't George Eliot, a Gentile and a woman, create a male Jew? The sportswriter has a lot more chutzpah than the rabbi."

"Relax," Mottele said, "the man had a column to write, it's just business. Anyway, your ballplayer is not exactly the Moor of Venice."

"The principle is the same," Max said.

"Every time someone in a newspaper criticizes you, you're ready to call in Shakespeare as a character witness. He's a journalist. Don't forget we tried that too."

To calm him down, Mottele helped Max recall their first journalism assignment—an investigation of beef barbecue. When Max accepted that job Mottele turned up his nose and kept it in the air. Throughout East Texas, where they inspected pits, Max interviewed, Mottele sniffed. Max quoted happy eaters, adults in paper bibs tearing into their dripping meat with two hands and a clean shirt. Mottele took in the beef and mesquite aromas.

In a switch from their usual roles, Max leaned toward the meat and potatoes while Mottele hankered for the spiritual. He even quoted one of Max's favorites, John Keats: "Heard melodies are sweet / Unheard sweeter still."

"He was talking about poetry," Max said, "not barbecue."

"So what," Mottele said. "It's also true of beef. You can have the food, I'll take the hunger. Do you think Kafka was the only Jew who understood hunger?"

While Max talked to cooks and managers who thought he was from the health department, Mottele analyzed smoke and emptiness. Max concocted a tomato, Worcestershire sauce, and onion recipe. *Esquire* decorated their reportage with drawings of Texas longhorns and sizzling fat. Together they received this response from their sister: "So for a thousand dollars you ate *treyf.*"

"If our own sister didn't understand that our work is about aroma and hunger," Mottele said, "what can you expect from outsiders? The people who try to tell us what we should be doing are always 'ones.' They can be pious ones like the rabbi or politically correct ones like the sportswriter, but they're all singles, not a twosome like we are. They see one thing; they know one thing. How hard is it for one to be right? A one is always right. Anyway, they just have opinions; they don't do research like we do."

In their research they're sometimes subtle, like private detectives on the trail of a suspect emotion, but most of the time they're daydreaming, or at the ballpark studying statistics, or in the midst of nature staring at ants to sharpen their sense of destiny. But whatever else they do, they're always conducting their ongoing primary research. They eavesdrop so lasciviously that they are now required in certain public places to wear T-shirts emblazoned with the warning "I'm Listening."

Age has not altered them, nor has a half-century of squabbles caused them to consider breaking up. They understand how much they need each other. Without Mottele, Max knows that he would be a pale imitator, a John Updike without Protestants. And Mottele alone would be exactly that—Mottele alone. Born into Yiddish at the exact moment that murderers were extinguishing it, he would have the language without the people. He needs Americans to populate his shtetl.

Of course, these two are just a couple. The great ones like Shakespeare and Tolstoy aren't mere couples—they're more like corporate Japan: they take in a whole society and guarantee full employment. Max and Mottele resemble their recent ancestors, the peddlers, more than they resemble the great writers. With their wares they roam the neighborhoods: an essay, a story, a novel, a screenplay—they're just glad to have customers. Since they're a twosome they can't enjoy solitary pleasures, they can never be single-minded or even focused. Like all couples, they hold harmony as their highest goal, and they find it above all in the lively carnival of America, in the English language, in words like these, which are to their ears music.

MARVIN BARRETT

Praying in the World: A Case History
from Parabola

This is an account of the circumstances in my life that led me away and back again to prayer. Twice.

I

If I divided my prayer life into three stages—petitions, intercessions, and what came after—petitions stand first. They were the gut prayers of childhood—praying for a toy, for a pal to play with, to win at ball, for good weather, good health.

Next came childish intercessions introduced by the chilling quatrain of ancient and unknown origin:

Now I lay me down to sleep.
I pray the Lord my soul to keep.
If I should die before I wake,
I pray the Lord my soul to take.

This was followed by "God bless mother and father, grandmother and grandfather, and all the other grown-ups. God bless brother Dirk and all the other children." The list was soon augmented by those I grew up among in the Midwestern city that was my home, cousins, uncles and aunts, teachers, neighborhood and schoolyard favorites, and in my case, perhaps not so enthusiastically, my younger brother, Eddie, a recent arrival. I began my prayers at age three. Petitions and intercessions flourished, and if I didn't always get what I asked for, those on my prayer list seemed preserved from serious misadventure.

Then at age eight, petitions and intercessions converged, and prayer as I knew it was wiped out by one instant, unambiguous, and soul-destroying answer. The Deity had heard and granted a thoughtless request with a terrifying promptness.

To be blunt, and God was certainly that, I had prayed that my three-year-old brother, Eddie (Edwin Galbraith Barrett, Jr.), justifiably the family favorite, a glorious child with a head of auburn curls, a heart-melting smile, and loving disposition, would die, and I not only would be spared the inconvenience of his charge and his unquestioned priority in my parents' and everyone else's affections but would become the inheritor of all his toys, not a few of which I coveted. I could not hope to appropriate his looks or charm.

Within the hour he was struck down in the avenue at the top of the hill above our house while I, his inattentive custodian, stood on the curb helplessly looking on.

For a day or two my prayers continued, that he would be brought back, that what I had seen at the top of the hill was an evil dream, that he was there at the other end of our attic room asleep in his trundle bed. That God would understand I hadn't meant it and reverse the outcome of my fatal prayer.

Then at his funeral, my first funeral, and the first funeral to be held in a glistening new funeral home at the other end of town, the prayers stopped.

"How appropriate," friends and relatives were saying in hushed tones, surveying the splendors around them, "that the first funeral in this beautiful place should be for a beautiful child."

Past the plunking fountain, the forest of indoor greenery, the grieving relatives and friends, I was led up to the satin-lined coffin and forced, resisting, to look in.

"You must. You'll never see your brother again. It is your last chance. He looks just like he is sleeping, so peaceful, so beautiful. Now he'll never grow up." He *was* peaceful and beautiful and still, terrifyingly still. His auburn curls were more ordered than they ever had been in life, his lips fashioned into a seraphic smile, his cheeks flushed with an unearthly, waxy glow. No effigy of the Holy Infant of Prague was ever more angelic. I looked and was appalled. I screwed my eyes closed and vowed never to pray again.

Nor did I, at least until I was old enough to be concerned for the fate of my eternal soul and perhaps my skin. Fourteen years later. This time there would be no petitions, no intercessions.

II

I had survived childhood, adolescence, had wangled—that was the proper word—a scholarship to Harvard College, earned straight As, won multiple campus honors, all unacknowledged miracles, without so much as a whisper in God's direction. Then Pearl Harbor intervened, and most miraculous of all, in a dash to escape the infantry, I wangled, wangled again, a commission as an instant ensign, a provisional communications officer in the United States Naval Reserve.

It was in the vacuum between the sunny, ivy-clad study and play of college and the inscrutable darkness of the war that lay ahead that, not remarkably, the possibility of prayer returned. But not without outside prompting.

To while away the time, to distract me while waiting at home for the navy's next move, I looked up the recent writings of Aldous Huxley, the favorite of my agnostic adolescence, the troubadour of erudite triviality, the apostle of clever meaninglessness —Matthew Arnold's grand-nephew ("a darkling plain . . . where ignorant armies clash by night"), the grandson of Darwin's bulldog. And as I read his latest works, the cleverest, the most eloquent of privileged and learned nonbelievers became the promoter of wall-to-wall, center-to-circumference meaning, his preferred access to this dazzling revelation—prayer.

The person responsible for this regrettable defection from apparently impregnable skepticism was, a scornful informant told me, a disreputable English would-be philosopher named Gerald Heard.

Our hometown library seemed to be filled with Heard's crabbed, hard-to-read works, most of which I succeeded in reading before I was summoned to the Small Craft Training Station on Treasure Island in San Francisco Bay. It was, the local recruiting officer explained, a place to polish up Sunday sailors who had conned their own little star fish in yacht club regattas so that they would be up to navigating YMSs, SCs, LSTs (I wasn't sure what the acronyms represented except that they were all small) through hostile waters. As for me, I didn't know port from starboard, a yawl from a ketch. The only boat I had intimate acquaintance with was a flat-bottomed scow that bumped through the Tunnel of Love at Riverside Park, the fun fair across town.

I, the Harvard Phi Beta Kappa in English, the playboy magna cum laude who had signed on as a communications officer-in-waiting, was scheduled to be promoted to skipper of some tiny tub steaming into a sea of trouble. And there was, I knew from the accounts in the papers, plenty of trouble, an ocean, more than one ocean of trouble.

III

The next act took place at the bottom of an opulent southern California garden, on a terrace cantilevered into the brilliant sun, over a churning, thumping, liquid malachite surf, me facing full front, eye contact riveted in place by the bearded, denim-clad philosopher, Heard himself.

I was there against my better judgment. Every religious crackpot who could manage the fare gravitated to the lower end of California. I was there against multiple navy regulations—no travel outside the Bay Area, no use of naval transportation by ensigns-in-training, etc., etc. All of it making me prime bait for a deck court-martial. And yet I sat there in the sun in my blue dress uniform, my white-covered cap beside me, at the fashionable end of Laguna Beach, mouth open, eyes wide, listening to this spellbinder tell me that the world was too much with me, that the reason I was there to learn about prayer was the shock and guilt of my brother's death, which had silenced my prayers fourteen years before, that the spiritual life was the only life worth living, that it could make sense of that early tragedy and of the chaos I was obviously heading into. Only prayer could redeem me, sustain me. But did I really want to be redeemed? He fixed me with his laser blue glare.

I had never met a true evangelist before, someone who could scare the living daylights out of you and then convince you there was one certain way back into the sun. Prayer again. Heard himself prayed six hours a day.

When I left two days later I was praying an hour every day myself, a half hour in the A.M. and a half hour in the P.M., carrying north in my head instructions for a new kind of prayer, not for things or friends and relatives, but for a state of being. Sit still in a quiet place, breathe deeply, and pray a kind of prayer, if I had only known it, that was infinitely more potent and dangerous than that which cost my brother Eddie his life.

Also there was the knowledge that up in the California foothills was Trabuco College, a religious commune conceived by Heard and Huxley with some input from Christopher Isherwood, to accommodate genuine seekers, to accommodate me, when I completed my service. Heard made it quite clear that, although he himself had been a conscientious objector in World War I, I must follow Krishna's advice to Arjuna—

> Slain you will go to heaven; victorious,
>   You will enjoy the earth.
> Therefore stand up, O Son of Kunti,
>   And resolve to fight!

I must resist the temptation to resign my commission, must persist as a naval officer and take the consequences—come hell or high water, both more than likely.

In my Brooks Brothers double-calf shirt case, left over from my earlier incarnation as a varsity dude, I carried away copies of *The Cloud of Unknowing,* the Bhagavad Gita, the sermons of Meister Eckhart, and Heard's own small pamphlet, *Training for the Life of the Spirit.*

On the first page of a daybook intended for an account of my adventures at the wars, naval and romantic, he had written, in his elegant Spencerian hand, three quotations to help me in my new commitment. They should have alerted me to the perils that lay ahead. Perils that had nothing to do with foul weather, an unpredictable sea, or enemy aircraft.

"The right relation between prayer and conduct is not that conduct is supremely important and prayer may help it; but that prayer is supremely important and conduct tests it."

The words of William Temple, Archbishop of Canterbury, seemed innocuous enough.

The second, from Louis XIV's saintly archbishop, Fénelon, was a little more demanding—a lot more, if one chose to explore beyond the elegant, apparently redundant words:

"Lord, I know not what I ought to ask of Thee, Thou only knowest what I need; Thou lovest me better than I know how to love myself. O Father! give to Thy child that which he himself knows not how to ask. I dare not ask either for crosses or consolations; I simply present myself before Thee. I open my heart to Thee. Behold my need, which I know not myself; see and do according to Thy tender mercy. Smile or heal, depress me, or raise me up; I adore all Thy purposes without knowing them: I am silent; I offer myself in sacrifice; I yield myself to Thee, I would have no other desire than to accomplish Thy will. Teach me to pray. Pray thyself in me."

And there was number three.

"O God! If I worship Thee in fear of Hell, burn me in Hell, and if I worship Thee in hope of Paradise, exclude me from Paradise: but if I worship Thee for Thine own sake, withhold not thy Everlasting Beauty!"

The words of Rabi'a, the eighth-century Sufi saint, ringing across an intervening millennium and several thousand miles— enough to chill the enthusiasm of a stronger, more perceptive man than I—and with a peculiar appropriateness to my condition, they gave me only temporary pause.

Still I got the idea. This was a totally different kind of prayer. There was no question of petitions or intercessions. I was, if I properly applied myself, heading for the "prayer of simplicity," "the prayer of quiet," illumination, ecstasy, "practicing the presence," "the life of union with God." And once sanctified—that was what Heard told me I must aspire to, sanctity, for "If you reach for excellence you may achieve mediocrity"—I could devote my life to the unremitting, incomparable service of my fellowman. Prayer could do all that. Could demand all that of me.

At the same time I was off to World War II, the proposed skip-

per, God help me, of a tiny boat on a huge embattled ocean. God
did help me.

IV

Could I have inadvertently launched a petition to be spared the
hopeless challenge of conning a "small" craft through towering
seas, amid whizzing torpedoes, bobbing mines, falling bombs? After two months' tuition at the Small Craft Training Station I still
didn't know fore from aft, what "red light returning" really meant,
which stars were essential in determining one's whereabouts on
the trackless waters.

Without knowing it, could I have asked to be spared these challenges during my ardent prayers in a locked cubicle in the training
station head, on an inverted pail in the broom closet down the
hall from our crowded, noisy dormitory? Treasure Island was not
particularly friendly to the requirements of silence and solitude,
certainly not the base chapel, which bustled with the activities of
a half dozen conflicting creeds.

Whether I unconsciously petitioned it or not, a thousand miles
north, at the Navy Yard in Bremerton, Washington, waiting for
my small craft to be commissioned and ordered to the wind-
wracked, enemy-infested Aleutians, volunteers were requested for
temporary duty at a desk in the Thirteenth Naval District communications office in downtown, enemy-proof, well-heated Seattle. I
volunteered for the job I had been enlisted to do, and the Bureau of
Naval Personnel thereupon lost me.

When they ferreted me out a year later I was up to six hours of
prayer a day. Perhaps I had experienced a bit of the prayer of quiet,
practiced a little of the presence at the keyboard of my clacking,
rattling Electric Coding Machine (top secret) or when sliding

frayed coding strips back and forth in aluminum frames or just sitting at attention for hours on end in my rented room back on Capitol Hill.

Certainly I had experienced the dark night of the senses, if not of the soul. No meat, no alcohol, no newspapers, no casual distractions, no movies, no novels, no dating, dancing, or carousing, the natural pursuits of a young naval officer in wartime. No sex. Especially no sex. Just prayer, a little food, a little sleep, and a lot of reading. The books Heard had given me and the ones he kept recommending—Poulain's *Graces of Interior Prayer,* de Caussade's *Abandonment to Divine Providence,* St. John of the Cross, St. Francis de Sales, Father Baker, Father Faber, William Law, William James, the Dhammapadda, the Yoga Sutras of Patanjali—the list lengthened and grew ever more dangerous.

Finally the Bureau of Naval Personnel found me out and ordered me not to the frigid Bering Strait but to the balmy South Pacific. No more rented rooms on Capitol Hill safe from prying eyes. I was on my way to the eye of the storm. The prayers continued at the same rate with possibly a little more clarity, a little more oomph. Adversity and inconvenience, I was learning, were great promoters of prayer. On the transport en route to the South Seas there were ten of us in a stateroom meant for a honeymooning two, ten noisy, apprehensive, keep-your-spirits-up-with-loud-profane-talk-and-hollow-laughter shipmates. Still I managed my six daily hours.

In a crowded hut in the holding station at Nouméa I managed as well. No sweat. I climbed the hill behind the camp, line upon line of Quonset huts filled with waiting officers below me, a turquoise sea, majestic purple mountains. I sat on a rock among the cowering sensitive plants, their little leaves folded inward against my presence, my eyes closed to the spectacular view, praying.

Then one day we were lined up at a desk at headquarters and

asked in sequence if we had ever been Boy Scouts. I replied with customary humility, only a tenderfoot, too inept to pitch a tent, to produce fire by rubbing two sticks together. I laughed at my honest appraisal. The officer looked at me sternly and said, "Next."

God at work once more. All Scouts Second Class and up—a single merit badge would do it—were sent off to the bloody landings at Bougainville. I was sent instead to an idyllic island on the border of the Coral Sea, a "staging area" where the scenery was even more glorious, swaying palms, towering volcanoes (extinct), no Japanese or hungry cannibals within hundreds of miles. Actually there were cannibals just fifty miles away; two botanizing Anzacs had been cooked and eaten only a few months back. But hungry Melanesians represented no threat to me, since I was by now, thanks to my diet, skin and bones.

Three or four inches of rain fell every day, and the anopheles mosquitoes were ravenous. But I outfitted myself with a rubber poncho, marine landing shoes, a folding stool, and a pith helmet with a mosquito net to drop over my face and plunged into the dense, dripping, buzzing tropical undergrowth.

There were a few comments by my hut mates when I returned soaked and pink cheeked and holy but no more than those made in the officers' mess when I turned down the rare offerings of beef, rare in both senses of the word, and ignored the privilege of whiskey or gin. Most men overseas, I was told, were lucky to get a beer.

But the prayers were going well—silence, a gray, faintly luminous field. Sometimes I even dreamed I was praying, a favorable sign, said Heard, who wrote me weekly letters gently urging me on.

So I spent a year and a half praying and reading edifying books and watching ships full of soldiers and sailors and marines steam off to one bloody landing after another: the upper Solomons, Tarawa, Kwajalein, Saipan, the Marshalls, the Marianas, New Guinea, the Philippines.

When I was moved to the dry side of the island I found a spot among the pandanus roots overlooking the harbor where only an occasional land crab, the size of a dinner plate, interrupted my devotions. If four hours were all I could squeeze in during daylight, I found the remaining two lying flat on my back on my bunk, inviting the spirit, ignoring my snoring hut mates, the cackling of flying foxes among the coconuts outside, and the scuttle of rats across the hut deck.

From time to time the way ahead of me seemed to open, to clarify. My hut mates, who might have found me a likely victim for ragging or worse, seemed inclined rather to view me as a mascot, a lovable oddball, their inoffensive junior in age and worldly experience. Different strokes for different folks. Live and let live. Sooner or later Lieutenant (j. g.) Barrett—I had been promoted —will come to his senses. My scramble to fill my daily prayer time left me little energy to correct their estimates or pass judgment on them and their feckless ways even if I had had the inclination. Actually, they were remarkably good-hearted, just dissatisfied with their lot. Eager for combat or dreading it, it was hard to tell, killing time instead of their fellow men.

Back in Pearl Harbor where I finally was sent, ostensibly for transshipment back to the States for rest and recreation, I stared from my top bunk into a bird-filled banyan tree and, waiting for release, prayed on.

Finally the war caught up with me. Instead of proceed orders to the nearest mainland station, I was given an assignment of maximum predictable peril, a combat communications unit designated to accompany the marines on their next major landing, D minus three days on some bomb-blasted beach at the far end of the Pacific—those were the days of the kamikazes. We would be issued a short-handled spade to dig a hole in the sand and a pup tent to cover it. I comforted myself with more prayers and spiritual reading, Suzuki's *Essays in Zen Buddhism* still available, despite the hostilities, in the Honolulu public library.

Then at the last possible minute God intervened again, and I was detached from my disaster-bound unit and returned to the States. While my buddies were storming the beaches of Okinawa, the bloodiest battle of the Pacific war, I was back praying in the chapel at Mare Island, at the quiet end of San Francisco Bay. Finally the Enola Gay dropped its hideous cargo on Hiroshima, and the war was over.

V

I was still wearing my khakis when I climbed the hill to the Heard-Huxley commune and what I intended to be the rest of my life—a life of prayer and, if prayer did its job, of enlightened service to my fellowman.

I lasted twelve months, nine happy, dedicated ones plus three of black desperation.

In the most peaceful spot on earth, surrounded by admiring like-minded young men and women—I was, after all, the famous praying ensign, six hours a day dodging bursting bombs, torpedoes, praying on in the machine gun's rattle and the rocket's red glare, while they and their active imaginations were safe at home—my spirits failed.

There I was at last, eating what everyone else ate, praying when everyone else prayed, praying, not that I'd get out of the godless mess I had gotten myself into and back to a spot where everyone was sane in mind and body and spirit. I was there. But praying simply that God's will be done, that I grow in knowledge and grace.

In a landscape that surpassed in beauty anything that the South Pacific offered, where the climate was superb, where charity prevailed and the goat's name was Rabi'a, with no adversity to overcome, no hut mates to urge me on by their negative example, surrounded by ardor and earnestness, with a lifetime of prayer and good works stretching before me, I lost heart. I more than lost heart, the bottom went out of my stomach. There, within me, was the abyss, black and bottomless. This, after all, was where I was heading. What I had prayed for and now was getting. The next step. The dark night of the soul and worse. I toppled in, fell, and kept falling. Six hours of prayer were intolerable. One minute even was not possible, nor one page of edifying reading.

The horror I felt on the curb watching my brother Eddie destroyed—peering into his casket—returned a hundredfold; and the comfort of my immediate surroundings, the sympathy of my fellows, the beauty we were embedded in became an accusation rather than a blessing.

Whatever God willed, I didn't want it. I was too weak, too cowardly, I knew it now, to sustain his knowledge and grace. I was unworthy.

I fled with him in pursuit. In the nick of time I escaped—I thought. In place of six hours of prayer a day and the world before me to serve, I now had the world to distract me from the memory of my failure. That, after all, was what the world and all its enticements, innocent and otherwise, was for—to distract me, to compensate me for my inability to pray.

Still under all this misery, this willful self-delusion, there was, remarkably, the dim buried acknowledgment that what I had given up would always remain an option. I had failed, but my failure didn't invalidate the experiment, make what I had aspired to any less desirable. Just for me, the miserable one, unattainable. Let others do it and God bless them. I couldn't. This wasn't a comfortable admission, but it somehow sustained me, kept me from complete despair.

For a few months I was in irons, then I was released shakily facing the other way. My name once again was Marvin Barrett (at the ranch in the interests of anonymity I had been known as Brother Benedict) and Manhattan and a job on a major magazine was my destination.

VI

Fade to the 1960s, one marriage, four children, and a half dozen magazine jobs later. The children are entering their teens, our marriage is entering its difficult period, the world has entered the Vietnam War and the psychedelic revolution, and in its vanguard have been my old gurus, Heard and Huxley, dropping acid.

Miraculously, perversely, inevitably, I find myself praying again. At the end of my rope, or one rope, I didn't seem to have any choice. I finally acknowledged that I had never really properly given up on prayer. That whatever his current behavior, what Heard had recommended in the past still applied. Prayer was there again in the midst of my hectic, harassed, worldly, responsibility-heavy life. At its center and on its edges. Settling in as if it had never been absent. Maybe it was not for six hours a day or even a specified number of minutes, but it was back, a recognizable part of my life. Perhaps its most important part. Fitted willy-nilly into a crowded apartment, a crowded burdensome schedule. I was back in church where I hadn't been since I was a teenager myself. Singing hymns, dropping bills into the collection plate—at a lively flower children's church in the city, a dull middle-class church in the country, in an upper room in the East 60s, a zendo, a temple, the world's largest Gothic cathedral. Anywhere two or three were gathered together trying to pray.

"Salvation shopping," Gerald would have called it. But the goods were genuine.

At home, late at night when the homework and the dishes were done, early in the morning before the first school bus arrived, I prayed.

If I didn't knowingly petition for particular favors or dispositions—that lesson was permanent—I did intercede for a growing list of relatives, friends, and a few enemies, needful and otherwise, giving them what I hoped was a helpful push into the light that I was wishing might somehow seep through and around them to me. If I didn't climb back to the prayer of simplicity, or quiet, that had gotten me through World War II and deserted me on my California hilltop, I did manage from time to time an inner silence in my busy, distracted life, especially, almost inevitably, when I lay back and closed my eyes as I had during those long nights in the South Pacific or drifted out of sleep in the early morning or just sat silently waiting in a doctor's, a dentist's, a headmaster's, a would-be employer's office, for a train, a bus, a plane, a child at dancing class, in a line at the supermarket.

It is now almost thirty years since I admit to returning to prayer. There have been El Salvador, Nicaragua, Uganda, Somalia, East Timor, Cambodia, the Gulf, the end of the Cold War, Bosnia, several heart attacks, a couple of cancers, a stroke, five grandchildren, a dozen or so books written and published.

Our wrinkled marriage has long since smoothed out. The children have left their teens, and the grandchildren have yet to enter theirs. Old friends have died, suddenly or peacefully. Gerald and Aldous have departed in a whiff of acid and sanctity.

Perhaps my conduct has improved as the Archbishop Temple would have it, but there was much room for improvement and age may have contributed. There are even moments when, as the great and good Archbishop Fénelon suggested, I seem to be taught to pray, even to be prayed in by something other than myself, particularly in sickness or anxiety for a loved one, one of my many hostages to fortune.

In times of optimism I think my intention may become pure and strong enough to get a glimpse through the paradise Rabi'a turned her back on, to a blinding resurrecting terrain inhabited by God alone, a consummation that should be every prayer's hope.

Meanwhile my prayers are calm and sweet and unavoidable, unlike those of my early manhood, which came from stubborn effort, were storm-ridden with an occasional patch of brightness, of peace breaking through, enough to keep me praying, to keep me afloat in my sea of trouble.

Prayer, I find, as I grow older is no longer a matter of choice or indeed of necessity. It is inevitable, even to those who would make a concerted effort to avoid it. It is the bare and glistening shingle stripped by Huxley's great-uncle's "long, receding roar," by the decades of skepticism and disbelief urged by his grandfather Thomas, by the tides and tempests of a tragic century nearing its end. The sand and pebbles have been swept away, and there on the naked rock at the edge of a great ocean we and all those praying around us—and there are many—stand staring out to sea with a small flimsy craft, our prayers, to carry us through the breakers.

Now I lay me down to sleep.
I pray the Lord my soul to keep.
If I should die before I wake,
I pray the Lord my soul to take.

In my seventy-ninth year, three-quarters of a century after I first recited them, those ancient words are back with their attendant catalogue of names recited without fear or apprehension, reinforced with an ever more hopeful meaning.

WENDELL BERRY

The Rejected Husband
from Chronicles

After the storm and the new
stillness of the snow, he returns
to the graveyard, as though
he might turn back the white coverlet,
slip in beside her as he used to do,
and again feel, beneath his hand,
her flesh quicken and turn warm.
But he is not her husband now.
To participate in resurrection, one
first must be dead. And he goes
back into the whitened world, alive.

S. PAUL BURHOLT

Sacred Threshold
from Parabola

On Christmas Eve of 1999, the pope will take a golden hammer and begin dismantling the bricks that presently seal the Holy Door to St. Peter's Basilica in Rome. When the debris has been cleared away, he will lead cardinals, bishops, and, in the course of the following year, many thousands of pilgrims from all over the world into what will be both a sacred space and a new era. The Holy Door is normally open only for one year at the turn of the centuries and the quarter-centuries. Recalling the birth of Jesus Christ as the beginning of new life for the world, the solemn opening of the Holy Door signifies special periods of renewal and divine grace for each generation.

As we approach the turn of the millennium and cast around for some symbol to help us understand this powerful but intangible change in our time, the image of the sacred threshold seems to beckon to us. One does not have to be a Roman Catholic to feel the significance of this almost violent act of breaking through to new life and possibilities. We realize that it is our spiritual vision that will enable us to thrust forward into the uncertain future, tearing down the barriers erected by ego and by attitudes that have long outlived their value. Yet we know that what lies ahead will be in some kind of continuity with the past and even reveal its meaning in terms of the tradition that we have received. This confidence stands in stark contrast with that part of us that would rather not cross the threshold, seeing in the new millennium only the projections of our self-doubt and secret paranoia.

The custom of passing through the Holy Doors in the four major Basilicas of Rome goes back to the year 1500, but the first year of each century has been seen as spiritually significant in western Europe since at least 1300, when Pope Boniface VIII proclaimed the first Holy Year. Boniface invoked biblical precedent for the idea of consecrating whole calendar years. God commanded the Jews not only to keep the weekly Sabbath holy by abstaining from work but also to observe every seventh year as a time of rest for the Land of Israel: the earth was to lie fallow, slaves were to be freed, and debts were to be canceled. Furthermore, every fiftieth year was to be a Jubilee, when the land was returned to its ancestral owners if it had been rented or sold to someone else. These laws forcefully reminded the people that they were but stewards of the earth, which ultimately belonged to God, and that there was a fundamental equality among the children of Israel, who had all been freed from slavery by their Lord.

The Catholic Holy Year, at first every fifty years but soon every quarter-century, was likewise to be a time of communal reconciliation and inner renewal, ideally expressed by going on pilgrimage, a task that would take many months and could be dangerous. Vast numbers of people flocked to Rome, whose soil contained the bones of the first Christian martyrs in the catacombs and where the tombs of St. Peter and St. Paul had been venerated down the centuries. Even if extra Holy Years were sometimes proclaimed, the normal feature was to mark the date since the birth of Christ, and for this reason they began on the feast of Christmas.

In this tradition, the present pope has proclaimed the year 2000 a Great Jubilee. Since 1979, Pope John Paul II has been focusing attention on the coming change of the millennium. In 1994 he announced a series of annual themes for meditation and discussion to help Roman Catholics deepen their Christian faith and prepare for what he sees as a profoundly important historical moment, when the world enters a new millennium and a new era. The pope's underlying thought is that human beings are cooperators with the movement of history. He sees the millennium as challenging everyone, whatever their religious position, to move into the future consciously. This means taking responsibility for our time, rather than letting ourselves be carried along passively by events—as has happened so often in the past and especially in the twentieth century, with its mindless succession of world wars, genocides, and inhuman political and economic systems. Part of taking responsibility for our time will involve a searching examination of conscience, both individual and communal.

The goal in John Paul's perspective is the building of a civilization of love, based on respect for the inviolable dignity of the human person, created in God's image and likeness. Invoking the ancient themes of the Jubilee, he pleads for a substantial reduction of the international debt, which effectively holds many nations in slavery and thus forms the basis of future resentment and conflict. Catholics are to purify themselves by repentance and to enter more deeply into their life in Christ as they prepare to enter the third millennium since the birth of their Lord. The Roman Church in particular is to acknowledge wrongs committed in the course of the past millennium, for example against other Christians and the Jews, and to reflect on how these sins came to pass and to seek a change of mentality and conduct.

Vitally important as these considerations are, they presuppose some basic questions about the relationship between Christianity and the millennium—and, indeed, between Christianity and time in general. Obviously, the year 2000 has a particularly Christian significance. If the world were now using the Jewish or Islamic calendars, we would be several centuries from a new millennium, and so it is possible that we would have no special sense of an approaching historical watershed. And even if for many people today our calendar signifies a Common Era rather than Anno Domini, its point of departure remains the theoretical date of Christ's birth two thousand years ago.

Yet all this in no way means that the year 2000 has some intrinsic importance in Christian belief. The New Testament does not refer to the two thousandth anniversary of Jesus' birth, nor has Christian worship traditionally dealt with such large periods of time as centuries and millennia. The papal concept of the Holy Year, as we have seen, is relatively late and is based on an analogy with the Jewish Jubilee; there never has been a similar marking of centuries among the Eastern Orthodox. Even after the conversion of the empire under St. Constantine in the fourth century, Christians remained content to use the Roman calendar, which dated years since the founding of Rome more than seven hundred years before the birth of Christ. Furthermore, when eventually the Christian calendar was drawn up, it was wrongly calculated, so that probably Jesus was born in 4 B.C. (as it were): in which case, from a strictly Christian perspective we have already entered the third millennium.

What, then, is the Christian tradition's relationship to time and history? The basis is the central belief in the Incarnation, which is primarily an event in history, not a timeless metaphysical category. God, more precisely the Son of God who is essentially one with his Father, took on our human nature and made it his own. This happened at a particular moment in time—in the days of Herod, king of Judea, and during the reign of the Roman Caesar Augustus. Eternally being brought forth from God, the Son was brought forth in time from the womb of the Virgin Mary as one of us and given the name Jesus. This is understood to be an entirely free, one might almost say unexpected, act of love on the part of God, who is good and loves mankind and has thus drawn near to us in a unique and ultimately ineffable way. The apostle Paul comments that God sent forth his Son born of a woman "in the fullness of time." Elsewhere the New Testament says that God spoke through the prophets in the past but has now addressed us through his own Son "at the end of the days." Christianity is thus profoundly bound up with time and history, although it reaches beyond them. This was what amazed the young Augustine, who tells us in his *Confessions* that as a philosopher he was quite familiar with the concept of God's eternal Logos or Son, but that he was astounded by the Christian claim that "the Logos became flesh and dwelt among us."

Eternity is thus believed to have entered time. Without ceasing to be eternal, the eternal God became part of historical contingency. The implication is that the Incarnation brings a new value not only for the material world and for humankind in particular but also for time itself, which is now permeated with God's presence and divine meaning. Rather than an eternally recurrent series of cycles, as taught by Greco-Roman sages, time was viewed by Christianity as linear and, one may say, goal oriented and purposeful. The point of departure was the very act of creation, which ushered in time along with the changing world of our experience.

Time is thus a progression, and, as we have seen, it reaches its "fullness," or *pleroma,* with the Incarnation, the birth of Jesus Christ. The present time, after the Incarnation, when Christians await the second and glorious coming, or *Parousia,* of their Lord, is called "the last hour" in the New Testament. Christ's birth, therefore, is both a midpoint in history and the beginning of the fullness of time and the last hour. In this perspective, we are now moving toward the goal of this fullness, the consummation of time when Christ will come again and "God will be all in all." For many centuries the Church saw this consummation not so much in terms of wrath and judgment but rather as a cosmic fruitfulness, a vindication of matter and the restoration of the world in Christ, when nothing will be lost, a vision that is still prominent in the Orthodox world.

But how does this understanding of time relate to the calendar—and to the millennium in particular? Clearly, if the present era between the two comings of Christ is termed "the last hour," we are being confronted with a way of thinking about time and its measurement that is very different from our own notions. In the ancient world, the term *hour* could mean any period of time, for instance a season of the year. Although daylight was commonly divided into twelve hours, there was no sense that these divisions ought to be of uniform length. Only with the comparatively recent proliferation of timepieces has time been objectively measured, and since Einstein we know that our pretensions to measuring the mysterious dimension of time are highly dubious. For the ancients, as for many traditional cultures even today, it was impossible to stand outside time so as to measure time abstractly, as if it were a commodity that we have or don't have or can "save." Instead, time had a more human, existential quality. Things took as much time as they took to be completed. Measurements of time were not abstract but part of the warp and woof of human experience, such as the setting of the sun, the phases of the moon, the tides, the crowing of the cock, the pattern of the seasons.

Closely connected with this concrete understanding of time is the sense of the right moment, the propitious time, what the Greeks called *kairos*. In our life it is critical for us to know the right time. A thing that is good at the right time may be bad at some other time. We cannot know this right time merely by looking at our watch. It is in this sense, surely, that the apostle Paul spoke of God sending his Son into the world in the fullness of time. Christ himself refused to be drawn out when his disciples asked him about the time of his Second Coming, saying that the Father alone knows the day and the hour. Instead he warned:

Stay awake therefore, for you do not know on what day your Lord is coming . . . be ready, for the Son of man is coming at an hour you do not expect.

The Christian attitude to time, then, is essentially a state of keeping watch and readiness. In monastic writings this state is often referred to as vigil (αγρυπνια) and sobriety (υηψιζ). It is the explicit goal of monastic and lay asceticism in the Church. The focus is on the present moment, or rather on the Lord Jesus who is present even now. It is a sustained spiritual alertness that is diametrically opposed to the state of the person who is fast asleep or drunk. The latter is likely to miss the opportunity, the right moment. Such a one, even if he or she is continually busy, truly "wastes" time.

If, because of the Incarnation, time really is permeated with God's presence and divine meaning, each moment will have its own unique mode, one might almost say flavor, of divine encounter. Several times, referring to the Kingdom of God and things lying in the future, Jesus said, "The hour is coming and is already come." It is as if we are being warned against a certain unhealthy extroversion that would always pitch our attention into some other time and place than the one we are being offered now. Rather than relying on calculations and projections of time into the future, the apostle Paul declares, "Now is the acceptable time, now is the day of salvation."

It is perhaps for these reasons that, although various Christian groups down the centuries have tried to calculate the dates of the Second Coming and of the mysterious prophecies of the book of

Revelation, the mainstream of the tradition has preferred to live the present moment in the spiritual tension of sustained alertness. Even St. Augustine of Hippo, himself no mean numerologist, saw the promise of the thousand-year reign of Christ and his saints as referring to the present era of the Church Militant. Referring to the biblical six days of creation, Augustine says that they are obviously very different from the kind of days we experience, as they preexisted the sun and the moon. And in the third century, Origen, pondering the Sabbaths and Jubilees of the Law, suggests that they are shadows of many other days and that "there must be new moons occurring at intervals of time determined by the conjunction of some other moon and some other sun." For Origen, the Jubilee Year symbolizes the consummation of the vast expanse of ages in which created beings come to their fullness in God.

According to this vision, our experience of the passing of time can be profoundly symbolic and anticipatory. The daily rising and setting of the sun, the weekly cycle beginning with the Lord's Day, and the rotation of the solar year crowned by the glorious feast of the Lord's resurrection at Pascha—all these are special moments of encounter with Christ, an encounter that is divine and unceasing. Although the secular mind may try to co-opt the Church's holy days for commerce or at best assimilate them to the cycle of the seasons, the true meaning of the festivals of the Lord and his saints is very different. They portray time and the seasons themselves always as something more, as symbols of heavenly archetypes, enabling us to participate even now in the life of the world to come.

This vision is offered to us in the Divine Liturgy of the Eastern Church, when the priest crosses the threshold of the Royal Doors and proclaims, "Blessed be the entrance of thy holy ones always, now and forever, and unto the ages of ages. Amen." And it is also shown in the sacred icons, which present Christ and the saints even now in the glorified humanity that will be ours at the Second Coming. In other words, the future, and not merely the past, gives form to our present reality. The saints, those who fully enter into the grace of the Holy Spirit, experience time as more than a linear sequence determined by the past, since they are granted even now to taste God's eternity and the future fullness of creation that the Jubilee foreshadows.

DOUGLAS BURTON-CHRISTIE

Living on the Edge of Eternity
from Weavings

This was not a journey I wanted to make. One of my oldest and dearest friends, Donald Nicholl, was dying of cancer in England. Traveling there to see him meant, I knew, saying good-bye. And this was something I did not want to do. I did not want to face up to the stark fact of his impending death. I did not want to consider how I would live with the immense hole that I knew his passing would create. Somehow, from a distance, I had been able to sustain the illusion that he would not die, that his disease would go into remission, that we would again walk the Pennines together, talking excitedly of our latest discoveries, of our hopes for the future. But now, handing my ticket to the flight attendant and boarding the plane, I no longer harbored such illusions. Embarking on this journey brought home to me the harsh reality I had so far been evading: my friend was dying. In doing so, it also wakened me in a new way to Donald's journey, to his struggle amidst much physical pain and loneliness to make his way along the narrow, steep path toward death, toward God.

This was a path in many ways unimaginable to me. Certainly, I have faced up to the reality of death, struggled with it in my own way. But to be on the edge of death, to know that the end of life is near? No, I have not known that reality. But perhaps this was one of the reasons for my journey to see Donald in England: to be brought into the presence of this mystery in a way that I never would have discovered on my own. It is strange to consider this. I imagined I was coming to see Donald to express my love for him, to be present to him, and perhaps be of some comfort to him in a difficult time. All of this was, I think, true. But already I was beginning to see another more fundamental reason for my trip: I was being drawn to journey with him for a time along that lonely path, to dwell with him in the liminal space between life and death that he now occupied, in order to learn something about my own life. I was being invited to receive from him another, final gift: to learn, as he himself was learning, to live on the edge of eternity.

An Immense and Mysterious World

The world on this early spring day seemed so vivid, so richly detailed, so precious. The gentle rocking motion of the train as it made its way north from London; the pale gray sky stretching over an endless green expanse; masses of daffodils blooming along the roadside; brilliant golden blossoms of forsythia against a red brick wall; tiny newborn lambs skirting across a field; crows circling; white, purple, and yellow pansies in huge mounds; two small boys running out to play soccer. It seemed important, somehow, to take note of all this, to register how the world looked and felt at this particular moment. I suppose I was seeing, or trying to see, all of this through Donald's eyes. Imagining taking it all in as if for the last time. Trying not to miss anything. Trying to stay awake. This too was part of the journey.

As the train rolled north I recalled my first encounter with Donald more than twenty years earlier. I was a student at the University of California at Santa Cruz. Donald was my teacher in a class on Russian religious thought. We were reading Dostoevsky's

The Brothers Karamazov. One day we read aloud a passage from the section "Cana of Galilee," about Alyosha's terrible disillusionment following the death of the elder Zossima. Alyosha had hoped and expected that the elder's body would be suffused with the odor of sanctity. This would have confirmed the elder's stature as a holy man and secured Alyosha in his own life path as a monk and disciple of the elder. But the elder's body instead stank with the odor of corruption, a sure sign that he had not in fact achieved holiness in his life. Alyosha's hopes were confounded by this turn of events, and he found himself plunged into a deep crisis of faith.

But then something strange and unexpected happens. Alyosha, wearied and broken, nevertheless goes to kneel in vigil in the church beside the body of his beloved elder. Another monk, sitting nearby, is reading aloud the story of the wedding feast at Cana from John's Gospel. Alyosha drifts off to sleep with these words ringing in his ear and finds himself dreaming of the wedding feast. Suddenly, Zossima is present to him, vividly present, reaching out to him. Alyosha can hardly believe it: "Can it be that he, too, is at the banquet, that he, too, has been called to the marriage in Cana of Galilee . . . ?" Indeed, against all expectation, the elder *has* been called. Somehow, even in his dream, Alyosha senses the significance of this. "Something," Dostoevsky says, "burned in Alyosha's heart, something suddenly filled him almost painfully, tears of rapture nearly burst from his soul. . . . "[1]

What this "something" was Dostoevsky does not say. But he notes that Alyosha emerged from the dream transformed. After pausing for a moment over the elder's coffin, he walked firmly and surely out of the church and into the night. Overhead the heavens pulsed with quiet shining stars. The night seemed to envelop the earth. The white towers and gilded domes of the church shone against the sapphire sky. "The silence of the earth," says

Dostoevsky, "seemed to merge with the silence of the heavens, the mystery of the earth touched the mystery of the stars. . . . Alyosha stood gazing and suddenly, as if he had been cut down, threw himself to the earth."

Alyosha did not know why he was embracing the earth, why he longed to kiss it and water it with his tears. Only that he did, and that in that moment "it was as if threads from all those innumerable worlds of God all came together in his soul, and it was trembling all over, 'touching other worlds.' "

I cannot say with certainty why this passage read aloud that day moved me so deeply. Was it because I sensed almost immediately the truth of the story? Because it touched upon and gave voice to my own longing to embrace and be embraced by "all those innumerable worlds of God?" Because through it I glimpsed an immense and mysterious world opening up before me—a world in which the wedding feast, the communion of saints, and the "sapphire sky" all pulsed and moved together in a single numinous reality; a world where the borders between heaven and earth, this world and the next were permeable and porous? It was all this and more. I was left wondering: could I learn to dwell in such a world? Could I taste, even for a moment, what Alyosha had tasted: eternity breaking into this mundane world?

That these questions should have become so real, so pressing to me in that moment, was due in no small part to my conviction that the one reading the passage knew it to be true. Somehow I discerned in the very tone of Donald's voice the truth of Alyosha's dream, the significance of his ecstatic embrace of the earth and of his spiritual transfiguration. This tall Yorkshireman, who had given himself for so many years to the study of Russian language and thought, seemed utterly suffused by Dostoevsky's luminous vision, seemed himself to inhabit a world in which "threads from all those innumerable worlds of God" came together.

Alyosha "felt clearly and almost tangibly something as firm and immovable as this heavenly vault descend into his soul. . . . Never, never in his life would [he] forget that moment." I sensed the same was true for me. Something momentous was unfolding within me at that moment. I was being drawn out of myself toward the very edge of a new world, a world suffused with Spirit. And I knew that my journey into this world would somehow be connected intimately and deeply with this man standing before me. More than twenty years later, as I journeyed north to see him for the last time, I was still plumbing the depths of its mystery.

A Spacious Sense of Time

Proshloe ne proshlo—"the past has not passed away." These were among the first words Donald spoke to me upon my arrival at his home in the little village of Betley. He had been thinking a lot about the past, about those who had gone before him but who were still intimately present to him in his final struggle. It was Pavel Florensky, the brilliant Russian philosopher and priest, who had first used this phrase in 1919: "The past has not passed away," he said, "but is eternally preserved somewhere or other and continues to be real and really influential. . . . Everybody and everything is so closely interwoven that separation is only approximate, with continuous transition taking place from one part of the whole to another part."[2] For Florensky, this was not merely an idea but a truth he felt called to live into. Which is why, when Florensky was falsely accused of organizing a nationalist-fascist conspiracy against the Soviet regime, he deliberately incriminated himself in order to save the others accused of conspiracy. As a result he was imprisoned and eventually executed at the hands of the NKVD. For Donald, it was Florensky's witness—his martyr-dom—that gave his words such power. "The past has not passed away." Florensky's witness was not wasted. It did not amount to "nothing in the end." Rather, it "is eternally preserved somewhere or other and continues to be real and really influential." As it was for Donald, who was striving to witness in his own way to the truth of the Spirit in his life.

One afternoon during my visit, I went upstairs with Donald into his "dugout." This small room had been for many years his study, and the walls were still lined with books—of early British and Irish history, Russian philosophy and religion, theology, bib-lical studies, Buddhist, Islamic, and Hindu thought—traces of a life's work of scholarship and pursuit of the truth. But the desk had recently been moved aside to make room for a bed. And the shelves near his bed had been cleared of books to make room for images of some of his beloved "witnesses"—Saint Seraphim of Sarov, Edith Stein, Raman Maharishi, the Cistercian monks of Atlas, Thubten Yeshe, Maximilian Kolbe, Saint Thérèse of Lisieux, and others. Here, in the company of this "great cloud of witnesses," as he called them, he was spending his final days and weeks, preparing for his final passage. Seeing Donald in the presence of these witnesses, hearing him speak slowly and softly of what they meant to him, I began to feel in a new way the truth of Florensky's words: "The past has not passed away."

For Donald, I know these words were both deeply consoling and challenging. It was consoling for him, in the midst of what was a lonely and painful time, to know himself as living within and sustained by this communion of saints. "We are," he said, "one in the Spirit with all our ancestors and especially with those who lived by the Spirit whilst on this earth—the martyrs in par-ticular, the supreme witnesses to the Spirit." To take this seriously is to discover the present moment as almost unimaginably rich and full, shot through with traces of life past and future. How is it, he wondered, that we have arrived at such a narrow, diminished sense of time? How is it that we have come to value the "contemporary" above all else and to underestimate the power of the Spirit to expand our sense of the contemporary? Facing death in the company of so many witnesses altered Donald's sense of time. "I realized . . . that I am contemporary with all who try and have tried and will try, as I myself do, however weakly, to live by the Spirit. All such people, from our earliest ancestors till the very last human being on this earth, dwell in the same world, breathe the same Spirit. We are one in the Spirit."

This is a truth we have known and carried within us ever since that first Pentecost when the Spirit kindled in those gathered a new awareness of the truth of the resurrection. But too often, it seems, we underestimate the power of the Spirit. We sense our unity with those who are living but find it harder to imagine the ongoing influence upon us of those who have gone before or our relationship with those still to come. We struggle to understand what it might mean to say that everything, from the alpha to the omega, is woven together as part of a single continuous whole, what it might mean to understand ourselves as living within that whole. One thing it might mean, as it seems to have meant for my friend and for so many of the witnesses in whose company he found himself journeying, is learning to live in the awareness that "everybody and everything is so closely interwoven that separation is only approximate."

This means recognizing that our own inner lives are infinitely richer than we often imagine them to be, filled as they are with the presence of so many witnesses who have gone before us. But with this fullness comes a challenge. For if these witnesses continue to live on in our midst and shape us, are we not also called to bear witness to the truth of the Spirit with our own lives? In the larger economy of salvation might not the witness of our lives be necessary, even crucial, to others? Even if in ways utterly hidden from us?

This was part of the burden my friend Donald carried with him during his final days. If he himself was buoyed up by the witness of others, he was also conscious of the need to bear witness with his own life. Not so much through words—he could speak very little at this point—as through the disposition of his entire being. Could he realize, in some measure anyway, the transparency and purity of heart that would allow the Spirit to breathe through his life and touch the lives of others? On an even more personal and fundamental level: would he be able, as he moved closer to the threshold between life and death, to abandon himself completely to God? To hold back nothing? "Pray for me," he implored, "that I may be faithful to Jesus to the end."

SECURE IN JOY

I was startled to hear him utter these words. It was not his request for my prayer that shook me, but the stark expression of uncertainty it revealed. What kind of attitude had I been expecting to see in him? Certainly not utter equanimity. I knew he was engaged in a fierce struggle. But this plea from the heart caught me up short. It compelled me to consider more carefully what kind of struggle my friend was facing. How much physical pain was he in? Did he feel lonely? Was he sad at the prospect of departing from his beloved wife and children, from a world he loved so deeply? I wondered too whether he felt fear or anxiety during the long, dark hours of the night.

His sense of isolation was, I began to realize, one of the most difficult struggles he faced. Not isolation from friends and loved ones, who were near at hand and who were a constant source of consolation to him. Rather, it was the sense of isolation that arose from his recognition that no one really knew what he was contending with. "I am bound to feel much isolation," he said, "because for everyone I meet or speak with my death represents one event among many others—tomorrow's engagement or the holiday planned for Christmas. Whereas for me my death is *the* event." Not that it really could have been otherwise. But this isolation made him realize that no one among the living could really teach him about the most important question facing him: how to approach death. Only those who had experienced it, and borne witness to it—the martyrs especially—could do that. "What they teach us, above all, is to go into death wholeheartedly, to embrace the experience with one's whole heart and in *joy.*"

This note of joy certainly permeated his final days and weeks. During that last Christmas, he found himself struck again by the characteristic note of joy that resounds through this feast. He himself was coming to know this joy ever more deeply. And coming to know, through this joy, a taste of eternity. "We have to be secure in joy," he said. "We have to be full of joy. . . . This joy is never going to end. Joy is eternal, which is why human beings have always felt they have been in eternity when they have received such a touch of joy."

But how to be "secure in joy"? How to know oneself as living on the edge of eternity when one is facing death, struggling through a period of intense suffering? Only by embracing that suffering and becoming purified by it. To put it in these terms cannot help but sound glib and pat. But that is not at all what I saw in my friend during these last days. Rather, he was *struggling* to accept and embrace his own suffering and anxiety and hoping through it to become a witness, a bearer of compassion for others. Central to this struggle for him was the attempt to cultivate a greater sense of intimacy with Jesus, especially by following him toward the cross. His own illness had helped him to begin relating to Jesus less distantly, less in the third person, and more, as he said, as a You or Thou. "Jesus becomes our intimate personal friend," he noted, "when we *share* his suffering for the redemption of the world. Perhaps only then can we also share his joy."

Many years earlier, in his book *Holiness,* he had already begun reflecting on the intimate relationship between suffering and joy, on the *necessity* of suffering in the journey to God. At the time, he had observed: "The nearer we get to the Holy One the more intense the demands made on us if our course is to be sustained."[3] Nowhere was this more apparent than in the demands made upon Jesus, demands that left him toward the end "bewildered and distressed," hoping that his own suffering might somehow be circumvented, his heart "breaking unto death" (Mark 14:32–35).[4] But not, in spite of everything, broken. Why? Because in his self-sacrifice, his heart was becoming purified, suffused with compassion for all those broken and fragile beings whom he loved even unto death. And therefore suffused with joy. I think Donald had an intimation of this joy even then. Now, however, as he found himself being drawn ever more deeply into the mystery of suffering, so too did he find himself being drawn into a more profound joy.

He had taken to heart the words of the letter to the Colossians during these last months: "I am now rejoicing in my sufferings for your sake, and in my flesh I am completing what is lacking in Christ's afflictions for the sake of his body, that is the church" (Col. 1:24 NRSV). He had begun living intimately and palpably in the mystery of this truth as his own body gradually diminished in strength. "The word that came to me this morning," he said, "was *ekenosen*—he emptied himself (Phil. 2). It is a word which helps me make sense of the fact that my muscles are losing their power; they are being emptied of power. I must try . . . to take it as part of the emptying of my self, the fibers of my *being* being taken apart by God so that I may become a 'new creature.' " As his own suffering intensified, so did his awareness of and compassion for everyone else's. "Each time I pass a crucifix now," he noted, "I touch the feet of Jesus and call to mind the words of Pascal: *Jesus Christ est en agonie jusqu'au fin du monde.* And I think of the suffering people throughout the world, especially now in Zaire. And I try to place myself amidst them." Here too, perhaps, one can hear the resonance of Florensky's words: "Everybody and everything is so closely interwoven that separation is only approximate." God's redemptive work in us, especially the growth of compassion that comes through suffering, makes the idea of separation from one another unimaginable.

Intimations of the New Creation

This growth of compassion in us also makes the idea of separation from God unimaginable. This is the great gift of the martyrs to us, the truth they bear witness to: that our entire lives are suffused with God's love; that we are already living at the edge of eternity. In those last days, my friend Donald seemed to have become intensely aware of this truth. Not as something altogether new or unexpected; he had, after all, been striving to live into this truth for most of his life. Now, however, came a new clarity brought about by his continual and radical relinquishment of everything but God.

Like his beloved Alyosha, Donald seemed already to be living in a new, transfigured world. "I have received intimations of what the 'new creation' might be, and what it might be to live unconditionally," he said. But unlike Alyosha, his life was drawing to a close. He was looking out onto a different horizon, already walking toward it. "I realize that such unconditional love is not altogether possible in this world for most of us. . . . I need to be bathed in the unconditional love of God which is heaven, plunged in the ocean of pure love so that my whole being is cleansed of my selfishness; and my ego is swept away entirely. I have a longing for that boundless love. . . ."

During our last afternoon together, we walked outside in the garden for a few minutes in silence. The sun was low in the sky. The birds had recently returned and were filling the trees with their song. The new spring grass was deep green and soft beneath our feet as we trod together the path that Donald had been walking alone these past few months. As we passed by the side of the house on one of our turns, Donald paused and motioned with his arms outstretched toward the sun, the trees, and the fields beyond. As if to say, "Look! Look! Isn't it magnificent?" As if "threads from all those innumerable worlds of God" were all coming together in his soul, and "it was trembling all over, 'touching other worlds.'" We continued walking, and he motioned again and again, now toward the birds, now toward the garden, bursting with daffodils, crocus, tulips, now toward me. His face was radiant with joy.

ENDNOTES

1. Fyodor Dostoevsky, *The Brothers Karamazov,* trans. Richard Pevear and Larissa Volokhonsky (San Francisco: North Point Press, 1990). This and subsequent citations are from pp. 361–63.

2. Cited in Donald Nicholl, *Triumphs of the Spirit in Russia* (London: Darton, Longman and Todd, 1997), p. 190.

3. Donald Nicholl, *Holiness* (London: Darton, Longman and Todd, 1981), p. 129.

4. See discussion in *Holiness,* pp. 130–32.

LÉONIE CALDECOTT

Harrowing Hell
from Parabola

> *All that most maddens and torments; all that stirs*
> *up the lees of things; all truth with malice in it; all*
> *that cracks the sinews and cakes the brain; all the*
> *subtle demonisms of life and thought; all evil, to*
> *crazy Ahab, were visibly personified, and made*
> *practically assailable in Moby-Dick. He piled upon*
> *the whale's white hump the sum of all the general*
> *rage and hate felt by his whole race from Adam*
> *down; and then, as if his chest had been a mortar,*
> *he burst his hot heart's shell upon it.*
>
> Herman Melville, *Moby-Dick*

It was during Holy Week 1998 that our small corner of England became a flood crisis area. All week it rained, such hard and copious raining as made the rivers, already overfull from a long wet winter, burst their banks and fill the low-lying areas of Oxfordshire. The audience watching *Titanic* in a local cinema suddenly found itself ankle deep in water. Less amusingly, a milkman and his youthful assistant were swept away as the swirling waters seized their small electric van. Friends of ours, trying to reach their home village from Stratford-on-Avon, were diverted countless times. A journey that should have taken half an hour took three or four. The worst thing, said the mother, was the fear. "I hate it when water gets out of control," she said. "You just never know what's going to happen next."

We, meanwhile, watched as the meadow behind our house began to fill with water from the Cherwell River. Normally this field, which has for centuries retained the undulating shape of Roman times, acquires no more than a few wet troughs at the far end, obliging the horses that graze upon it to move closer to the houses, even in the worst of the winter weather. Between it and the river there is another meadow, the true wet meadow, which in winter takes on the look of an oriental rice paddy, with spiky vegetation that bursts through the water to the grey winter sky as if to defy the imposition of the new element that swamps it. This time, however, the upper meadow filled as inexorably as the lower one, and the residents of our street gazed in amazement as the grassy banks between the wet troughs disappeared to leave a smooth, shiny lake across half the field, and the cycle path to town was entirely submerged, only the row of Narnian lampposts along its track showing above the expanse of water.

All through Maundy Thursday it rained. I kept vigil until midnight after the Mass of the Lord's Supper, the small candlelit chapel of repose feeling like an oasis amidst an increasing threat, and thought about fear. I thought about His fear, how He sweated blood and asked that the cup pass from His lips. I thought about my fears, fear of pain, fear of disaster, fear of rejection, fear of failure, fear of betrayal by one I have trusted. I tried to submerge my fears in His and only partially succeeded. Fear is not an easy thing to control. *Yet Thy will, not mine, be done.* The will is one thing. The feeling another.

I returned home just after midnight: it was the beginning of Good Friday, and it was my birthday. I felt a strange peace. This is the worst day of the year, I thought, the one day when the sacred

mysteries cannot be celebrated. There is only the Cross to contemplate: the mystery of darkness. It is the low point. Things cannot get worse than this. The floods are rising about our home, and
evil appears to have won the day. The best, the most lovely, the
man who is God incarnate, is being betrayed, tried, condemned,
scourged, driven through the streets in agony and humiliation,
carrying the instrument of his final torture, and then put to death
in the most painful fashion possible. And yet once it has begun,
the torture itself seems almost better than the anticipation, the fear.
The disciples responded to the imminent horror with the classic
response: fight or flight. They fled into sleep whilst their master
kept his lonely agonizing watch. Peter attacked the high priest's
guard as he approached, only to flee from the challenge of the true
enemy later in the night. "One of the servants of the high priest, a
kinsman of the man whose ear Peter had cut off, asked, 'Did I not
see you in the garden with him?' Peter again denied it; and at once
the cock crowed" (John 18:26–27).

All through Good Friday it rained. "Why do they call it good,
when it's so bad?" asked my smallest daughter, after she had followed the Stations of the Cross for children in the church, gazing
in amazement as the illuminated alabaster carvings were explained one by one. "Because something gooder than all the badness came out of it," I said. *Then why do I still fear the badness?* I
wondered, privately. In the afternoon, I sang the long service of
the Lord's Passion. The choir sits above the congregation at the
back, and we could see the long line of people as they queued to
kiss the feet of the crucified one displayed at the entrance to the
sanctuary. There was nothing perfunctory about this rite, everyone took his or her time, the mourning was not rushed. We sang
motet after motet, unable to join the throng as we filled the air
with the solemn notes, and yet not apart from their slow shuffle to
the altar, their reverent obeisance to that delicate flesh pierced by

the nails, their acknowledgment of the gift. *You took my place, you suffered the worst any man could suffer, so that I would not be alone with my fear, alone against the rising floods, any longer. What better gift could I have than this?*

The next day, Holy Saturday, dawned equally wet and grey. The flood swept into the bottom of our street. I went with my eldest daughter to the church to decorate the shrine of St. Thérèse of Lisieux for the Easter Vigil. We took all the child's symbols of Easter—a real bird's nest found abandoned last summer, painted eggs, fluffy chicks—and we made a small tomb out of stones from our garden, which we left sealed for the moment. We tried to be as quiet as possible, being close to the chapel of repose where people had come to pray on this mysterious day when all of creation holds its breath and wonders, *Where is the Lord and what is He doing?* He is not even to be seen asleep in the back of the boat: he sleeps somewhere else and will not be woken until the appointed moment. He is lost from sight, whilst the storm rages and the floodwaters rise, inexorably.

Back home, the water continued to creep up the street towards our house. Then the electricity failed. Darkness was approaching, the evening of Holy Saturday, as the children dressed and brushed their hair by candlelight and were taken to the darkened church, where the tabernacle stood empty and the congregation sat, in hushed anticipation, waiting for the paschal fire to be rekindled.

I have always been simultaneously fascinated by and terrified of water, and in particular the vast expanse of the sea. It happens that I first visited Martha's Vineyard shortly after I had seen Steven Spielberg's seaside horror movie, *Jaws*. Consequently, I could not persuade myself to do more than paddle in the ocean. At one point I had nearly succeeded in overcoming my fear, telling myself it was ridiculous to be so influenced by a movie, and was bobbing about not far from the shore when I caught sight of some teenagers reeling in something on their fishing lines. It was a small shark.

In his *Philosophy of History,* Hegel speaks of how, for the Mediterranean peoples, the drive to do philosophy arises out of the relationship to the ocean, which reminds us of the infinite within ourselves. The ability to navigate this ocean that we long to cross requires both wisdom, for the construction of the craft, and courage. Homer's *Odyssey* charts the seemingly interminable voyage of that great seafarer, Odysseus, whose wisdom gave the Greeks victory over the Trojans and yet did not save him from making mistakes that lost the lives of his crew and delayed his homecoming for many years.

In the nineteenth century, Melville's *Moby-Dick* charted the obsession of one man with a near-legendary white whale, in whose pursuit he literally exhales his life, pitting himself against evil, as he perceives it. In this era when whaling is universally condemned, and parties of people go out in ships not to hunt, but to watch and wonder at the presence of the great natives of the deep, it is perhaps more difficult to empathize with Captain Ahab's vendetta against the leviathan whose pursuit has partially dismembered him. We are no longer hunter-gatherers; the logic of the chase, the triumph of man over the beast at bay, has less and less meaning for a culture obsessed with other thrills. And yet, as the reaction to *Jaws* (and a score of other modern monster movies) shows, we are still preoccupied by the confrontation with the source and locus of fear: the dead eye of the shark rising out of the unseen depths with its maw agape still expresses a primordial anxiety that we are far from exorcising. Those "subtle demonisms of life and thought," those images that stir up "the lees of things," which Ahab projected onto the great whale, are still with us, are still an issue, are still a locus of terror.

I sometimes wonder, seeing the pictures of the late Diana, Princess of Wales, stepping slowly and deliberately through a minefield, whether this was not as much an exercise in the confrontation of fear as a philanthropic venture on behalf of the victims of mines. For what evokes horror, ultimately, is not so much the monster under the bed, the dragon in the woods, the jaws that snap, as the fact that these things invade places that *ought to be safe*. We bask on the surface of the sea, enjoying the buoyancy and freedom of movement the element affords us. We walk on terra firma, not expecting to have our legs blown off by an unseen device in the dirt. We take refuge, as children, in our home, our bed, to rest or nestle. But what if there is no safe place? What if *an alien has taken over my mother?* What if all my nearest and dearest have fallen prey to an invasion of body snatchers? Our dreams, at their most anxious, are full of such images. If we do not dream of unseen enemies in the depths of the ocean, we dream of the underworld, the dark cellar of our house, the implacable enemy down below.

You are in the orderly, sunlit, upper area of a house, when from the interstices of the dwelling there rise up people unknown to you, invaders with dead eyes and sharp teeth: a vampire visitation of alien voyeurs. They stare at you with those loveless eyes. You make off down the stairs from which they themselves issued. In the cellar of the house you find a man, tortured and desperate, stretched out on a rack. He begs you to release him, but you are afraid of him, of his ugliness, and instead of releasing him you turn away and run out into the street. You find yourself in a derelict landscape, with not a soul in sight. At the end of the street is a barricade, over which you climb, before looking back to see the sign that is attached to it: CONTAMINATED ZONE. You realize with horror that you have been living in a place from which you were never supposed to escape, a ghetto. You will never be *able to live among ordinary people, if it is known where you come from. You flee, into the busy heart of the city, into anonymity. You haunt the most public places, where you can be inconspicuous. You manage, somehow, to live, to eat, to take shelter—but all the time you fear the discovery of your secret, the fact that you have issued from the gates of hell. And then one day, you realize that you are sick and in urgent need of medical care. You hail a taxi and ask the driver to take you to the hospital. He says nothing, does not acknowledge your presence, but begins to drive. As you stare at the back of his head, a terrible suspicion begins to gnaw at you. As he stops at some traffic lights, you crane your neck to get a glimpse of his face. He turns his head and looks at you. He is one of them, one of the vampires: and he is driving you, not to hospital, but back to the zone you have been trying to escape.*

In C. G. Jung's posthumous *Man and His Symbols,* editor Marie-Luise von Franz wrote: "In the unconscious, one is unfortunately in the same situation as in a moonlit landscape. All the contents are blurred and merge into one another, and one never knows exactly what or where anything is, or where one thing begins and ends. (This is known as the 'contamination' of unconscious contents.)" No amount of analysis, however, will dispel the very real fear that stems from the knowledge that something evil can apparently creep into any and every situation and render itself indistinguishable from what is good. Jungians try to deal with this by reference to the "shadow." Indeed von Franz continues: "When Jung called one aspect of the unconscious personality the shadow, he was referring to a relatively well-defined factor. But sometimes everything that is unknown to the ego is mixed up with the shadow, including even the most valuable and highest forces."

What element in the story I described earlier could correspond with this? Who is exempt from the evil-eye disease that seems to afflict the inhabitants of the contaminated zone? There is one figure who stands in stark contrast to the rest: who cries out and begs for help, who communicates his being rather than staring in cold and parasitical silence. It is the disfigured and suffering man stretched out on the rack.

By watching horror movies we may be trying to blunt our response to fear by overexposing ourselves to its more ludicrous manifestations; for ours is an age that wants to tame, not slay, the dragon. If we can turn the inhabitants of the haunted house into the Addams Family, perhaps we can pooh-pooh our childhood fears and allay the ghosts of the uneasy adult conscience. And yet there is perhaps a warning in that curious tale told by the brothers Grimm, "The Youth Who Wanted to Learn How to Shiver." A young man, the simpleton of his family who would never amount to much, has only one ambition in life: to learn how to shiver. To this end, he goes through many horrific experiences, culminating in a trial that has killed or driven mad everyone else who has attempted it: spending three nights in an abandoned castle full of the most foul fiends imaginable. He plays bowls with some of them, first planing the skulls they are using for balls in order to make them rounder, and he fastens the long white beard of Death himself to an anvil with a single blow of his axe, obliging the ghoul not only to beg for his own life, but to make the young man rich in the process. But all of this is a shallow victory, for the youth has not learned to shiver. He has not had to summon courage in order to overcome fear: he has simply behaved as his own nature dictated, violently and without feeling. It is finally his wife, the princess he wins by means of his feats, who teaches him. As he sleeps in his bed, she pours a bucket full of little fish all over his body. *Then* he shivers.

Bruno Bettelheim, in *The Uses of Enchantment,* analyzes this tale in terms of sexual anxiety, stressing the humanizing influence of the woman who shares the marriage bed. Certainly, it is only she who can take the man by surprise and bring him into the realm of those who know how to feel emotion, away from the inhuman ghouls, the Undead, with whom he has been on such comfortable terms hitherto. She has an intimacy with him that permits her access to his most vulnerable point, and she uses it, for his benefit. But there are other, deeper lessons to be learned from this denouement. There is the fact that it is, once again, the element of water that causes him to wake up to fear. And in the water are the bodies of fishes, however small. Why should water, and fish, be the means to awaken the soul?

There is little merit in the kind of detachment that plays bowls with the Undead. Ahab may have known fear, and overridden it, but he still perished, sacrificing most of his crew along with him, as he hurled himself against the adversary. Odysseus could not resist taunting the Cyclops in his moment of victory: stand in front of Turner's painting of this moment, and you will see all the warning signs of disaster amid the crash of the elements, the boiling of earth, air, and sea illuminated in a blaze of brazenness. True courage, ultimately, the facing of fear, has to be something more profound, as Odysseus learned to his cost. On the flag of the ship is a white horse, seemingly the Trojan horse, which gave victory to the Greeks and proved the intellectual might of Odysseus to be more effective than the arms of his comrades. And yet there is another moment in the hero's life when a horse stood in a field: it was the moment when he tried to avoid the encounter altogether by feigning madness and ploughing his fields in the place of that horse. They put his infant son in front of the plough, and he was obliged to stop, revealing that he was sane. Love for his child undermined his ruse and sent him on the journey he knew would keep him from his loved ones for many decades. His wife's love kept his kingdom safe, nonetheless, from the potential usurpers. Odysseus, for all his difficulties, is not cursed, as many of the returning heroes are, by reason of this deep familial love.

"Hell," wrote that most non-family-oriented philosopher, Jean-Paul Sartre, "is other people." Though we may not agree with such a categorical statement, we have all experienced, to some degree, that interior hell—the existential imposition by the "other" who does not empathize with us and who foists upon us his own agenda. At the extreme point of human consciousness, this unloving other, this ambitious suitor at Penelope's table, manifests himself as one of the Undead, those who appear for a time to be alive because they are walking about but who are empty inside. (Yet we are busy constructing machines that will do exactly that.) The Undead erupt into the midst of normal life and turn it into a nightmare. They come from the margins of the world, the graveyard and the basement, the places we want to forget. But someone has been in that basement before us, not just symbolically but literally: someone who told his generation that they would not get the signs and wonders they required, for the eyes of love do not require them. (Signs and wonders will never satisfy even the most rapacious of voyeurs.) The only sign of His presence is the sign of Jonah—to be lost from sight for the space of three days in the belly of the Terror, to be humiliated and rendered powerless, to be counted among the dead. This is the great subversion of Love: to use the crushing annihilation of the Undead to redeem their own realm. Even dry bones can be made to speak. We release the tortured Prisoner in our basement so that He may guide us out to good pastures. *Though I walk in the valley of the shadow of death, no evil will I fear, for you are with me, your rod and staff give me comfort.*

It is dark outside the church, but the rain has, miraculously, stopped. The people gather in the courtyard around a burning brazier. I think of Moses and his burning bush. Silently, the priests and deacons, vested in gold, process out carrying the paschal candle and encircle the fire. After the opening prayer, the celebrant cuts a cross in the wax of the candle, carving the Alpha above the cross, the Omega below, and the numerals of the current year between the arms of the cross. He inserts five grains of incense into the arms of the cross, saying: *By his holy and glorious wounds may Christ our Lord guard us and keep us. Amen.* Then he lights the candle from the new fire, saying: *May the light of Christ, rising in glory, dispel the darkness of our hearts and minds.*

The priests then lead the way back into the church, with the deacon pausing three times to chant *Lumen Christi.* The rest of us sing out the response: *Deo Gratias.* As the procession reaches the sanctuary, the acolytes light their candles from the paschal candle and step into the body of the church to pass the Easter fire on to the congregation. The deacon sings the proclamation: *Rejoice, heavenly powers! Sing, choirs of angels! Exult, all creation, around God's throne! Jesus Christ, our King, is risen!* Neighbor turns to neighbor, each lighting the candle of the other, and gradually the little flames spread their gentle glow across the darkened space. The proclamation continues. . . . *The power of this holy night dispels all evil, washes guilt away, restores lost innocence, brings mourners joy.* . . . By now everyone holds a lighted candle. From the choir loft, I can see the profiles of my children, lit up as they gaze at their candles or at the softly illuminated lilies on the great pulpit, the dimly perceived gold of the statues now unveiled from their passiontide purple, the gleaming paschal lamb embroidered onto the altar frontal. *May the Morning Star which never sets find this flame still burning: Christ, that Morning Star, who came back from the dead, and shed His peaceful light on all mankind.* . . .

The readings follow: the story of creation, the story of Abraham and Isaac, the story of Moses leading the Israelites through the Red Sea. We sing the responding psalm: *I will sing to the Lord, glorious his triumph!* and think of tidal waves, walls of water, held back, this time, to give safe passage. And then comes Isaiah.

Unhappy creature, storm-tossed, disconsolate, see: I will set your stones on carbuncles, and your foundations on sapphires. . . . You will be founded on integrity; remote from oppression, you will have nothing to fear; remote from terror, it will not approach you.

Soon, the tall paschal candle, from which we have taken the new light into our own trembling hands, is immersed in a great vat of water, like Jesus standing in the Jordan River. The very element that has been the source of fear, the fear of chaos, of invisible evil rising inexorably to devour, the fear of drowning, of being annihilated in the depths, has been sanctified. It has been made safe by the One who has harrowed those depths. These waters are now a fountain of life, the holy waters Ezekiel saw running out from beneath the Temple to cleanse the land, fertile waters in which everything thrives and multiplies once more. These are the waters in which my husband's little goddaughter is now baptized. Her name is Talitha Rose Marina. *Behold, little child, I take you by the hand. Rise up, rise up, little lamb, little flower, little star of the ocean, and live.*

Later, much later, we shepherd our own tired but jubilant children home to what by all rational calculation should still be a cold, dark house. The sky is clear, the moon full, and the stars benign. We draw up outside the house. The lights are on.

TRACY COCHRAN

My True Home Is Brooklyn
from Tricycle

On the first night of my seven-year-old daughter Alexandra's first Buddhist retreat, Thich Nhat Hanh smiled and looked into her eyes as few adults ever look at children. Although he sat very still on a stage, the Vietnamese teacher seemed to bow to her inwardly, offering her his full presence and inviting her to be who she really is.

Alexandra threw her jacket over her head.

"Children look like flowers," said the man who was nominated for the Nobel Peace Prize by Martin Luther King, Jr., in 1967. His voice was soft and bittersweet. "Their faces look like flowers, their eyes, their ears . . ."

Surrounded by scores of monks and nuns who had traveled with him from Plum Village, the French monastic community that has been his home since his peace activism caused his exile from Vietnam, he lifted his eyes from the little flower who was huddled, hiding her face, in the front row. Before him sat 1,200 people who had gathered in a vast white tent on the wooded campus of the Omega Institute for Holistic Studies in upstate New York. Thay, as he is affectionately known, had convened us for a five-day retreat dedicated to cultivating mindfulness through practices such as sitting meditation, walking, and sharing silent meals.

As the Master talked about the "freshness," or openness and sensitivity of children, I couldn't help but be struck by the way Alexandra was ducking for cover. He extolled freshness as one of the qualities that each of us possesses in our essence, our Buddha-nature. Alexandra, shrouded in nylon, was reminding me that true freshness isn't limited to those moments when we feel happily and playfully open. It often means feeling raw and vulnerable. I wondered if it had been a mistake to bring her here, to risk exposing her to the way we really are.

During the retreat, children and adults came together during different parts of the day. In addition to sharing meals and a daily mindfulness walk, the children clustered at the front of the stage for the first twenty minutes of Thay's dharma talks, which he carefully framed in simple, poetic images that children could remember. I brought Alexandra, hoping that contact with Buddhist practice would stimulate her imagination and awaken her own wisdom. I thought she could be inspired by the various techniques Thay described, such as listening to the sound of a bell that can call us back to "our true home."

"My true home is in Brooklyn," Alexandra whispered. She had peeled off her covering and lay stretched out on the floor with her head in my lap, jittering her foot to convey how bored and impatient she was. On the first night, most of the other children nearby were sitting cross-legged, quietly, and listening with what seemed to me preternatural attention. Alexandra was muttering to herself and writhing around on the floor like a big, unhappy baby. I wondered if she had some mild form of autism that had escaped detection.

Seventy-three-year-old Thich Nhat Hanh was sitting directly above me, embodying a mountainlike stability and compassion. A monk on the stage winked at Alexandra, and a pretty young nun dimpled up in a fit of silent giggles. The people around me were friendly and relaxed. I felt like a terrible mother to be judging and comparing my daughter in these gentle conditions. It was almost as if the spirit of nonjudgmental acceptance that surrounded me was triggering a perverse reaction, drawing out my darkest, meanest thoughts. I felt like a vampire who had stepped out into the sunlight.

As we made our way back to our little cabin, the power went out all over the Omega campus. And a light turned on inside Alexandra. We stopped on the path, unsure which way to turn. I had left the flashlights behind.

Alexandra took charge.

"Let's go back to the visitors' office," she said, leading the way. A kindly man on the Omega staff gave Alexandra a candle and walked us to our cabin.

"You knew just what to do," I said as I tucked Alexandra into bed. "That was good thinking."

"I hated to think of you wandering around in the dark," she said, beaming in the candlelight.

The next day Alexandra asked, "Mommy, is Thich Nhat Hanh a man? Like, does he have a penis?"

Yes, I offered, he was an ordinary man, but he was a monk. That meant that he lived for the happiness of others, so he might seem different.

My answer felt vague and wimpy, not as real as the question.

The following day in the dining hall, I discovered how deeply traveling with your own pint-sized Zen master makes you feel aware of yourself, and how apart. The majority of the people there were moving about with a kind of underwater grace, practicing silence. We parents struggled with the task of filling trays and settling children while trying to remember to stop and breathe consciously when the mindfulness bell sounded.

Alexandra and I sat at a table in the dining hall facing a table decorated with pumpkins.

"Mommy!"

I whispered to her that we were supposed to try eating silently together.

"This is not my experiment," Alexandra reminded me. "I don't want to do it, because I have a question."

"What's your question, Alexandra?"

"Is a pumpkin a fruit or a vegetable?"

"A vegetable."

"Why are you being so mean? Aren't you supposed to be happy?"

The interconnection of all phenomena is a constant theme of Thich Nhat Hanh's. He speaks often of "interbeing," the actual state of reality that, once recognized, nurtures compassion and empathy. As people ate in silence around us, I remembered an incident that had happened several weeks earlier. Alexandra was going through a phase of pondering how she was related to the first person who ever lived and to all other people.

"Every living being is connected," I had told her as I was putting her to bed one night. "The whole universe is alive, and what you put out in the world is what you get back. If you put out love and kindness, you tend to get love and kindness in return."

Alexandra and I had decided to put the little purple bike with training wheels that she had outgrown down on the street for someone to take. She crayoned a sign that read, "Whoever takes this bike, please enjoy it, love, Alexandra."

She had been full of anticipation. The next morning she bolted out of bed and ran to the window.

"Mommy, my bike is gone!" she'd said, as radiant as on Christmas morning. "Somebody took my bike!"

The concept of the web of life was alive and breathing that morning. But by the end of the day, not surprisingly, she had moved past the shimmering magic and was applying the cause-and-effect practicality of a kid.

"So when do I get something back?" she asked.

David Dimmack, a longtime student of Thay's, was the volunteer in charge of the children's program on the retreat. He taught the kids the "Flower Fresh" song, the theme song of the Community of Mindful Living. At the beginning of a dharma talk one morning, they all got up on the stage together and sang to Thich Nhat Hanh and the rest of the sangha.

"Breathing in, breathing out," sang Dimmack and the children. *"I am blooming like a flower, I am fresh as the dew.*

"I am solid as a mountain, I am firm as the earth. I am free."

When I stood in the back of the tent, watching the children onstage, it was impossible for me not to compare it to Sunday school.

Dimmack has called the songs "entrainment," matter-of-factly acknowledging that sometimes teaching just comes down to presenting ideas in a way that gently and gradually makes an impression, like water wearing away rock. At the same time, though, he emphasized that there was a constant creative tension in the children's program between teaching and allowing, between imposing structure and letting the kids be.

Mark Vette, another student of Thay's, works as an animal psychologist and lives on a ranch in New Zealand. Vette had the inspired idea of teaching the kids to use dowsing rods made of bent coat hangers and pendulums made of little pieces of wood.

"Here's the dowsing prayer," he said to the group of us gathered on a big meadow in the center of the campus. "May I let go of the things that are known and embrace the things that are unknown." After the kids tired of looking for water and chasing one another ("Lead me to a dork!"), many of them settled down to find their place of "inner power." (The kids liked the word *power* better than *peace.*)

"Pendulums and dowsing rods seemed to be a perfect way to introduce them to their own intuitive sense," said Vette, a sandy-haired, athletic man who by the end of the week had completely captured my daughter's heart. "In the bush, these things work because we really already know where that lost animal is or where north is. And the kids can use it in the same way to learn to meditate, to find their center or their true home."

One day, during walking meditation, I began to get an inkling of what it is to find my true home. Every day the children, who left the dharma talk after the first twenty or thirty minutes, were invited to meet up with Thich Nhat Hanh and the grown-up students as they flowed out of the dharma hall to walk toward the lake. On one beautiful azure day in late October, those of us who were with the children watched Thich Nhat Hanh walking toward us from the dharma tent, leading his multitude: 1,200 tall Americans dressed in bright Polartec colors following a small figure in brown.

No sooner had Alexandra and several other children joined to walk up front with Thay than she split off to scamper to the top of a leaf-carpeted hill.

"I'm going to roll down this hill!" she shouted to another girl. "Come on!"

It actually awed me that she was so unselfconscious about shattering the silence. Alexandra rolled down the hill, sounding like a bear crashing through the forest.

I dropped my head and trudged along. Suddenly, I noticed Thich Nhat Hanh gliding along, like a mountain on rails, almost next to me. His face looked calm and fresh, while mine ached like a clenched fist. Alex had raced ahead to the water's edge, where she stood waving and smiling at me. I felt a pang of love for her and really experienced how the voice of my heart was being drowned out by a welter of negative thoughts that seemed to come from somewhere in my brain that didn't even feel organic—more like a robot, a split-off part of me mechanically repeating bits of old programming.

Aware as I now felt, I was haranguing myself that really good mothers didn't get swamped by nasty reactions. Good mothers, my mind chided, were capable of unconditional love.

The bell calling for mindfulness sounded. I knelt down in the warm sand. The bell rang again, and a third time. I picked up my head to see an old man's hand gently stroking a familiar head of thick ash-blond hair. Thich Nhat Hanh and my daughter were sitting side by side. It slowly dawned on me that it was Alexandra who had just rung the bell calling the rest of us back to our true homes. Thay had been inspired to pick Alexandra, the loudest kid there that particular day, to sound, or "invite," the bell that called everyone else to silence.

At that moment, the ideal of unconditional love seemed nothing but a brittle concept, a fetter. I felt I finally comprehended what Thich Nhat Hanh meant when he said that acceptance is understanding and understanding is love.

"I was throwing sand and I looked up and he was looking at me," she explained later. "He was kind of smiling. He waved for me to come over and sit by him. He didn't say anything, he just showed me how to ring the bell."

Back in Brooklyn, as Alexandra and I slipped back into our daily routines, I wondered from time to time what effect, if any, a week of mindfulness training might have. Then, one night many months later, I was fuming about some frustration.

"Breathe, Mommy," said Alexandra. "Just relax and breathe and return to your true home."

ROBERT CORDING

Sam Cooke: "Touch the Hem of His Garment"
from DoubleTake

As if he cannot help himself
from adding up what's lost to the good times
so difficult to have in this world,

Cooke's throaty voice warbles
up out of his reed-thin, man-child body,
half balm, half aching need,

his trademark whoa-ooh-oh-oh-oh
lingered over, drawn out until it hangs in air,
honey-tongued, heavenly, fragile

as consolation. I'm listening
to a 1956 recording, and Cooke, twenty-five,
has already discovered his gift

for making women tremble
and shake with the spirit in church aisles.
He's retelling the Gospel story

of a woman who wants only
to touch the hem of Christ's robe, a song
that will sell twenty-five thousand copies,

propel Cooke into a gospel star,
and begin the long chain of small decisions
that ends with a bullet in his lungs.

Still eight years away—
the $3-and-up motel, the hooker charging
assault, Cooke's cherry red Ferrari

purring in the parking lot
as he slumps to the floor, naked save for
an overcoat and one expensive shoe—

but I can't keep from hearing
the urgency in his voice as the woman, pushed
by the terror of self-recognition,

her flesh dying from the inside
out, staggers through the crowd around Jesus,
and, with only the slightest brush

of her fingers, touches
his robe, believing it will make her whole.
"Who has touched me?" Jesus asks,

and Cooke sings, "It was I-I-I,"
extending the moment in his clear, sustained
yodel, pulling us into the miracle

of how, after night-long drifts
from bar to bar, the slur of zippers and
whiskeyed words dimming the nameless

———————

landscapes of a hundred
identical blackened factories stuck between
billboards and railway bridges,

after a week of days piling
one on another like dirty laundry, Sunday arrives,
and everyone rises and testifies

and sways under the wings
of notes that swoop and glide and make us whole,
if only for the duration of the song.

ANNIE DILLARD

Acts of God
from Northeast

"Memoirs of a Cape Breton Doctor" describes, among many more dramatic incidents, the delivery of a transverse-presenting baby. "I looked after the baby . . . I think I had the most worry because I had to use artificial respiration for a long time. I didn't time how long I was using mouth-to-mouth breathing, but I remember thinking during the last several minutes that it was hopeless. But I persisted, and I was finally rewarded when Anna MacRae of Middle River, Victoria County, came to life." She came to life. There was a blue baby-shaped bunch of cells between the two hands of Dr. C. Lamont MacMillan, and then there was a person who had a name and a birthday, like the rest of us. Genetically she bore precisely one of the 8.4 million possible mixes of her mother's and father's genes, like the rest of us. On December 1, 1931, Anna MacRae came to life. How many centuries would you have to live before this, and thousands of incidents like it every day, ceased to astound you?

Now it is a city hospital on a Monday morning. This is the obstetrical ward. The doctors and nurses wear scrubs of red, blue, or green, and white running shoes. They are, according to the tags clipped to their pockets, obstetricians, gynecologists, pediatricians, pediatric nurse practitioners, and pediatric RNs. They consult one another on the hoof. They carry clipboards and vanish down corridors. They push numbered buttons on wall plaques, and doors open.

There might well be a rough angel guarding this ward, or a dragon, or an upwelling current that dashes boats on rocks. There might well be an old stone cairn in the hall by the elevators, or a well, or a ruined shrine wall where people still hear bells. Should we not remove our shoes, drink potions, take baths? For this is surely the wildest deep-sea vent on earth: This is where the people come out.

Here, on the obstetrical ward, is a double sink in a little room— a chrome faucet, two basins and drains, just like any kitchen sink. There is a counter on the left, and a counter on the right. Overhead, a long heat lamp lights and warms the two counters and the sink.

This is where they wash the newborns like dishes. A nurse, one or another, spends most of an eight-hour shift standing here at the sink.

Different nurses bring in newborns, one after another, and line them down the counter to the sink's left. The newborns wear flannel blankets. Knit hats the size of teacups keep sliding up their wet heads. Their faces run the spectrum from lavender through purple and red to pink and beige.

Nurse Pat Eisberg wears her curly blond hair short in back; her thin neck bends out of a blue collarless scrub as she leans left for the next bundle. The newborn's face is red.

"Now you," she says to it in a warm voice, unsmiling. She slides it along the counter toward her, plucks off its cap, unwraps its body, and leaves the blanket underneath. This baby is red all over. His tadpole belly is red; his scrotum, the size of a plum, is fiercely red, and looks as if it might explode. The top of his head looks like a dunce cap; he is a conehead. He gazes up attentively from the nurse's arms. The bright heat lamp does not seem to bother his eyes, nor do the silver nitrate eyedrops, which prevent gonorrhea.

His plastic ID bracelet, an inch wide, covers a full third of his forearm. Someone has taped his blue umbilical cord—the inch or so left of it—upward on his belly. A black clamp grips the cord's end, so it looks like a jumper cable.

The nurse washes this boy; she dips a thin washcloth again and again in warm water. She cleans his head and face, careful to wash every fold of his ears. She wipes white lines of crumbled vernix from folds in his groin and under his arms. She holds one wormy arm and one wormy leg to turn him over; then she cleans his dorsal side, and ends with his anus. She has washed and rinsed every bit of his red skin. The heat lamp has dried him already. The Qur'an says Allah created man from a clot. The red baby is a ball of blood Allah wetted and into which he blew. So does a clown inflate a few thin balloons and twist them lickety-split into a rabbit, a dog, a giraffe.

Nurse Pat Eisberg drains the sink. She drops the newborn's old blanket and hat into an open hamper, peels a new blanket and hat from the pile on the right, and sticks the red baby on the right-hand counter. She diapers him. She swaddles him: she folds the right corner of the blanket over him and rolls him back to tuck it under him; she brings up the bottom blanket corner over his chest; she wraps the left corner around and around, and his weight holds it tight as he lies on his back. Now he is tidy and compact, the size of a one-quarter Thermos. She caps his conehead, and gives the bundle a push to slide it down the counter to the end of the line with the others she has just washed.

The red newborn looks up and studies his surroundings, alert, seemingly pleased, and preternaturally calm as if enchanted.

"We move between two darknesses," E. M. Forster wrote. "The two entities who might enlighten us, the baby and the corpse, cannot do so."

How I love Leonardo da Vinci's earliest memory! "As I was in my cradle a kite came to me and opened my mouth with its tail and struck me several times with its tail inside my lips." The European kite, two feet long, has a deeply forked tail. Soaring like a swallow, it swoops hawklike to snatch reptiles; it also eats corpses.

Every few minutes another nurse comes in to pick up whichever washed baby has reached the head of the line. The nurse returns the parcel to its mother. When the red boy's number is up, I follow.

The mother is propped on a clean hospital bed. She looks a bit wan. When I was on the ward a few hours ago, I had heard her cry out, thinly, *aaaa!*—until the nurse shut the door. Now the mother is white as the sheets, in her thirties, puffy, pretty, and completely stunned. She accepts compliments on the baby with a lovely smile that costs her such effort it seems best not to address her further. She looks like the cartoon Road Runner who has just had a steamroller drive over it.

The skinny father is making faces at his son. He keeps checking his watch. "You are thirty minutes old," he tells him. The nurse has put the baby on his back in a bassinet cart. Americans place infants on their backs now—never on their stomachs, lest they smother in their sleep and die. Ten years ago, Americans placed infants on their stomachs—never on their backs, lest they choke in their sleep and die.

There are six of us in this room—the parents, the baby, two nurses, and I. Four of us cluster around the baby. The mother, across the room, faces ahead; her eyes are open and unmoving. Winter light pours through a big window beyond her bed. Everyone else is near the door, talking about the baby.

A nurse unwraps him. He does not like it; he hates being unwrapped. He is still red. His fingernail slivers are red, as if someone had painted nail polish on them. His toenails are red. The nurse shows the father how to swaddle him.

"You're forty minutes old," the father says, "and crying already?"

"*Aaaa,*" says the baby.

"I'd just as soon not go through that again, ever," says the mother to the air at large. Presently she adds that it was an easy labor, only twelve hours.

". . . and then you wrap the last corner tight around the whole works," the nurse says. As she finishes binding him into his proper Thermos shape, the baby closes his mouth, opens his eyes, and peers about like a sibyl. He looks into our faces. When he meets our eyes in turn, his father and I each say "Hi," involuntarily. In the nurses, this impulse has perhaps worn out.

A hole in the earth's crust releases clear water into the St. John's River of central Florida at the rate of one hundred million gallons a day. Saltwater issues from deep-sea mouths as very hot water and minerals. There iron and sulfur erupt into the sea from under the planet's crust, and there clays form black towers. In Safad, the kabbalist Isaac Luria began prayers by saying, "Open thou my lips, O Lord, and my mouth shall show forth thy praise."

I visit neonatal intensive care. A nurse lifts a baby from a clear plastic isolette. She seats the tiny girl on her lap and feeds her. This baby needs only an ounce more weight to go home. I watch her drain a little milk bottle, three ounces' worth. She sucks it down in a twinkling. "Did you ever taste that stuff?" one nurse asks another. "Isn't it awful?" he says. "Bitter. I don't know what they put in it."

The male nurse is holding a boarder baby—a baby whose mother abandoned it in the hospital, saying she would be back.

Social workers try to track down such women, who often leave false addresses. This boarder baby is a boy the nurses call Billy. Billy has lived here for two weeks; his fifteen-year-old mother visited him once, early, and never returned. Unlike many boarder babies, Billy is free of fetal alcohol syndrome; he is a healthy, easygoing redhead. Every nurse totes Billy around whenever possible, and the male nurse is now holding him up to his shoulder as he hurries from room to room, fetching and carrying. Billy is awake, looking over that shoulder at the swirling scene. His eyebrows have not yet come in, but I can see the fine furrows where they will sprout. He will soon join a foster family. The nurses will not let me hold anyone.

Outside the viewing window, a black woman in her fifties is waving, and with her a white woman in her twenties is jumping up and down. They are trying to attract the attention of what looks to be a baked potato but is in fact a baby wrapped in aluminum foil. This baked potato weighs three pounds, a nurse tells me; his body is a compressed handful. The aluminum foil is "to keep the heat in." Intravenous feeding lines, a ventilator tube, and two heart monitor wires extend into the aluminum foil. He is doing well.

Above this baby a TV screen hooked to his monitors traces their findings in numbers. The nurses read these numbers once a minute.

Behind the window, in the hall, the black woman, dressed to the nines, has been reduced to pointing and exclaiming. The jumping white woman, wearing jeans, has been reduced to waving. After all, the baby is plainly asleep. The nurse reaches into the isolette and lifts the baby—and foil, wiring, tubes—to display him to his visitors. She pushes his knitted cap back, so a bit more of his face shows. His face is the size of a squash ball. Both visitors tilt their heads to match his angle. Just above the nurse's head, four Mylar balloons strain against the ribbons tied to the isolette:

"It's a boy!" the balloons say. There on a shelf with syringes and thermometers is a carton of Reynolds Wrap.

The sculptor Alberto Giacometti said, "The more I work, the more I see things differently, that is, everything gains in grandeur every day, becomes more and more unknown, more and more beautiful. The closer I come, the grander it is, the more remote it is."

Generations of physicians have, in their witty way, given jocular names to our defects. Happy-puppet syndrome produces severely mentally retarded adults who jerk and laugh. "The laughter," admonishes the physician, "is not apparently associated with happiness."

Whistling-face syndrome, leopard syndrome, and *cri-du-chat* syndrome are terms to vivify diagnosis. Whistling-face people are, fortunately, rare: Their faces are thickened masks. Their eyes cross and roll up; their mouths and chins pucker. Leopard-syndrome people grow dark spots; their sharp ears protrude. The *cri-du-chat* babies, mentally deficient, mew. Leprechaunism babies suffer a metabolic defect. Wrinkled and tiny as leprechauns, they have big lips, big ears, and appealing full heads of hair. They fail to thrive, and die.

In sirenomelia sequence, the infant, usually stillborn, looks (to a delivery room wag, and then only somewhat) like a mermaid. That is, the sirenomelia infant has only one leg, the knee and foot of which point backward, so that if these people lived to hop around—which they do not—they would never see which way they were going. Isn't this kind of fun, once you get used to it? No. Outstandingly no fun are the dying or dead infants who look like frogs—no eyelids, gaping mouths, scaling skin. "Consanguinity," the text notes of their etiology: incest produced them.

Many damaged infants die in a few days or weeks. The majority of those who live are mentally deficient. In *Smith's Recognizable Patterns of Human Malformation,* the infants' visible anomalies—their crushed or pulled faces, their snarled limbs and wild eyes—signal, or rather express in skin and bones, their bollixed brains.

Here they are, page after page, black-and-white photographs, frontal and profile, of infants and children and adults at every age, naked or wearing briefs. The photographer stands these people, if they can stand, against a wall. A black-and-white grid marks squares on the wall, so we can see how off plumb their bodies are.

From Degas's notebooks: "There are, naturally, feelings that one cannot render."

Turn the page. Here she is. Of the thousand or so photographs in this book, this one most terrifies me. She is an ebulliently happy and pretty little girl. She is wearing a pair of cotton underpants. She has dark hair, bangs, and two wavy ponytails tied with yarn bows. Sure of her charm, she smiles directly at the camera; her young face shines with confidence and pleasure: Am I not cute? She is indeed cute. She is three. She has raised her arms at the elbows as if approaching the photographer for a hug. Actually, a physician has likely asked her to raise her arms to display them. Symptomatically, she cannot straighten her elbows; no one who suffers femoral hypoplasia—short legs—can. Her legs are pathologically short. (A photograph of an infant victim of this disorder shows feet sticking directly from loins and diaper.) If this child lowered her arms, her hands would extend well below her knees. No plastic surgery could help. Intelligence: normal. She is, in the photograph, delighted with her world and herself. Someone brushes her hair. Someone ties her hair bows. Someone adores her, and why not? "Someone loves us all," Elizabeth Bishop wrote.

On the facing page stands another short-legged kid, a crooked boy who is five. His malformed legs are short as fists—so short that his fingers, could he extend his elbows, would graze his ankles. His body is otherwise fine. He can grow up and have children. He has a handsome young face, this boy; he stands naked against the black-and-white grid wall. He looks grim. He tilts his head down and looks up at the camera. His eyes accuse, his brows defy, his mouth mourns.

The confident girl and the sorrowing boy, facing each other on opposite pages, make it appear as if, at some time between the ages of three and five, these kids catch on. Their legs are short, and it is going to be more of a problem than buying clothes.

"Rise at midnight," said a Hasid master, "and weep for your sins." But we have said that all nature disregards our sins. Our sins have nothing to do with our physical fates. When you shell peas, you notice that defective germ plasm shrivels one pea in almost every pod. I ain't so pretty myself.

This hospital, like every other, is a hole in the universe through which holiness issues in blasts. It blows both ways, in and out of time. On wards above and below me, men and women are dying. Their hearts seize, give out, or clatter, their kidneys fail, their lungs harden or drown, their brains clog or jam and die for blood. Their awarenesses lower like lamp wicks. Off they go, these many great and beloved people, as death subtracts them one by one from the living—about 164,300 of them a day worldwide, and 6,000 a day in the United States—and the hospitals shunt their bodies away. Simultaneously, here they come, these many new people, for now absurdly alike—about 10,000 of them a day in this country—as apparently shabby replacements.

At the sink in the maternity ward, nurse Pat Eisberg is unwrapping another package. This infant emerged into the world three weeks early; she is lavender, and goopy with yellow vernix, like a channel swimmer. As the washcloth rubs her, she pinks up. I cannot read her name. She is alert and silent. She looks about with apparent concentration; she pays great attention, and seems to have a raw drive to think.

She fixes on my eyes and, through them, studies me. I am not sure I can withstand such scrutiny, but I can, because she is just looking, purely looking, as if she were inspecting this world from a new angle. She is, perhaps for the first time, looking into eyes, but serenely, as if she does not mind whose eyes she meets. What does it matter, after all? It is life that glistens in her eyes; it is a calm consciousness that connects with volts the ocular nerves and working brain. She has a self, and she knows it; the red baby knew it too.

This alert baby's intensity appears hieratic; it recalls the extraordinary nature of this Formica room. Repetition is powerless before ecstasy, Martin Buber said. Now the newborn is studying the nurse—conferring, it seems, her consciousness upon the busy nurse as a general blessing. I want to walk around this aware baby in circles, as if she were the silver star's hole on the cave floor, or the Kaaba stone in Mecca, the wellspring of mystery itself, the black mute stone that requires men to ask, Why is there something here, instead of nothing? And why are we aware of this question—we people, particles going around and around this black stone? Why are we aware of it?

What use is material science as a philosophy or worldview if it cannot explain our intelligence and our consciousness? The paleontologist Teilhard de Chardin gave a lot of thought to this question. "I don't know why," he wrote disingenuously, "but geologists have considered every concentric layer forming the Earth except one: the layer of human thought." Since, as he said, "There is no thought but man's thought," how could we credit any philosophy that does not make man "the key of the universe"? A generation ago, biologists scorned this view as anthropocentrist. Today some dismiss it as "speciesist." For are we not evolved? And primates?

By this reasoning, somewhere around eleven thousand years ago, some clever hunting human primates—who made stone spears, drew pictures, and talked—had another idea. They knocked ripe seeds from transplanted wild barley or einkorn wheat and stored the seeds dry at their campsite in the Zagros Mountains. Since eating ground seeds kept the families alive when hunting failed, they settled there, planted more seed, hunkered down to wait its sprouting, and, what with one thing and another, shucks, here we be, I at my laptop computer, you with a magazine in your hands. We are just like squirrels, really, or, well, more like gibbons, but we happen to use tools, speak, and write; we blundered into art and science. We are one of those animals, the ones whose neocortexes swelled, who just happen to write encyclopedias and fly to the moon. Can anyone believe this?

Yes, because cultural evolution happens fast; it accelerates exponentially and, to put it less precisely, explodes. Biological evolution takes time, because it requires biological generations; the unit of reproduction is the mortal and replicating creature. Once the naked ape starts talking, however, "the unit of reproduction becomes"—in the words of anthropologist Gary Clevidence—"the mouth." Information and complexity burgeon and replicate so fast that the printing press arrives as almost an afterthought of our 10 billion brain neurons and their 60 trillion connections. Positivist science can, theoretically, account for the whole human show, even our 5.9 billion unique shades of consciousness, and our love for one another and for books.

Science could, I say, if it possessed all the data, describe the purely physical workings that have enabled our species to build and fly jets, write poems, encode data on silicon, and photograph Jupiter. But science has other fish to fry. Science (like philosophy) has bypassed this vast and abyssal fish of consciousness and culture. The data are tighter in other areas. Still, let us grant that our human world is a quirk of materials. Let us ignore the staggering truth that you hold in your hands an object of culture, one of many your gaze meets all around you. If, then, the human layer in which we spend our lives is an epiphenomenon in nature's mechanical doings, if science devotes scant attention to human culture, and if science has scrutinized human consciousness only recently and leaves other disciplines, if any, to study human thought—then science, which is, God knows, correct, nevertheless cannot address what interests us most: What are we doing here?

Teilhard's own notion, like the Hasids', moves top-down, and therefore lacks all respectability: No one can account for spirit by matter (hence science's reasonable stance), but one can indeed account for matter by spirit. Having started from spirit, from God, these and other unpopular thinkers have no real difficulty pinning down, or spinning out, or at least addressing, our role and raison d'être.

A standard caution forbids teaching Kabbalah to anyone under forty. Recently, an Ashkenazi Orthodox immigrant to Guatemala advised his adult, secular American grandson, "If you want to learn Kabbalah, lock yourself in a room with the Zohar and a pound of cocaine." This astounded the grandson and infuriated his father, the old immigrant's son.

When the high priest enters the Holy of Holies on the Day of Atonement, other men tie a rope to his leg, so that if he dies they can haul him out without going in themselves. So says the Zohar. For when the high priest recites the holy name and the blessing, the divine bends down and smites him.

Nurse Pat Eisberg, a small young woman, wears big green-and-white jogging shoes; the shoes nearly match in size the alert lavender baby. The baby, firm in the nurse's hands, turns her bottomless eyes slowly in every direction, as if she is memorizing the nurse, the light, the ceiling, me, and the sink. Pat Eisberg's fingertips are wrinkling in water. She washes the baby carefully, swaddles her, and slides her down the counter on the right.

When Krishna's mother looked inside his mouth, she saw in his throat the night sky filled with all the stars in the cosmos. She saw "the far corners of the sky, and the wind, and lightning, and the orb of the Earth . . . and she saw her own village and herself." Wordsworth's "trailing clouds of glory" refers to newborns; they trail clouds of glory as they come. These immediate newborns—those on the left counter, and those washed ones on the right—are keenly interested. None cries. They look about slowly, moving their eyes. They do not speak, as trees do not speak. They do seem wise, as though they understood that their new world, however strange, was only another shade in a streaming marvel they had known from the beginning.

The Talmud states that fetuses in the womb study Torah, and learn it by heart. They also see, moments before birth, all the mingled vastness of the universe, and its volumes of time, and its multitudes of peoples trampling the generations under. These unborn children are in a holy state. An angel comes to each one, however, just before he is born, and taps his lips so he forgets all he knows and joins the bewildered human race. "This 'forgetting' desanctifies him, of course," Lis Harris notes, so to "console" him, his "fellow fallible mortals" throw him a party.

In a few hours, this oracular newborn here in the hospital will lose her alertness. She will open her eyes infrequently. She will be quite obviously unable to focus. Her glee will come later, if she lives, and her love later still. For now, she will sleep and cry and suck and be wonderful enough.

The nurse wipes her forehead on a sleeve. The lights are hot. She reaches for another one.

"Now you," she says.

BRIAN DOYLE

Eating Dirt
from Orion

I have a small daughter and two smaller sons, twins. They are all three in our minuscule garden at the moment, my sons eating dirt as fast as they can get it off the planet and down their gullets. They are two years old, they were seized with dirt-fever an instant ago, and as admirably direct and forceful young men, quick to act, true sons of the West, they are going to *eat some dirt,* boy, and you'd better step aside.

My daughter and I step aside.

The boys are eating so much dirt so fast that much of it is missing their maws and sliding down their chicken chests. It is thick moist dirt, slightly more solid than liquid. I watch a handful as it travels toward the sun. It's rich brown stuff, almost black, crumbly. There are a couple of tiny pebbles, the thin lacy bones of a former leaf (hawthorn?), the end of a worm, the tiny green elbows of bean sprouts. I watch with interest as Son Two inserts the dirt, chews meditatively, emits the wriggling worm, stares at it—and eats it again.

"Dad, they're *eating the garden,*" says my daughter.

So they are. I'll stop them soon, but for this rare minute in life we are all absorbed by dirt, our faces to the ground, and I feel that there's something simple and true going on here, some lesson they should absorb, and so I let them absorb it. In spades.

Eventually my sons, filled with fill, turn their attentions to the other vigorous denizens of the garden: bamboo, beetles, black-

berry, carrots, dockweed, cedars, camellias, dandelions, garlic, hawthorn, jays, moles, shrews, slugs, snails, spiders, squirrels—all made
of dirt, directly or indirectly. As are mugs, vases, clothes, houses,
books, magazines. We breathe dirt suspended in the air, we crunch
it between our teeth on spinach leaves and fresh carrots, we wear it
in the lines of our hands and the folds of our faces, we catch it in
the linings of our noses and eyes and ears. We swim in an ocean of
dirt, yet we hardly ever consider it closely, except to plumb it for
its treasures, or furrow it for seed, or banish it from our persons,
clothes, houses.

I am hardly handy about the house and garden, and spend my
hours on other matters, but enough of me feels responsible for the
dirt that surrounds my home that I have often regretted the general abandonment of my garden, and felt a certain guilt that it is
not productive, that the land lies fallow. But now, cradling my
daughter, grinning at the mud monkeys, I see that the garden is *itself* hard at work, hatching honey ants and potato bugs, propelling
bamboo and beans into the air, serving as a grocery store for
shrews. I imagine it in one of those sped-up film clips, madly roiling with animals and plants, the sun and rain baking and ham-
mering it at a terrific pace, the banks of clouds sliding over like
vast battleships.

Such busy dirt.

The children tire, the sun retreats, in we go to baths and beds. I
wash the garden off my sons. It swirls down the bath-drain, into
the river, eventually to the ocean. So some of my garden ends up
as silt, some sinks to the ocean floor, some becomes kelp and sea
otters, some is drawn up again into rain; and maybe some returns
to the garden, after an unimaginable vacation.

My daughter and I discuss dirt journeys.

And when the rain begins that evening, the first of the rains
that define fall and winter here, she and I draw a map for our dirt,

so that it will know how to come home, and we leave the map on the back porch for the dirt to read.

"Maybe there are dirt fairies," says my daughter. "Or maybe the dirt can read. Who knows?"

Maybe my daughter is right about this. Maybe the dirt *can* read. Certainly, in a real sense, the dirt can write: Consider, for example, this essay, made by dirt worked in wondrous ways into bone, blood, protein, water, and a heartbeat. So grizzled dirt leans against a fence with lovely dirt in his lap, and watches dirt demons devour dirt, and the world spins in its miraculous mysterious circles, dust unto dust.

Such busy dirt, such a blizzard of blessings.

ANDRE DUBUS III

Fences & Fields
from Hope

For my daughter Ariadne, and in loving memory of my father, Andre Dubus.

It was a dry summer, and so hot it was a mistake to go barefoot on the sidewalk. When a rare breeze blew off the ocean, one or two miles east, we could hear the rattle of leaves in the tree branches, and smell the soft rubber and hot metal of cars in the street and driveway. Every Saturday I would drive to my father's house to cut his grass, but last summer I could wait three weeks or more before the yellowed lawn needed a trim. Joggers exercised only after dark. Dogs slept all day in the shade of maples and beech, or under parked cars I'd worry would drive over them the way I drove over my own dog, Dodo, when I was nineteen. At night we kept all our windows open and I put two fans in my son's room, one to suck hot air out the screen, the other directed at his crib, where he slept in only a diaper, his curly hair matted in wet ringlets to his temples and neck. In the other bedroom I lay alongside my wife, and waited for sleep with my hand on her swollen belly, the olive skin there stretched tight. Our second child's due date had come and gone two weeks earlier; my wife's mother and aunt had stayed with us then, but no contractions came, and my mother-in-law had to go back to work. So now we waited.

Those days I was doing carpentry work just two blocks from our house, building a gate and fence in a treeless yard. Between post holes, I had to dig a trench a foot deep, and by mid-morning I'd be wearing only shorts and boots, headband and bug spray, my torso slick with sweat, my hair as wet as if I'd just gotten cool. Every time I heard the ring of a phone coming from someone's house I would pause in my work and look up, and whenever a car drove slowly by, I'd wait for it to stop, expecting to see my lovely pregnant wife, her belly a full curved promise, come to tell me it was time.

One morning, as I was setting in my second post, holding my level to it, poised to kick more dirt into the hole once I'd found plumb, I heard breathing that wasn't my own and turned to see a little girl squinting up at me in the sunlight. She was thin, her pale arms and legs poking out of clothes that didn't match: a sleeveless green and yellow flowered shirt, faded pink shorts with white ruffles on the hem, red sneakers with no socks, and white ankles coated with dust from the street and dry back yards. Her hair was dusty too, and so straight and fine that her normal ears stuck out. I think I blurted out a startled hello but she just pointed to the four-foot level I was still holding to the post: "So what are you doing with *that?*"

"Trying to make the post straight up and down."

"I'll help you," she said, and kicked in some dirt before I was ready. It was after coffee break, the morning shade from the house gone now, and the cool dark soil I'd shoveled earlier was already dry and cracked and flaking under my boots. My headband was saturated, the sweat beginning to burn my eyes, and this trench was taking longer than I'd estimated; I was beginning to fear I'd given too low a price for the work. At home there was a whole new cycle of bills coming in and I still didn't have another job lined up after this one and I felt sure our new baby would come any minute. I wanted to get this fence done as soon as I could; I wanted this little girl to go play somewhere else.

I asked her not to kick in any dirt until I said to. She stood quickly, looked over the job site, then picked up the spade shovel, its handle twice as long as she was.

"Now?"

I found myself nodding and she squatted and scraped a small mound of dirt into the hole, the shovel knocking against the post. I pushed in more and tamped it with my boot. She dropped the shovel and began to stomp around the base of the four-by-four, her thin leg fitting all the way into the hole, her red sneaker leaving nothing more than light prints in the soil. But we got into a rhythm. We set that post, then another, and I knew the job wasn't going any faster with her, but not slower, either, and as we worked I asked her name and told her mine. I asked if she lived in one of the houses nearby, and did her parents know where she was.

"My mom thinks I'm at my friend's. I don't have a father, just a stepfather. Well, he's not really my stepfather, just my mother's boyfriend. They're gonna get married when they save enough money."

A jug of spring water sat near my tool bag and she walked over, uncapped it, and drank. The jug was half empty but she had to hold it with two hands and she spilled some water onto her flowered shirt. She put the cap back on, then left it leaning against the tools and hurried back to the new post hole. "I was *thirsty*."

I was holding the level to the four-by-four. I considered telling her it's polite to ask someone for a sip of their water before drinking it, but I was glad I'd had the water when she needed it, so let it go. "Do you ever see your father?"

"He died when I was little." She looked up at me and made a sad face, as if she were no longer sad but felt she still should be, that it wouldn't be right to say her father was dead without showing me her downturned lips.

"Do you remember him?"

Now she did look sad, her gray-blue eyes looking off into the dry brush at the yard's edge. "Know what I wish?"

"What?"

"That he was here and my mom was with *him* and she didn't even *know* her *boy*friend."

Something fell away inside me. I began to get an image I didn't want of this tiny girl lost under some man. I said her name and she looked at me, her eyes not quite seeing me.

"Does your mother's boyfriend treat you okay? Is he good to you?"

She shrugged her shoulders. "Nah, he doesn't even look at us." She began to kick more dirt into the post hole and I let out a breath.

"He doesn't?"

"He hardly remembers our *names.*"

A breeze picked up. It blew a feathering of sawdust into the trench. It cooled my back and legs. The girl's fine hair blew sideways in her face and as she worked she reached up with her finger and stuck a loose strand behind one ear. I guessed her to be eight or nine years old, but at that moment, pulling the hair from her face so she could keep working and not stop, her eyes on what she was doing but not really, she looked for a moment like every hard-time girl and woman I'd ever worked with in halfway houses and group homes and pre-parole. They were either lean and scrappy or else obese and resilient; they moved with intent or didn't move much at all, but smoked cigarette after cigarette, drank too much coffee or Diet Coke, talked too loud or kept silent—all of them, it seemed, doing essentially this: stomping dirt into a hole with a tiny red shoe, trying to cover and bury and hide their solitary hearts.

I called her name.

"What?" She pulled her leg out of the hole, picked up the too-long shovel, and began to push in more soil.

"Your dad will always be with you, you know."

She straightened and looked at me, the shovel hanging in her hands; her mouth hung partly open and in her eyes was a tentative light. I'd seen that look on my two-and-a-half-year-old son whenever I would try to explain away something common that frightened him, like a balloon or a clown's face; when each word I spoke was a step on the high wire over the valley of his normal fears and terrors. She blinked and looked at me harder, and for a second I was afraid my choice of words would be wrong, that I'd stumble and drop her into a worse place than she'd been before. But this doubt faded quickly; I began to imagine being dead, with my young child still on earth, and I felt sure I was telling her the absolute truth.

"Your father loves you too much to leave you alone. He'll watch over you your whole life."

"He will?" Now her eyes were bright and alert.

"Of course he will. He's probably watching over you right now."

"Can I *see* him?"

"Probably not."

She looked down at the shovel in her hands.

"But you might be able to feel him, sometimes." The breeze picked up again. It blew through the brush and high grass at the yard's edge. It began to dry the sweat on my neck and upper back. "Feel this wind? That could be him trying to cool you off."

She cocked her head at me, skeptical, standing as still as if her very body was in danger of plummeting into deep disappointment. I began to wish I'd kept quiet, once again in my life wrestling with the question of what true helping really was.

We continued working, the sun directly over us. The breeze died down, then blew in one last time. I felt a chill and knew it was sunburn. My post was leaning out of plumb and I put the level to it, then tamped the dirt at the base. She dropped the shovel for me to pick up and use, I thought, but as I reached for it I glanced at her and saw her standing there in the hot breeze, her eyes closed, her chin raised slightly, a solitary hair quivering against her cheek, her small dirty hands held up close to her chest.

We worked together until almost lunchtime. She abandoned the shovel and began to pull the dirt into the hole with her hands. The air was heavy and so hot my lungs felt tender. The girl's mother called her from the front stoop three doors down and out of sight. Her voice was shrill and coarse. From too much daily yelling, I imagined, too much alcohol and cigarette smoke, too much of some things and not enough of another, and I wanted to protect my young helper from it. She jerked at the sound, dropped the shovel, and without a word cut through the back yard the way she'd come, wiping her hands off on her pink shorts, leaving light footprints in the sawdust and dirt.

Soon after, I covered my tools with a tarp and walked home for lunch, and I think I knew then our second child would be a girl, that I would be the father of a son and a daughter. I think I made yet another silent prayer for our baby to be born safely, for my wife to come through it well, and if the baby was a *boy* to please not be hurt that I'd had the premonition of a girl. But as I walked down the shaded street, I began to sense deeply we *would* have a girl, and that loving a daughter would be different from loving a son, the way loving rivers is not the same as loving mountains, loving a half moon through the trees is different from loving the sun on your back.

And then she was born; early on an August afternoon when it was almost a hundred degrees and there was a full moon we couldn't see in the cloudless sky, she came. After twenty hours of labor there was the blinding light of the operating room, my exhausted wife's bright blood, our daughter coming headfirst out of the incision, her hazel eyes wide open and a nurse almost jumping back from the table. I held my tiny daughter and she cried and I cried and her valiant mother cried, lying on the table, the surgeons still working on her behind a raised blue sheet.

Later, as my wife began to recover in her room and our son played with his grandmother and aunts and our baby girl slept in the hospital nursery, a pink name tag attached to her clear plastic bassinet, I went outside into the heat with my brother and father. We drove to a package store, then to the river, two blocks from the hospital, its banks thick with trees. We sat in the shade at the edge of a jogging path, my father in his wheelchair, my brother and I sitting on a railroad tie. It was late afternoon and we were sweating under our clothes. A hundred yards away on the other side of the jogging path was a softball field, and people were playing, men and women, I think, though it could have been teenagers, their voices high with a winded purpose that sometimes sounded cruel to me. Already I wanted to keep that sound from ever entering my tiny daughter's ears, and her older brother's, too. We could see the bright sunlight on the water through the trees, and we drank beer and smoked our cigars. I began to speak, though I could not do it without crying, for the word *daughter* was ringing through my blood, her name already deep in my heart with her brother's, as if both had been there since my own delivery nearly thirty-six years earlier. With my son's birth, a love had opened up in me that forever left my small heart behind the way a flood scatters sandbags. And now the walls of my heart seemed to fall away completely and become a green field inside me. Through tears I told my father and brother how much I felt, and that even that faithless corner of my heart that worried about money, worried that once this fence job was through nothing would follow—even that part of me was assuaged. Because how can there be green fields inside us and no food on our tables?

My brother had a disposable camera and he was taking pictures of me, but I was seeing a picture of him, twenty-three years old, holding his blue-eyed baby boy, whispering to him, a mischievous and delighted smile on his son's face, playing imaginary games on the floor with him, eating cheese and crackers at the table, painting pictures, laughing, all before he had to drive him back home to his mother. I told my brother I loved him and grieved for his truncated fatherhood. I told him I knew his son would be in his life more fully one day, a presumptuous thing to say, and again I found myself on the verbal high wire over the depths of another's pain. But I was certain what I said was true, and as my brother, father, and I wept, I knew I would feel none of this certainty without my baby daughter and lovely son, without the horizonless love and attendant faith and hope that opens up in us when we are given the gift of children.

A woman jogged by, my age or older. Her T-shirt was wet with sweat, the wires of her bra were easy to see, and her hips wide beneath jogging shorts. I think she glanced in our direction as she passed, her flushed face a mask she'd chosen to give us—three men drinking and smoking in the mottled heat. It said: *I can take care of myself and I can outrun you and I will if I have to.* And I felt so keenly then that my new child was a female and not a male and I wanted to shield my daughter from all the forces that had ever put that look on that woman's face. I wanted to stand and say: "It's okay, we're *fathers.* We're *fathers!*" But I of course knew better; she could not see the green fields inside us—and how many fathers had torched their own fields and burned their children, leaving their own hearts nothing but ashen caves they continued to poke around in as if they were still living?

My beer can was empty. The sting of sweat was in my eyes, and I squinted out at the sun on the river through the tree trunks. I remembered last winter at a restaurant in Boston, a friend in his forties saying over a Thai dinner that he would never bring children into such a violent and ugly world. My wife was sitting pregnant beside me and he apologized, and his girlfriend, who is the mother of a twenty-year-old daughter, turned to him and said, "But you can't have a child without having hope, too. It comes with the birth."

I glanced over at my father. I am his second child of six, and he looked broad and handsome in the wheelchair that will be his legs the rest of his life. His forehead was beaded with sweat, his eyes ringed and moist. I saw pride and love in his eyes, pride and love for his two weeping sons. I believe he still grieves the three broken marriages behind him and knows the pain it caused us, his children, and he knows all too well the challenges facing our own young marriages. But sitting there then, his beard gray and white, I saw only hope in his eyes, hope for all of us.

But hope is one-dimensional without resolve, and in the last few moments I'd been picturing my baby girl still alone in the hospital nursery, swaddled in her clear plastic bassinet, her mother recovering from surgery while her father smoked and drank down by the river. Yet, I knew I was doing far more than that; I was communing with my father and only brother; I was sinking back into the arms of all the manhood I would need and more; I was celebrating the historic and ephemeral moment of my daughter's birth that was already fading away and becoming something else, the first hours of her infancy. I stood, and as we drove the two blocks back to the hospital, our windows open, the hot August air blowing in our faces, I thought of that fatherless girl who started coming daily to the job site to work with me, her dirty ankles thin and bony, her fine hair clinging to her skull, her small face already beginning to take on the same mask as the woman jogger. And I imagined her father's spirit fighting deep sky and rains and wind to be her breeze in the heat of a small dirty yard; to hold her up-turned face in his airy hands, to gently thumb a strand of hair from her eye, her face—in that moment, as open and vulnerable as a newborn's; and I could hardly sit still. I wanted to be in the hospital nursery cradling my baby daughter in my arms, her entire body fitting from my elbow to palm; I wanted to smell her new skin and hair; I wanted to kiss her sleeping eyes and rock her and hold her to my chest, her tiny ear and cheek pressed to where she could feel the beating of her father's heart—my grateful, hopeful heart.

ALMA ROBERTS GIORDAN

What This Old Hand Knows

from America

My husband of fifty-five years kissed my hand. I withdrew it in embarrassment. After all, he was never that demonstrative even in our courting days. "It's not a very pretty hand," I explained, passing the fruit bowl. "To me it is," he insisted.

I looked at my hand with candor. No, it wasn't at all pretty. And yet, it was fair and good to me. Gratefully I examined its five practical digits. (Most of my peers always had graceful "piano fingers.") Slowly I began to appreciate what this hand had been able to accomplish in response to my lifetime demands. For all my deprecation it bore me no malice, not even a twinge in an over-burdened knuckle.

How many microcosmic worlds has it moved about, naked of glove, as it urged beauty and food from a cooperative earth? How many fragile seedlings has it encouraged to fruition? How many tears has it wiped away with balled fist, or offered a paper tissue to another? How many Band-Aids has it applied to generations of minor abrasions? Questions. Answers.

This square hand still wears a thin gold band between a tiny diamond and family ring. Its nails are short, with deep half-moons. Wrinkles, testaments of eighty years, characterize it, with a scattering of freckles and liver spots, along a network of prominent veins. It certainly is not a pretty hand. But it has served me well—turning pages, picking blueberries, tossing salad, braiding a child's hair. It is everything to the old cat, who eagerly awaits the food and drink I provide. It has combed burrs out of hunting dogs' tails and extended fingers to blue budgies for convenient perches. It has rescued turtles, crickets, sparrows, and garter snakes from dry wells.

For how many years has this hand and its mate mounted the keyboard of a trusty typewriter, pounding out letters that become words that eventually filled drawers with poems, essays, and stories without complaint as to the worth of such mileage? And this but one more facet of my old hand's dexterity.

And so I proclaim it a wondrous hand, such a miracle, as Walt Whitman and others have acknowledged. To have filtered sunlight, caught fireflies, tested daisies for "he-loves-me, he-loves-me-not," held buttercups under a child's chin, and triggered jewelweed seeds into tomorrow is no slight accomplishment for any member. To have mastered a tugging knife, then released it, is a great piece of work for so humble a servant. How dexterous you are, Hand, I tell it, to dial a phone, crack a nut, catch a ball, push a swing, sew a seam, turn a wheel, apply a brake, feel textures of flesh and fabric, and sign my name.

To have grasped other hands in greeting or prayer or farewell, waved loved ones off, smoothed a beloved husband's brow as he entered eternity: Blest have you been, old Hand. To have stroked a long-needled pine bough, held a lens over a moth's wing—such experiences should never be discounted. O good and faithful Hand, I repeat, let me remember the fine things you've done. Here's water, here's soap to wash away deeds less than noble. Luxuriate in its cleansing joy. Here's food to maneuver to mouth, to the flesh and blood of me, to achieve growth and fulfillment.

Here's a key to unlock the door, a shell to hold to an ear, sand to sift, kindling to lay on a fire, a small torch to carry. Here's a knob, a switch, a button, a zipper, a bell, a guitar with strings to twang.

Here's a nail to pound into a wall on which a memory may be hung in exultation, praise, and thanksgiving. O Hand, you truly are exceedingly beautiful and worthy of recognition. Bless the faithful heart of the spouse who also found you so, and kissed your telltale lifeline.

BERNIE GLASSMAN

My Wife Died Unexpectedly Last March

from Tikkun

My wife died unexpectedly last March.

We had just arrived in Santa Fe, New Mexico, to begin a new life. We had moved the hub of the Zen Peacemaker Order, which we had cofounded, to Santa Fe and bought an old house which needed lots of work. But it had a central courtyard, hacienda-style, and lots of room for our dogs and a big garden. Nestled in the shadows of the Sangre de Cristo Mountains, it was a perfect refuge for a couple planning to be on the road for much of the year.

We arrived on Monday and moved into our house on Tuesday. The following Sunday, as we were hanging pictures on the wall, Jishu complained of chest pains. She was hurried to the hospital, where the doctors verified that she had suffered a major heart attack. For the next four days she seemed to get stronger and better. But on Thursday night Jishu suffered a second heart attack, and she left this form of existence on Friday night, March 20th, the first day of spring, four days shy of her fifty-seventh birthday.

People ask me how I'm doing. It takes a while for me to reply, for it's hard to answer them in words. Finally I tell them I'm bearing witness.

But how do you feel, they ask me.

I'm raw, I tell them.

Do you feel sad?

I shake my head. Raw doesn't feel good or bad. Raw is the smell of lilacs by the back door, not six feet away from her relics on the mantel. Raw is listening to Mahler's Fourth Symphony or the songs of Sweet Honey in the Rock. Raw is reading the hundreds of letters that come in, watching television alone at night.

Raw is letting whatever happens happen, what arises, arise. Feelings, too: grief, pain, loss, a desire to disappear, even the desire to die. One feeling follows another, one sensation after the next. I just listen deeply, bear witness.

I do some work; it's very little in comparison to former days. I am careful about how much time I spend with students and associates, for I know how easy and comfortable it is to let that raw state slip and let myself be distracted by work and talk with well-meaning friends. So I, long accustomed to being on the road, have stayed home. There are only a few people around me.

I live in a house chosen by my wife, reflecting her tastes and wishes. My own choice would be a studio in New York City's Bowery, not a house in a canyon overlooking a river. Those were the things Jishu wanted, and Jishu is gone. So I live in her house—I call it Casa Jishu—and do the things she would have loved. I greet the dawn coming over the mountains, watch the hummingbirds, prune the lilac bushes. Each time I think of the smile on her face had she been here to do these things. Instead I do them, bearing witness to her presence and her absence.

How am I doing?

I'm bearing witness. And the state of bearing witness is the state of love.

MARY GORDON

Still Life
from Harper's Magazine

In the year 1908, Pierre Bonnard painted *The Bathroom* and my mother was born. The posture of the young woman in the painting is that of someone enraptured by the miracle of light. The light is filtered through the lace curtains, and its patterning is reflected in the water that fills the tub into which she is about to step. Even the floral spread on the divan from which she has just risen is an emblem of prosperity and joy. Bonnard is famous for painting bathing women; in all her life my mother has never taken a bath. At three, she was stricken with polio, and she never had the agility to get in or out of a bathtub. She told me that once, after I was born, my father tried to lift her into a bath, but it made them both too nervous.

Ninety years after the painting of *The Bathroom,* ten days before my mother's ninetieth birthday, I am looking at the works of Bonnard at the Museum of Modern Art, a show I've been waiting for with the excitement of a teenager waiting for a rock concert. I was not brought to museums as a child; going to museums wasn't, as my mother would have said, "the kind of thing we went in for." It is very possible that my mother has never been inside a museum in her life. As a family we were pious, talkative, and fond of stories and the law. Our preference was for the invisible.

I can no longer remember how looking at art became such a source of solace and refreshment for me. Art history wasn't anything I studied formally. I think I must have begun going to museums as a place to meet friends. However and wherever it happened, a fully realized painterly vision that testifies in its fullness to the goodness of life has become for me a repository of faith and hope, two of the three theological virtues I was brought up to believe were at the center of things. It is no accident, I suppose, though at the time I might have said it was, that I've arranged to meet two friends at the Bonnard show at the same time that I'm meant to phone the recreation therapist at my mother's nursing home to plan her birthday party. Fifteen minutes after I arrive, I'll have to leave the show. The therapist will be available only for a specific half hour; after that, she's leaving for vacation.

Am I purposely creating difficulties for myself, a situation of false conflict, so that I can be tested and emerge a hero? There is the chance that I will not be able to leave the dazzle of the first room, to resist the intoxication of these paintings, so absorbing, so saturating, so suggestive of a world of intense color, of prosperous involvement, of the flow of good life and good fortune. There's the chance that I will forget to call the therapist. I do not forget, but my experience of the first paintings is poisoned by the fear that I will.

My mother has no idea that her ninetieth birthday is coming up. She has no notion of the time of day, the day of the week, the season of the year, the year of the century. No notion of the approaching millennium. And no idea, any longer, who I am. Her forgetting of me happened just a few months ago, after I had been traveling for more than a month and hadn't been to see her. When I came back, she asked me if I were her niece. I said no, I was her daughter. "Does that mean I had you?" she asked. I said yes. "Where was I when I had you?" she asked me. I told her she was in a hospital in Far Rockaway, New York. "So much has happened to me in my life," she said. "You can't expect me to remember everything."

My mother has erased me from the book of the living. She is denying the significance of my birth. I do not take this personally. It is impossible for me to believe any longer that anything she says refers to me. As long as I remember this, I can still, sometimes, enjoy her company.

The day before I go to the Bonnard show, I visit my mother. It is not a good visit. It is one of her fearful days. I say I'll take her out to the roof garden for some air. She says, "But what if I fall off?" I bring her flowers, which I put in a vase near her bed. She says, "But what if they steal them or yell at me for having them?" She asks me thirty or more times if I know where I'm going as we wait for the elevator. When I say we'll go to the chapel in a little while, she asks if I think she'll get in trouble for going to the chapel outside the normal hours for Mass, and on a day that's not a Sunday or a holy day. She seems to believe me each time when I tell her that she won't fall off the roof, that no one will reprimand her or steal her flowers, that I know where I'm going, that she will not get in trouble for being in church and saying her prayers.

I have brought her a piece of banana cake and some cut-up watermelon. There are only three things to which my mother now responds: prayers, songs, and sweets. Usually, I sing to her as we eat cake and then I take her to the chapel, where we say a decade of the rosary. But today she is too cast down to sing, or pray, or even eat. There is no question of going out onto the roof. She just wants to go back to her room. She complains of being cold, though it is ninety-five degrees outside and the air conditioning is off. It is not a long visit. I bring her back to her floor after twenty minutes.

On my mother's floor in the nursing home, many people in wheelchairs spend most of their days in the hall. There is a man who is still attractive, though his face is sullen and his eyes are dull. Well, of course, I think, why wouldn't they be? He looks at me, and his dull eyes focus on my breasts in a way that is still predatory, despite his immobility. I take this as a sign of life. It's another thing I don't take personally. In fact, I want to encourage this sign of life. So I walk down the hall in an obviously sexual way. "*Putana!*" he screams out behind me. I believe that I deserve this; even though what I did was an error, a misreading, it was still, I understand now, wrong.

In front of the dayroom door sits a legless woman. Her hair is shoulder length, dyed a reddish color; her lips are painted red. The light blue and white nylon skirts of her dressing gown billow around her seat, and she looks like a doll sitting on a child's dresser or a child's crude drawing of a doll.

My mother was once a beautiful woman, but all her teeth are gone now. Toothless, no woman can be considered beautiful. Whenever I arrive, she is sitting at the table in the common dining room, her head in her hands, rocking. Medication has eased her anxiety, but nothing moves her from her stupor except occasional moments of fear, too deep for medication. This is a room that has no windows, that lets in no light, in which an overlarge TV is constantly blaring, sending images that no one looks at, where the floors are beige tiles, the walls cream colored at the bottom, papered halfway up with a pattern of nearly invisible grayish leaves. Many of the residents sit staring, slack jawed, openmouthed. I find it impossible to imagine what they might be looking at.

It is difficult to meet the eyes of these people; it is difficult to look at their faces. I wonder if Bonnard could do anything with this lightless room. If he could enter it, see in these suffering people, including my mother, especially my mother, only a series of shapes and forms, concentrate on the colors of their clothing (a red sweater here, a blue shirt there), transform the blaring images on the TV screen to a series of vivid rectangles, and, failing to differentiate, insisting on the falseness of distinctions, of an overly rigid individuality, saying that we must get over the idea that the features of the face are the important part—would he be able to create a scene of beauty from this scene, which is, to me, nearly unbearable? He once told friends that he had spent much of his life trying to understand the secret of white. How I envy him such a pure preoccupation, so removed from the inevitable degradations of human character and fate. So he could paint wilting flowers, overripe fruit, and make of them a richer kind of beauty, like the nearly deliquescing purple grapes, the visibly softening bananas, of *Bowl of Fruit*, 1933. "He let the flowers wilt and then he started painting; he said that way they would have more presence," his housekeeper once said.

The people in the dining room are wilting, they are decomposing, but I cannot perceive it as simply another form, simply another subject or observation. I cannot say there are no differences between them and young, healthy people, no greater or lesser beauty, as one could say of buds or wilting flowers, unripe fruit or fruit on the verge of rotting. It is impossible for me to say that what has happened to these people is not a slow disaster.

And how important is it that when we read or look at a painting we do not use our sense of smell? The smells of age and misery hang over the common room. Overcooked food, aging flesh. My mother is kept clean, but when I bend over to kiss her hair, it smells like an old woman's. And there is the residual smell of her incontinence. My mother wears diapers. A residual smell that is unpleasant even in children but in the old is not only a bad smell but a sign of shame, of punishment: a curse. I cannot experience it any other way. My mother's body is inexorably failing, but not fast enough. She is still more among the living than the dying, and I wonder, often, what might be the good of that.

I thought that the women in the Bonnard paintings would all be long dead. As it turns out, at least one is still alive.

It is the day of my mother's birthday. Two of my friends, Gary and Nola, have agreed to be with me for this day. They are both very good-looking people. They are both, in fact, beauties. Gary is a priest; in another age, he might be called my confessor, not that he has heard my confession in the sacramental sense but because he is someone to whom I could tell anything, with no shame. Nola was my prize student, then she worked as my assistant for four years. We are proud that we have transformed ourselves from teacher/student, employer/employee, into, simply, friends.

When I thank him for agreeing to come to my mother's party, Gary says, "This will be fun." "No it won't," I say, "it won't be fun at all." "Well, it will be something to be got through. Which is, in some ways, not so different from fun." "It is," I say, "it is." "No, not really. It isn't really," he says, and we both laugh.

Gary's mother is also in a nursing home, in St. Louis, Missouri, a city I have never visited. She accuses his father, who is devoted to her, who has been devoted for years, of the most flagrant infidelities. All he says in response is, "I didn't do that, I would never do that." When we speak about our mothers, of our mothers' fears and sadnesses, particularly about the shape his mother's rage has taken, Gary and I agree that if we could understand the mystery of sex and the mystery of our mothers' fates we would have penetrated to the heart of something quite essential. We very well know that we will not. This is very different from Bonnard's secret of white.

Gary's father visits his mother in the nursing home every day. The end of Marthe Bonnard's life was marked by a withdrawal into a depressed and increasingly phobic isolation, so that the shape of a large part of her husband's life was determined by her illness, finding places for her to take cures, and staying away from people whom she feared, who she thought were staring at her, laughing at her. In 1931, Bonnard wrote, "For quite some time now I have been living a very secluded life as Marthe has become completely antisocial [*Marthe étant devenue d'une sauvagerie complète*] and I am obliged to avoid all contact with other people. I have hopes though that this state of affairs will change for the better but it is rather painful."

Did this forced isolation, in fact, suit Bonnard very well; was it the excuse he could present to a sympathetic world so that he could have the solitude he needed for his work? What is the nature of the pain of which he spoke? What was the nature of her "*sauvagerie complète*"? In the painting in which he suggests Marthe's isolation, *The Vigil,* although she sits uncomfortably in her chair, in a room empty of people, alienated even from the furniture, unable to take comfort even from her dog, she appears still young, still attractive, still someone we want to look at. In fact, she was fifty-two, and someone whose misery, if we encountered it in person, might have caused us to avert our eyes.

I do not shape my life around my mother's needs or her condition. I try to visit her once a week, but sometimes I don't make it, sometimes it is two weeks, even three. If life is pressing on me, it is easy for me to put the visit off, because I don't know how much it means to her, and I know that she forgets I was there minutes after I have left, that she doesn't feel a difference between three hours and three weeks. If I believed that visiting my mother every day would give something important to my work, as the isolation required by Marthe Bonnard's illness gave something to her husband's, perhaps I would do it. But when I leave my mother, work is impossible for me; the rest of the afternoon is a struggle not to give in to a hopelessness that makes the creation of something made of words seem ridiculous, grotesque, a joke.

Two weeks before my mother's birthday, Gary celebrated the twenty-fifth anniversary of his ordination. His father couldn't be there; he wouldn't leave Gary's mother, even for a day. That was a grief for Gary, but most of the day was full of joy, a swelling of love, a church full of all the representatives of Gary's life—musicians, artists, dancers, writers, the bodybuilders he came to know at the gym where he works out, to whom he is an informal chaplain, as well as the parishioners he serves. The music was mostly provided by a gospel choir, who brought everyone to tears, and whose music blended perfectly with the parish choir's Gregorian chant, with which it alternated. It was a day of harmony, of perfect blending, but with high spots of color, like the paintings of Bonnard. I bought for the occasion a red silk dress with a fitted waist and an elaborate collar. I wore gold shoes. On the altar, flanked by red and white flowers in brass vases, I read the epistle of St. Paul to the Galatians, which assures that in Christ there is neither male nor female, slave nor free—a blurring of distinctions like the blurring of boundaries in Bonnard, where the edge of an arm melts into a tablecloth, a leg into the ceramic of a tub, flesh into water, the sun's light into the pink triangle of a crotch.

Nola has the long legs, slim hips, and small but feminine breasts of Marthe Bonnard. I know this because a certain part of our relationship centers around water. We swim together in the university pools; afterward we shower and take saunas. She has introduced me to a place where, three or four times a year, we treat ourselves to a day of luxury. A no-frills bath in the old style, a shvitz, a place where we sit in steam, in wet heat, in dry heat, in a room that sounds like something from the *Arabian Nights:* the Radiant Room. We spend hours naked among other naked women, women who walk unselfconsciously, women of all ages and all ranges of beauty, in a place where wetness is the rule, where a mist hangs over things, as in the bathrooms of Bonnard. The preponderance of bathing women in Bonnard's work has been explained by Marthe Bonnard's compulsive bathing. She sometimes bathed several times a day. This may have been part of a hygienic treatment connected to her tuberculosis. But whatever the cause, her husband used it triumphantly.

Nola has just come from a friend's wedding in Maine. She was seated at the reception next to a German student, who became besotted with her. He grabbed her head and tried to put his own head on her shoulder. "You must come and have a drink with me at my inn," he said to her. She refused.

"You weren't tempted by all that ardor?" I ask her.

"No," she says. "I saw he had no lightness, that there was no lightness to him or anything that he did."

Bonnard's paintings are full of light, but they are not exactly about lightness, and his touch is not light, except in the sense that the paint is applied thinly and wetly. But he is always present in his paintings, and his hand is always visible. He has not tried to efface himself; he has not tried to disappear.

When I walk into the dining room on the day of my mother's birthday, I see that she has already been served lunch. The staff has forgotten to hold it back, though I told them a week ago that I would be providing lunch. She hasn't touched anything on her tray except a piece of carrot cake, which she holds in her hands. The icing is smeared on her hands and face. I don't want my friends to see her smeared with icing, so I wet a paper towel and wipe her. This fills me with a terrible tenderness, recalling, as it does, a gesture I have performed for my children. If I can see her as a child, it is easy to feel only tenderness for her. Bonnard paints children most frequently in his earlier period, in the darker Vuillard-like paintings, in which it is his natal family that is invoked. In the brighter pictures, children do not take their place as representatives of the goodness of the world. That place is taken up by dogs. In the painting *Marthe and Her Dog,* Marthe and a dachshund greet each other ecstatically in the foreground. In the far background, faceless, and having no communication with the woman and her dog, children run, leaving lime-colored shadows on the yellow grass.

As I wipe my mother's face, I see that her skin is still beautiful. I hold her chin in my hand and kiss her forehead. I tell her it's her birthday, that she's ninety years old. "How did that happen?" she asks. "I can't understand how that could happen."

I have brought her a bouquet of crimson, yellow, and salmon pink snapdragons. She likes the flowers very much. She likes the name. "Snapdragons. It seems like an animal that's going to bite me. But it's not an animal, it's a plant. That's a funny thing."

One reason I bought the flowers is that the colors reminded me of Bonnard. I don't tell my mother that. Even if she still had her wits, I would not have mentioned it. Bonnard is not someone she would have heard of. She had no interest in painting.

I have bought food that I hope will please my mother, and that will be easy for her to eat: orzo salad with little pieces of crayfish cut into it, potato salad, small chunks of marinated tomatoes. I have bought paper plates with a rust-colored background, upon which are painted yellow and gold flowers and blue leaves. I deliberated over the color of the plastic knives, forks, and spoons and settled on dark blue, to match the leaves. I am trying to make an attractive arrangement of food and flowers, but it's not easy against the worn gray Formica of the table. I think of Bonnard's beautiful food, which always looks as if it would be warm to the touch. It is most often fruit, fruit that seems to be another vessel

of sunlight, as if pressing it to the roof of your mouth would release into your body a pure jet of sun. Bonnard's food is arranged
with the generous, voluptuous propriety I associate with the south
of France, though Bonnard moved often, dividing his time between the south and the north. He places his food in rooms or
gardens that themselves contribute to a sense of colorful plenitude. Yet it is very rare in Bonnard that more than one person is
with the food; none of the festal atmosphere of the Impression-
ists, none of Renoir's expansive party mood, enters the paintings
of Bonnard in which food is an important component. The beautiful colors of the food are what is important, not that the food is
part of an encounter with people who will eat it, speak of it, enjoy
one another's company.

Nola and Gary and I enjoy one another's company; I do not
know what my mother enjoys. Certainly, the colorful food—the
pink crayfish in the saffron-colored orzo, the red tomatoes, the
russet potatoes punctuated with the parsley's severe green—is not
a source of joy for her. Joy, if it is in the room, comes from the love
of friends, from human communion—usually absent in the paintings of Bonnard. I do not think, though, that my mother feels
part of this communion.

I talk about the food a bit to my mother, but she isn't much interested in descriptions of food. She never has been. She always
had contempt for people who talked about food, who recounted
memorable meals. She doesn't join us in saying the grace in which
Gary leads us. Nor does she join us in singing the songs that, two
weeks ago, she still was able to sing: "Sweet Rosie O'Grady,"
"Daisy Daisy," "When Irish Eyes Are Smiling." Nothing focuses
her attention until the cake, a cheesecake, which she picks up in
her hands and eats messily, greedily. I wonder if it is only the
prospect of eating sweets that keeps my mother alive.

When we are about to leave, I tell my mother that I'm going on vacation, that I won't see her for three weeks, that I am going to the sea. "How will I stand that, how will I stand that?" she says, but I know that a minute after I'm gone she'll forget I was there.

I have bought the catalogue of the exhibition, and when I leave my mother I go home and look at it for quite a long time. I read that Bonnard once said that "he liked to construct a painting around an empty space." A critic named Patrick Heron says that Bonnard knew "how to make a virtue of emptiness." Illustrating Bonnard's affinities with Mallarmé, Sarah Whitfield, the curator of the show, quotes a description of a water lily in one of Mallarmé's prose poems. The lily encloses "in the hollow whiteness a nothing, made of intact dreams, of a happiness which will not take place."

Much of my mother's life is made up of emptiness. She does, literally, nothing most of the day. For many hours she sits with her head in her hands, her eyes closed, rocking. She is not sleeping. I have no idea what she thinks about or if she thinks, if she's making images. Are images the outgrowth of memory? If they are, I don't know how my mother can be making images in her mind, since she has no memory. And, if her eyes are mostly closed, can she be making images of what is in front of her? The beige walls and linoleum, her compatriots with their withered faces, thin hair, toothless mouths, distorted bodies? The nurses and caretakers, perhaps? No, I don't think so. I think that my mother's life is mostly a blank, perhaps an empty screen occasionally impressed upon by shadows.

Sarah Whitfield says that in the center of many of Bonnard's pictures is a hole or a hollow: a tub, a bath, a basket, or a bowl. A hole or hollow that makes a place for a beautiful emptiness. Nola once described her mother's life as having graceful emptiness so that a whole day could be shaped around one action. We both admired that, so different from the frantic buzz that often characterizes our lives. I am afraid that the emptiness at the center of my mother's life is neither beautiful nor graceful but a blankness that has become obdurate, no longer malleable enough even to contain sadness. An emptiness that, unlike Bonnard's or Mallarmé's or Nola's mother's, really contains nothing. And there is nothing I can do about it. Nothing.

I don't know what that emptiness once contained, if it once held Mallarmé's intact dreams; dreams of happiness, which, for my mother, will not now be realized. Perhaps she is experiencing the "emptying out" of which the mystics speak, an emptying of the self in order to make a place for God. I don't know, since my mother does not use language to describe her mental state. I try to allow for the possibility that within my mother's emptiness there is a richness beyond language and beyond visual expression, a truth so profound that my mother is kept alive by it, and that she lives for it. To believe that, I must reject all the evidence of my senses, all the ways of knowing the world represented by the paintings of Bonnard.

Bonnard's mistress, Renée Monchaty, killed herself. There are many stories that surround the suicide. One is that she killed herself in the bath, a punitive homage to her lover's iconography. Another is that she took pills and covered herself with a blanket of lilacs. I also have heard that Marthe, after the painter finally married her, insisted that Bonnard destroy all the paintings he had done of Renée. I don't know if any of these stories is true, and I no longer remember where I heard them.

In one painting that survives, *Young Women in the Garden,* Renée is suffused in a yellow light that seems like a shower of undiluted sun; her blonde hair, the bowl of fruit, the undefined yet suggestively fecund floral background are all saturated with a yellowness, the distilled essence of youthful hope. Renée sits, her head resting against one hand, a half smile on her face, her light eyes catlike and ambiguous; she sits in a light-filled universe, in front of a table with a striped cloth, a bowl of apples, a dish of pears. In the margins, seen from the rear and only in profile, Marthe peers, eclipsed but omnipresent. I am thinking of this painting as I stand in the corner of the dining room, watching my mother from the side, like Marthe, the future wife. How can it be, I wonder, that Renée— who inhabited a world of yellow light, striped tablecloths, red and russet-colored fruit, a world in which all that is good about the physical presented itself in abundance—chose to end her life? While these old people, sitting in a windowless room with nothing to look at but the hysterically colored TV screen, their bodies failing, aching, how can it be that they are fighting so desperately for the very life that this woman, enveloped in such a varied richness, threw away? I am angry at Renée; she seems ungrateful. At the same time I do not understand why these people whom my mother sits among do not allow themselves to die. Renée had so much to live for, to live in, and chose not to live. What do they have to live for? I often ask myself of my mother and her companions. And yet they choose, with a terrible animal avidity, to continue to live.

In a 1941 letter to Bonnard, Matisse writes that "we must bless the luck that has allowed us, who are still here, to come this far. Rodin once said that a combination of extraordinary circumstances was needed for a man to live to seventy and to pursue with passion what he loves." And yet the last self-portraits painted by Bonnard in his seventies are as desolate as the monologues of Samuel Beckett. *Self-Portrait in the Bathroom Mirror* portrays a nearly featureless face, eyes that are more like sockets, a head that seems shamed by its own baldness, the defeatist's sloping shoulders, arms cut off before we can see hands. In the *Self-Portrait* of 1945, Bonnard's mouth is half open in a gesture of desolation; his eyes, miserable, are black holes, swallowing, rather than reflecting, light. At the end of his life, Bonnard was deeply dejected by the loss of Marthe, of his friends, by the hardship of the war, which he includes in one of his self-portraits by the presence of a blackout shade. Is it possible that, despite his portrayal of the joy and richness of the colors of this world, despite his mastery and his absorption in the process of seeing, despite his recognition and success, his last days were no more enviable than my mother's?

RON HANSEN

Stigmata
from Image

At sunrise on the feast of the Holy Cross in 1224, a full month into a retreat of prayer and harsh fasting, the forty-two-year-old Saint Francis of Assisi knelt outside his hut on Monte La Verna and fervently contemplated Christ's Crucifixion. We read in the *Fioretti,* which records his life and sayings, that Saint Francis became so inflamed with love that he felt wholly transformed into Jesus himself, whence he saw a seraph with six fiery wings in front of him, which bore the form of a man nailed to a cross. At first he felt fright, then joy at seeing the face of Christ, who seemed so familiar to him and kindly, but when he viewed the nails in his hands and feet, Saint Francis was filled with infinite sorrow and compassion. Christ talked to him for a good while, about what we aren't told, after which

> *this marvelous vision faded, leaving . . . in his body a wonderful image and imprint of the Passion of Christ. For in the hands and feet of Saint Francis forthwith began to appear the marks of the nails in the same manner as he had seen them in the body of Jesus crucified.*

At first he tried to hide the five painful wounds—for his side, too, was pierced—but with his habit stained with blood and his feet so injured he could do no more than hobble, he was soon found out by the other friars with him, and he finally allowed them to look with awe on the wounds in his hands, where on the back the flesh was raised and blackened in the form of the head of an iron spike, and in the torn palm the flesh looked like the point of a spike hammered flat.

We do not know, of course, if Saint Francis of Assisi was the first person to receive the stigmata—a Latin derivation of the Greek for tattoo, scar, or mark—but he is the first to have that gift of Christ's wounds inspected and chronicled. Hundreds would have a comparable experience through the next seven centuries, generally getting the stigmata while in ecstasy, but in oddly differing ways.

Often, for example, their heads would bleed as from the Crown of Thorns, or mean welts would stripe their backs as if they'd been lashed forty times as Jesus was. While in a trance, Elizabeth of Herkenrode, a Belgian Cistercian nun, would strike herself on the jaw and roughly yank at her habit as if she were being hauled like Jesus from the house of Annas to the house of Caiaphas, and on to the praetorium. A farm girl in Brittany displayed in the flesh of her breast the words "O crux ave" ("hail O cross"). Therese Neumann of Bavaria bled frighteningly from the eyes. She and many other stigmatics seem to have had fairly healthy lives without any food but the Holy Eucharist. Wounds to the hands and feet are formed like nail heads on occasion, but also can be holes that are big enough for an examiner to read the page of a book through them. In Louise Lateau of Belgium, Saint Gemma Galgani of Italy, and, in 1972, the eleven-year-old Cloretta Robinson, a Baptist, blood would ooze up in their palms while being observed by physicians, but when the blood was wiped away, no laceration would ever be found. A few have been bruised on their right or left shoulder as if from carrying a heavy Cross. And Christ's wound from the centurion's lance journeys in size and shape, between many ribs, and also from side to side.

Women are seven times more likely than men to get the stigmata, and those in religious orders far outnumber all others who have received it. Age seems not to matter: an eight-year-old French girl has been given the wounds, and so has a sixty-five-year-old Sicilian nun. Occurrences of it are far more prevalent in Europe, and in particular Italy, than in other countries, and Catholicism is so typical in the phenomena that a stigmatic of another faith—there have been more than a few—is a genuine surprise.

Occasionally the stories of stigmata only fill one with pity. We read of a Mrs. H., a psychiatric patient in Australia, who claimed visions of Mary and wept tears of blood, but took her own life in 1963. Or Herr M., a businessman near Hamburg, a nominal Protestant who never went to church and whose stigmata was accompanied by intense headaches, confusion, and loss of weight, vision, and hearing. Saint Maria Maddalena de' Pazzi, a headstrong Carmelite nun in the sixteenth century, would tear off her habit and flamboyantly embrace a statue of Jesus while crying out orgasmically, "O love, you are melting and dissolving my very being! You are consuming and killing me!" Aldous Huxley's history *The Devils of Loudun* relates the case of Soeur Jeanne des Anges, the prioress of an Ursuline convent, who, frustrated in love, exhibited a bloody cross on her forehead, was publicly exorcised, and then, obviously craving more fame, became a florid spectacle throughout France as she flaunted the names of Jesus and the saints written in blood on her hand. And the Inquisition declared that Sor Maria de la Visitacion faked her hand wounds with paint, having been induced to do so by two Dominican friars who wanted the "holy nun of Lisbon" to augur Hell for the King of Portugal unless he fulfilled their wishes.

Reviewing the Roman Catholic Church's hundreds of investigations of stigmata in our far more skeptical age, it's quite easy to find hoaxes, delusions, misinterpretations, and a host of theatrical, masochistic neurotics, or sincere people who have fallen prey to a forlorn and fraudulent piety. And it's a fact that only in a few instances has the Church ever ruled an occurrence of stigmata to be genuine, even then encouraging a variety of causes and extenuations, none of which have anything to do with the supernatural.

In Germany, in 1928, when the thirty-year-old Therese Neumann was attracting international attention with Christ's bloody wounds, with a lifelong fast that included no food beyond the Communion Host, and with visions in which she talked to Jesus in Aramaic, a language she could not have known, Doktor Alfred Lechler, a psychiatrist, took into his consultation a mentally ill twenty-six-year-old woman whom he called Elizabeth K. Working in his house as a maid, she was available for continual observation and hypnotic suggestion, and Lechler found it irresistible to try to have Elizabeth K. imitate Therese Neumann's feats. While she was in a trance, the psychiatrist told Elizabeth that nails were being hammered into her hands and feet, and the next day, he said, she manifested red and swollen abrasions. She was shown magazine photographs of blood welling from Therese's eyes, and within hours she was shedding blood-stained tears. Elizabeth K. even went without food for a week and, through Lechler's hypnosis, managed to gain weight.

Of course, the fact that functions and symptoms can be replicated does not mean they have fundamentally the same source, and there is a world of difference between the fraught and uneasy lives of psychotics like Mrs. H. and Elizabeth K. and the health and serenity of those stigmatics whose holiness was the conduit for wonders.

Look, for example, at the famous Italian mystic Francesco Forgione, who took the name Pio after entering the Capuchin order of the Franciscans at the age of fifteen. Ordained a priest in 1910

and forced to serve as a medical orderly during World War I, Padre Pio finally took up residence in the friary of Santa Maria delle Grazie in the village of San Giovanni Rotondo, on the Adriatic Sea. There, on September 20, 1918, he was sitting in choir making his post-Communion thanksgiving when he saw a heavenly light containing the form of Christ on the Cross. Shafts of flame from the Cross pierced his hands and feet, and, he wrote his father guardian, the Capuchin superior:

I was suddenly filled with great peace and abandonment which effaced everything else and caused a lull in the turmoil. All this happened in a flash. Meanwhile I saw before me a mysterious person . . . his hands and feet and side were dripping blood. The sight frightened me, and what I felt at that moment cannot be described. I thought I should die, and indeed I should have died if the Lord had not intervened and strengthened my heart, which was about to burst out of my chest.

The vision disappeared and I became aware that my own hands and feet and side were dripping blood. Imagine the agony I experienced and continue to experience almost every day. The heart wound bleeds continually, especially from Thursday evening until Saturday. Dear Father, I am dying of pain because of the wound and the resulting embarrassment. I am afraid I shall bleed to death if the Lord does not hear my heartfelt supplication to relieve me of this condition.

The afflictions never healed, were never infected, and Padre Pio was soon famous. Hundreds of the faithful would line up to have him hear their Confessions, or fill the pews for his Masses just to receive Communion from his bleeding and half-mittened hands. Eminent physicians confirmed the authenticity of his wounds, but a wary Pope Pius XI—acting on misinformation, he later

said—effectively imprisoned Padre Pio within the friary while the Church investigated the stigmata, a harassment that would continue off and on throughout his life. And his reputation only increased.

Whole books have been filled with tales of his holiness and miracles during the fifty years of his stigmata. Wild dogs were reported to visit the friary during his Mass, quietly listen to his voice, and at the *Ite, missa est,* trot away. Mass with him would last three or four hours, so often did he fall into ecstasy in it, and he heard the thoughts of his congregation, offering their fears and prayers with his own. A hefty man, Padre Pio's only food was a few vegetables and a pittance of fish at midday, no more than three hundred calories. To a friend he confessed that the excruciating pain he constantly felt was only magnified if he slept, and so instead of sleeping, he prayed. Many claimed he was favored with the odor of sanctity, and wherever he went one could smell the exquisite perfume of a spice like cumin.

His was a gruff saintliness: he scowled at idiocies, chided whiners, hated television, brusquely answered most questions before they were asked, hotly refused to forgive sins that he knew were already confessed and forgiven, foresaw the future, fought with demons, healed people through touch, through ghostly visitations, through their dreams.

A teenaged girl with one leg in a thigh-high cast was horrified to find that her toes had turned black. Doctors feared she'd gotten gangrene and would have to have the leg amputated. She appealed to Padre Pio for help and he touched the cast, and when the hospital removed the hard plaster in preparation for surgery, the doctors were shocked to see that the formerly injured leg was fully healed and more beautiful than the other.

A baby girl was born who was such a grotesque and twisted mass of flesh that doctors didn't know how to begin treating her.

Signora Roversi, the mother, took the infant to church and dumped her in Padre Pio's lap, firmly insisting she wouldn't leave until the child was cured. The girl grew up to be as supple and tall as an Amazon.

Humiliated on the field of battle, an Italian general was about to kill himself with his revolver when a friar suddenly appeared in his tent and shouted, "What on earth do you think you're doing?" The friar gently counseled him until the general agreed to live out his full life, but when the friar left, the general went out and up-braided his sentry for letting a priest get past him. And he was flabbergasted to hear than no one had gone in or out. Much later, of course, he would find out that the friar was Padre Pio.

A farmer in Padova, three hundred miles north of the friary, was ailing with occlusions to the blood vessels in his lungs that no medical treatment could cure. Realizing he was dying, the farmer prayed for intercession and was surprised by a friendly apparition of a bearded friar who laid his hand on the farmer's chest, smiled, and disappeared. Completely healed, but so embarrassed by the weird circumstances that he told no one but his mother about them, the farmer went to a lunch months later and was amazed to find hanging on the wall of the house a photograph of a friar he'd thought was imaginary. That night he journeyed south by train to San Giovanni Rotondo, to offer his gratitude to Padre Pio who, after hearing the farmer's sins in Confession, asked quite naturally, "And tell me, what about the lungs now? How are they?"

In World War II an American Army Air Corps squadron leader disobeyed the order to bomb San Giovanni Rotondo because he saw the gigantic form of a friar in the sky, fiercely diverting the aircraft, and was chagrined to have to write that in an official re-port. Worried that he'd lost his faculties, the pilot found out about Padre Pio through offhand inquiries, and after the war visited Santa Maria delle Grazie, becoming one of Pio's "children."

One night the friars were awakened by hundreds of voices happily cheering Padre Pio, but when they looked in the hallways, no one was there. A friend asked Pio about it later and was frankly told that those were the souls in purgatory thanking him for his prayers.

Often he blessed holy gifts and, in a country of faulty mail service, packages, but once, shouting in wild anger, he forced a man to open a beautifully wrapped box. The friar then flung out its contents of books, holy pictures, and rosaries until he found hidden in the bottom a handful of lottery tickets. Tearing them into confetti, he thundered to his flock, "Get out! Get out! Devils, all of you!"

Karol Wojtyla, the bishop of Krakow, visited the friary in 1962 and in a letter written in Latin later requested healing for a mother of six who was dying of cancer. Padre Pio wrote back, saying the mother was free of the illness and as a postscript noted that the Polish bishop would be the pontiff someday. Karol Wojtyla would be ordained Pope John Paul II in 1978, ten years after Padre Pio's death.

A friar companion said of Padre Pio:

He was living in another dimension, with one foot here and the other in the supernatural world. He maintained a perfect balance and never let you know what was going on. One day, in this very hall, a woman whose son had recently died came up to him. She said, "Padre, please tell me if my son is in heaven." And he flashed back, as sharp as ever, "Why, yes, I've just come from there myself, this very moment."

A fool once told the friar that his wounds were caused by focusing too much on Christ's Crucifixion. To which Padre Pio hotly suggested, "Go out in a field and stare at a bull and see if you grow horns."

Questions and requests of all kinds were brought to Padre Pio by the villagers of San Giovanni Rotondo: whether to buy a car, sell a home, change jobs, take as a husband this man, give away this favorite rosary. Will you heal my wife's tumor? Will you give my old mother just one more year? Won't you please make Papa quit the Communist Party? When will I fall in love?

Would he have become so famous, so necessary, were it not for his stigmata? Wasn't it a sign that attracted the faithful to him, who himself was a further sign of God's fatherly concern for the humblest things that trouble us?

In *Mariette in Ecstasy* I told the story of a passionate and attractive seventeen-year-old who joins the religious order of the Sisters of the Crucifixion in upstate New York in 1906. At Christmas, the postulant's older sister, the convent's prioress, dies of cancer, and soon after the funeral Mariette Baptiste is favored with Christ's wounds. An investigation is begun within the Convent of Our Lady of Sorrows to find out whether Mariette is the real thing, or a schemer full of trickery, or a madwoman confusing sexual yearning with religious ecstasy.

Mother Saint-Raphaël, the new prioress, is troubled by the stigmata not only because Mariette's fame is hurting the tranquillity of the cloister, but also because she can't understand why God would give Christ's wounds in such a way. Confronting the postulant in her infirmary bed, Mother Saint-Raphaël says, "I see no possible reasons for it."

> *"Is it so Mariette Baptiste will be praised and esteemed by the pious? Or is it so she shall be humiliated and jeered at by skeptics? Is it to honor religion or humble science? And what are*

these horrible wounds, really? A trick of anatomy, a bleeding challenge to medical diagnosis, a brief and baffling injury that hasn't yet, in six hundred years, changed our theology or our religious practices. Have you any idea how disruptive you've been? You are awakening hollow talk and half-formed opinions that have no place in our priory, and I have no idea why God would be doing this to us. To you. I do know that the things the villagers have been giving us have not helped us in our vow of poverty. And all the seeking people who have been showing up have not helped our rule of enclosure. And there are breaches to our vow of obedience whenever you become the topic."

She sees that the postulant is staring at her impassively, with a hint, even, of amusement. She says in a sterner way, "I flatter myself that I have been extremely tolerant and patient, thus far. I have done so out of respect for your late sister, and in sympathy for the torment you have in her loss. But I shall not suffer your confusions much longer. And so I pray, Mariette, that if it is in your power to stop this—as I presume it is—that you do indeed stop it." She pauses and then stands. "And if it is in your power to heal me of the hate and envy I have for you now, please do that as well."

If the fruits of stigmata are truly the esteem of the pious, the humiliation for the favored one, and hollow talk, confusion, hate, and envy, one may indeed wonder why God would grace the world with them. I do have some possible reasons for it. We are so far away from the Jesus of history that he can seem a fiction, a myth—the greatest story ever told, but no more. We have a hint of his reality, and the shame and agony of his Crucifixion, in those whom God has graced with stigmata. Conversions of life have come from them. We are taught the efficacy of prayer, the joy that can be found even in suffering, and the enormous, untapped powers of the human body and mind. That some who have been given stigmata are irreligious only confirms the fact that they are favors freely given, not earned. That such a high proportion of stigmatics are women may be God's way of illustrating the importance of women in Christ's ministry and of correcting the imbalance in holy scripture where a far higher proportion of men have their voices heard.

Cynics may find in stigmata only wish fulfillment, illness, or fakery, but the faithful ought to find in them vibrant and disturbing symbols of Christ's incarnation and his painful, redemptive death on the Cross.

I think of an English biochemist named Cecil who was in Italy when he fell asleep at the wheel of his car and woke up in a hospital, floating near death, his arms, legs, ribs, and skull fractured. A Franciscan friar walked into his room, forced him to confess his sins, gave him Communion and Last Rites, and went away. Like others, Cecil would find out the friar was Padre Pio, and he would visit Santa Maria delle Grazie, and while the old friar celebrated Mass, Cecil felt transported to Calvary, as if he were really present at the Crucifixion. "I was utterly overcome," the Englishman said.

> *Padre Pio made me visualize Christ's agony in the garden, with all its horror and revulsion. . . . He made me understand the extent of the pain and anguish, the price of sin and of saving souls. He showed me what the Crucifixion cost God—as far as any human being can grasp its magnitude.*

We cannot grasp that magnitude, so it may be that God on occasion grants us witnesses.

SEAMUS HEANEY

A New Work in the English Tongue
from The New Yorker

On first reading Ted Hughes's "Birthday Letters"

1

Post-this, post-that, post-the-other, yet in the end
Not past a thing. Not understanding or telling
Or forgiveness.
     But often past oneself,
Pounded like a shore by the roller griefs
In language that can still knock language sideways.

2

I read it quickly, then stood looking back
As if it were a bridge I had passed under—
The single span and bull's eye of the one
Over the railway lines at Anahorish—
So intimate in there, the tremor-drip
And cranial acoustic of the stone
With its arch-ear to the ground, a listening post
Open to the light, to the limen world
Of soul on its lonely path, the rails on either side
Shining in silence, the fretful part of me
Stepped in so deep in unshadowed apprehension
I felt like one come out of an upper room
To fret no more and walk abroad confirmed.

3

Passive suffering: who said it was disallowed
As a theme for poetry? Already in Beowulf
The dumbfounding of woe, the stunt and stress
Of hurt-in-hiding is the best of it—

As when King Hrethel's son accidentally kills
His older brother and snaps the grief-trap shut
On Hrethel himself, wronged father of the son
Struck down, constrained by love and blood
To seek redress from the son who had survived—

And the poet draws from his word-hoard a weird tale
Of a life and a love balked, which I reword here
Remembering night-tremors once on Dartmoor,
The power station wailing in its pit
Under the heath, as if we'd stepped from Devon
Into *King Lear,* and that king's breaking heart
And Cordelia's breaking silence called to you,
Chooser of poem light, ploughshare of fields unsunned.

4

"Imagine this pain: an old man
Lives to see his son's body
Swing on the gallows. He begins to keen
And weep for his boy, while the black raven
Gloats where he hangs: he can be of no help.
The wisdom of age is worthless to him.
Morning after morning he wakes to remember
That his child has gone; he has no interest

In living on until another heir
Is born in the hall, now that this boy
Has entered the door of death forever.
He gazes sorrowfully at his son's dwelling,
The banquet hall bereft of all delight,
The windswept hearthstone; the horsemen are sleeping,
The warriors under earth; what was is no more.
No tune from harp, no cheering in the yard.
Alone with his longing, he lies down on his bed
And sings a dirge, suddenly without joy
In his steadings and wide fields.
                                      Such were the woes
And griefs endured by that doomed lord
After Herebeard's death. The king was helpless
To set right the wrong committed . . . "

5

Soul has its scruples. Things not to be said.
Things for keeping, that can keep the small hours gaze
Open and steady. Things for the aye of God
And for poetry. Which is, as Milosz says,
"A dividend from ourselves," a tribute paid
By what we have been true to. A thing allowed.

EDWARD HIRSCH

Zora Neale Hurston
from DoubleTake

A lot of racial uplifters, "Negrotarians,"
have come to observe one of "The New Negros"
who was rocked in the cradle of Negroism,
talking about love, that universal subject
of speculation. Well, listen up, subject:
I'm here as the "Queen of the Niggerati,"
and I don't belong to the school of Negro-
hood sobbing for help from Negrotarians.

I'm black, but I'm not "tragically colored"
since I came up in Eatonville, a pure Negro
town without "helpful" southern white folks.
(We weren't the first all-black community—
we *were* the first "incorporated" community.)
I'm fortunate to have studied the folklore and folk-ways of the southern Negro,
crayoning in a book wonderfully colored.

At home I ate the steaming dish of love—
nourishing, plentiful, astoundingly hot.
I thrived on a diet of men and even women
swapping stories—or "lies"—on the porch
of a town store, which was the front porch
of the wide world to me, since those women

and men fed me something astoundingly hot—
spicy tales of life, lessons in love.

I fattened on folk-tales of Br'er Rabbit,
Br'er Fox, the Devil, Ole Massa and his wife
walking the earth just like the good Lord.
I should have learned one essential lesson
a little better, since it's the basic lesson
of human equality: when the good Lord
sanctifies the union of husband and wife,
it shouldn't be a marriage of a fox and a rabbit.

Tell that to my first husband who never
wanted me to have a headlong career—
can you imagine? He also taught me
that marriage itself does not make love
or even guarantee anything for lovers. . . .
The death of my romantic dream taught me
to become a woman and have a career:
some contracts may not last "forever."

But love when it starts over again
between equals, makes its own sense,
its blossoming trees and aromatic herbs;
it creates its own version of summertime,
an Eden beyond everything, even time,
where we are drenched in God's own herbs
and overwhelmed by the sweetest scents
of forgotten existence remembered again.

The fiend of Hell extends a special gift
to lovers—the slithering serpent of doubt.

I've eaten his apple more than just a few times
and it's bitter—I'd just throw it away.
Better to let old Venus have her own way
with you, taking her sweet southern time
to lead you to a Caribbean beyond doubt. . . .
Well, listen to me woofing about the gift.

Clothed in mystery henceforth and forever,
love ain't nothing but the easy-going
heart disease, nothing but the journey
to a country from which no one returns
the same. We're pilgrims taking turns
in the holy land, signed up for a journey
to the Mysteries. I, too, shall be going
on this pilgrimage, henceforth and forever.

PICO IYER

Why We Travel: A Love Affair with the World

from The Shambhala Sun

We travel, initially, to lose ourselves; and we travel, next, to find ourselves. We travel to open our hearts and eyes and learn more about the world than our newspapers will accommodate. We travel to bring what little we can, in our ignorance and knowledge, to those parts of the globe whose riches are differently dispersed. And we travel, in essence, to become young fools again—to slow time down and get taken in, and fall in love once more.

The beauty of this whole process was perhaps best described, before people even took to frequent flying, by George Santayana in his lapidary essay, "The Philosophy of Travel." We "need sometimes," the Harvard philosopher wrote, "to escape into open solitudes, into aimlessness, into the moral holiday of running some pure hazard, in order to sharpen the edge of life, to taste hardship, and to be compelled to work desperately for a moment at no matter what."

I like that stress on work, since never more than on the road are we shown how proportional our blessings are to the difficulty that precedes them; and I like that stress on a holiday that's "moral," since we fall into our ethical habits as easily as into our beds at night. Few of us ever forget the connection between "travel" and "travail," and I know that I travel in large part in search of hardship—both my own, which I want to feel, and others', which I need to see. Travel in that sense guides us towards a better balance of wisdom and compassion—of seeing the world clearly, and yet feeling it truly. For seeing without feeling can obviously be uncaring; while feeling without seeing can be blind.

Yet for me the first great joy of traveling is simply the luxury of leaving all my beliefs and certainties at home, and seeing everything I thought I knew in a different light, and from a crooked angle. In that regard, even a Kentucky Fried Chicken outlet (in Beijing) or a scratchy revival showing of *Wild Orchids* (on the Champs-Elysées) can be both novelty and revelation: in China, after all, people will pay a whole week's wages to eat with Colonel Sanders, and in Paris, Mickey Rourke is regarded as the greatest actor since Jerry Lewis. If a Mongolian restaurant seems exotic to us in Evanston, Illinois, it only follows that a McDonald's would seem equally exotic in Ulan Bator—or, at least, equally far from everything expected. Though it's fashionable nowadays to draw a distinction between the "tourist" and the "traveler," perhaps the real distinction lies between those who leave their assumptions at home and those who don't: among those who don't, a tourist is just someone who complains, "Nothing here is the way it is at home," while a traveler is one who grumbles, "Everything here is the same as it is in Cairo—or Cuzco, or Kathmandu." It's all very much the same.

But for the rest of us, the sovereign freedom of traveling comes from the fact that it whirls you around and turns you upside down, and stands everything you took for granted on its head: if a diploma can famously be a passport (to a journey through hard realism), a passport can be a diploma (for a crash course in cultural relativism). And the first lesson we learn on the road, whether we like it or not, is how provisional and provincial are the things we imagine to be universal. When you go to North Korea, for example, you really do feel as if you've landed on a different planet—and the North Koreans doubtless feel that they're being visited by an extraterrestrial, too (or else they simply assume that you, as they do, receive orders every morning from the Central Committee on what clothes to wear and what route to use when walking to work, and you, as they do, have loudspeakers in your bedroom broadcasting propaganda every morning at dawn, and you, as they do, have your radios fixed so as to receive only a single channel).

We travel, then, in part just to shake up our complacencies by seeing all the moral and political urgencies, the life-and-death dilemmas, that we seldom have to face at home. And we travel to fill in the gaps left by tomorrow's headlines: when you drive down the streets of Port-au-Prince, for example, where there is almost no paving and women relieve themselves next to mountains of trash, your notions of the Internet and a "one world order" grow usefully revised. Travel is the best way we have of rescuing the humanity of places, and saving them from abstraction and ideology.

And, in the process, we also get saved from abstraction ourselves, and come to see how much we can bring to the places we visit, and how much we can become a kind of carrier pigeon—an anti–Federal Express, if you like—in transporting back and forth what every culture needs. I find that I always take Michael Jordan posters to Kyoto, and bring woven ikebana baskets back to California; I invariably travel to Cuba with a suitcase piled high with bottles of Tylenol and bars of soap, and come back with one piled high with salsa tapes, and hopes, and letters to long-lost brothers. But more significantly, we carry values and beliefs and news to the places we go, and in many parts of the world, we become walking video screens and living newspapers, the only channels that can take people out of the censored limits of their homelands. In closed or impoverished places, like Pagan or Lhasa or Havana, we are the eyes and ears of the people we meet, their only contact with the world outside and, very often, the closest, quite literally, they will ever come to Michael Jackson or Bill Clinton. Not the least of the challenges of travel, therefore, is learning how to import—and export—dreams with tenderness.

By now all of us have heard (too often) the old Proust line about how the real voyage of discovery consists not in seeing new places but in seeing with new eyes. Yet one of the subtler beauties of travel is that it enables you to bring new eyes to the people you encounter. Thus even as holidays help you appreciate your own home more—not least by seeing it through a distant admirer's eyes—they help you bring newly appreciative—distant—eyes to the places you visit. You can teach them what they have to celebrate as much as you celebrate what they have to teach.

This, I think, is how tourism, which so obviously destroys cultures, can also resuscitate or revive them, how it has created new "traditional" dances in Bali, and caused craftsmen in India to pay new attention to their works. If the first thing we can bring the Cubans is a real and balanced sense of what contemporary America is like, the second—and perhaps more important—thing we can bring them is a fresh and renewed sense of how special are the warmth and beauty of their country, for those who can compare it with other places around the globe.

Thus travel spins us round in two ways at once: it shows us the sights and values and issues that we ordinarily might ignore; but it also, and more deeply, shows us all the parts of ourselves that might otherwise grow rusty. For in traveling to a truly foreign place, we inevitably travel to moods and states of mind and hidden inward passages that we'd otherwise seldom have cause to visit: on the most basic level, when I'm in Thailand, though a teetotaler who usually goes to bed at 9:00 P.M. each night, I stay up till dawn in the local bars; and in Tibet, though not a real Buddhist, I spend days on end in temples, listening to the chants of sutras. I go to Iceland to visit the lunar spaces within me, and, in the uncanny quietude and emptiness of that vast and treeless world, to tap parts of myself generally obscured by chatter and routine.

We travel, then, in search of both self and anonymity—and, of course, in finding the one we apprehend the other. Abroad, we are wonderfully free of caste and job and standing; we are, as Hazlitt puts it, just the "gentleman in the parlor," and people cannot put a name or tag to us. And precisely because we are clarified in this way, and freed of unessential labels, we have the opportunity to come into contact with more essential parts of ourselves (which may begin to explain why we may feel most alive when far from home).

Abroad is the place where we stay up late, follow impulse, and find ourselves as wide open as when we are in love. We live without a past or future, for a moment at least, and are ourselves up for grabs and open to interpretation. We even may become mysterious—to others, at first, and sometimes to ourselves—and, as no less a dignitary than Oliver Cromwell once noted, "A man never goes so far as when he does not know where he is going."

There are, of course, great dangers to this, as to every kind of freedom, but the great promise of it is that, traveling, we are born again, and able to return at moments to a younger and a more open kind of self. Traveling is a way to reverse time, to a small extent, and make a day last a year—or at least forty-five hours—and traveling is an easy way of surrounding ourselves, as in childhood, with what we cannot understand. Language facilitates this cracking open, for when we go to France, we often migrate to French, and the more childlike self, simple and polite, that speaking a foreign language educes. Even when I'm speaking pidgin English in Hanoi, I'm simplified in a positive way, and concerned not with expressing myself, but simply making sense.

So travel, for many of us, is a quest for not just the unknown, but the unknowing; I, at least, travel in search of an innocent eye that can return me to a more innocent self. I tend to believe more abroad than I do at home (which, though treacherous again, can at least help me to extend my vision), and I tend to be more easily excited abroad, and even kinder. And since no one I meet can "place" me—no one can fix me in my résumé—I can remake myself for better, as well as, of course, for worse (if travel is notoriously a cradle for false identities, it can also, at its best, be a crucible for truer ones). In this way, travel can be a kind of monasticism on the move: on the road, we often live more simply (even when staying in a luxury hotel), with no more possessions than we can carry, and surrendering ourselves to chance.

This is what Camus meant when he said that "what gives value to travel is fear"—disruption, in other words (or emancipation), from circumstance and all the habits behind which we hide. And that is why many of us travel not in search of answers, but of better questions. I, like many people, tend to ask questions of the places I visit, and relish most the ones that ask the most searching questions back of me: in Paraguay, for example, where one car in every two is stolen, and two-thirds of the goods on sale are smuggled, I have to rethink my every Californian assumption. And in Thailand, where many young women give up their bodies in order to protect their families—to become better Buddhists—I have to question my own too-ready judgments. "The ideal travel book," Christopher Isherwood once said, "should be perhaps a little like a crime story in which you're in search of something." And it's the best kind of something, I would add, if it's one that you can never quite find.

I remember, in fact, after my first trips to Southeast Asia more than a decade ago, how I would come back to my apartment in New York City and lie in my bed, kept up by something more than jet lag, playing back in my memory, over and over, all that I had experienced, and paging wistfully through my photographs and reading and rereading my diaries, as if to extract some mystery from them. Anyone witnessing this strange scene would have drawn the right conclusion: I was in love.

For if every true love affair can feel like a journey to a foreign country, where you can't quite speak the language, and you don't know where you're going, and you're pulled ever deeper into an inviting darkness, every trip to a foreign country can be a love affair, where you're left puzzling over who you are and whom you've fallen in with. All the great travel books are love stories, by some reckoning—from the *Odyssey* and the *Aeneid* to the *Divine Comedy* and the New Testament—and all good trips are, like love, about being carried out of yourself and deposited in the midst of terror and wonder.

And what this metaphor also brings home to us is that all travel is a two-way transaction, as we too easily forget, and if warfare is one model of the meeting of nations, romance is another. For what we all too often ignore when we go abroad is that we are objects of scrutiny as much as the people we scrutinize, and we are being consumed by the cultures we consume, as much on the road as when we are at home. At the very least, we are objects of speculation (and even desire) who can seem as exotic to the people around us as they do to us.

We are the comic props in Japanese home movies, the oddities in Maliese anecdotes, and the fall guys in Chinese jokes; we are the moving postcards or bizarre *objets trouvés* that villagers in Peru will later tell their friends about. If travel is about the meeting of realities, it is no less about the mating of illusions: you give me my dreamed-of vision of Tibet, and I'll give you your wished-for California. And in truth, many of us, even (or especially) the ones who are fleeing America abroad, will get taken, willy-nilly, as symbols of the American Dream. That, in fact, is perhaps the most central and most wrenching of the questions travel proposes to us:

how to respond to the dreams that people tender to you? Do you encourage their notions of a Land of Milk and Honey across the horizon, even if it is the same land you've abandoned? Or do you try to dampen their enthusiasm for a place that exists only in the mind? To quicken their dreams may, after all, be to matchmake them with an illusion; yet to dash them may be to strip them of the one possession that sustains them in adversity.

That whole complex interaction—not unlike the dilemmas we face with those we love (how do we balance truthfulness and tact?)—is partly the reason why so many of the great travel writers, by nature, are enthusiasts: not just Pierre Loti, who famously, infamously, fell in love wherever he alighted (an archetypal sailor leaving offspring in the form of Madame Butterfly myths), but also Henry Miller, or D. H. Lawrence, or Graham Greene, all of whom bore out the hidden truth that we are optimists abroad as readily as pessimists at home. None of them was by any means blind to the deficiencies of the places around them, but all, having chosen to go there, chose to find something to admire.

All, in that sense, believed in "being moved" as one of the points of taking trips, and "being transported" by private as well as public means; all saw that "ecstasy" ("ex-stasis") tells us that our highest moments come when we're not stationary, and that epiphany can follow movement as much as it precipitates it. I remember once asking the great travel writer Norman Lewis if he'd ever be interested in writing on apartheid South Africa. He looked at me astonished. "To write well about a thing," he said, "I've got to like it!"

At the same time, as all this is intrinsic to travel, from Ovid to O'Rourke, travel itself is changing as the world does and, with it, the mandate of the travel writer. It's not enough to go to the ends of the earth these days (not least because the ends of the earth are often coming to you); and where a writer like Jan Morris could, a few years ago, achieve something miraculous simply by voyaging to all the great cities of the globe, now anyone with a Visa card can do that. So where Morris, in effect, was chronicling the last days of Empire, a younger travel writer is in a better position to chart the first days of a new Empire, postnational, global, mobile, and yet as diligent as the Raj in transporting its props and its values around the world.

In the mid-nineteenth century, the British famously sent the Bible and Shakespeare and cricket round the world; now a more international kind of Empire is sending Madonna and the Simpsons and Brad Pitt. And the way in which each culture takes in this common pool of references tells you as much about them as their indigenous products might. Madonna in an Islamic country, after all, sounds radically different from Madonna in a Confucian one, and neither begins to mean the same as Madonna on East 14th Street. When you go to a McDonald's outlet in Kyoto, you will find Teriyaki McBurgers and Bacon Potato Pies. The place mats offer maps of the great temples of the city, and the posters all around broadcast the wonders of San Francisco. And—most crucial of all—the young people eating their Big Macs, with baseball caps worn backwards, and tight 501 jeans, are still utterly and inalienably Japanese in the way they move, they nod, they sip their Oolong Teas—and never to be mistaken for the patrons of a McDonald's outlet in Rio, or Morocco, or Managua. These days a whole new realm of exotica arises out of the way one culture colors and appropriates the products of another.

The other factor complicating and exciting all of this is people, who are, more and more, themselves as many tongued and mongrel as cities like Sydney or Toronto or Hong Kong. I am, in many ways, an increasingly typical specimen, if only because I was born, as the son of Indian parents, in England, moved to America at seven, and cannot really call myself an Indian, an American, or an

Englishman. I was, in short, a traveler at birth, for whom even a visit to the candy store was a trip through a foreign world where no one I saw quite matched my parents' inheritance, or my own. And though some of this is involuntary and tragic—the number of refugees in the world, which came to just 2.5 million in 1970, is now at least 27.4 million—it does involve, for some of us, the chance to be transnational in a happier sense, able to adapt anywhere, used to being outsiders everywhere, and forced to fashion our own rigorous sense of home. (And if nowhere is quite home, we can be optimists everywhere.)

Besides, even those who don't move around the world find the world moving more and more around them. Walk just six blocks, in Queens or Berkeley, and you're traveling through several cultures in as many minutes; get into a cab outside the White House, and you're often in a piece of Addis Ababa. And technology, too, compounds this (sometimes deceptive) sense of availability, so that many people feel they can travel around the world without leaving the room—through cyberspace or CD-ROMs, videos and virtual travel. There are many challenges in this, of course, in what it says about essential notions of family and community and loyalty, and in the worry that air-conditioned, purely synthetic versions of places may replace the real thing—not to mention the fact that the world seems increasingly in flux, a moving target quicker than our notions of it. But there is, for the traveler at least, the sense that learning about home and learning about a foreign world can be one and the same thing.

All of us feel this from the cradle, and know, in some sense, that all the significant movement we ever take is internal. We travel when we see a movie, strike up a new friendship, get held up. Novels are often journeys as much as travel books are fictions; and though this has been true since at least as long ago as Sir John Mandeville's colorful fourteenth-century accounts of a Far East he'd never visited, it's an even more shadowy distinction now, as genre distinctions join other borders in collapsing. In Mary Morris's *House Arrest,* a thinly disguised account of Castro's Cuba, the novelist reiterates on the copyright page, "All dialogue is invented. Isabella, her family, the inhabitants and even la isla itself are creations of the author's imagination." On page 172, however, we read, "La isla, of course, does exist. Don't let anyone fool you about that. It just feels as if it doesn't. But it does." No wonder the travel writer narrator—a fictional construct (or not)?—confesses to devoting her travel magazine column to places that never existed. "Erewhon," after all, the undiscovered land in Samuel Butler's great travel novel, is just "nowhere" rearranged.

Travel, then, is a voyage into that famously subjective zone, the imagination, and what the traveler brings back is—and has to be—an ineffable compound of himself and the place, what's really there and what's only in him. Thus Bruce Chatwin's books seem to dance around the distinction between fact and fancy. V. S. Naipaul's last book, *A Way in the World,* was published as a nonfictional "series" in England and a "novel" over here. And when some of the stories in Paul Theroux's half-invented memoir, *My Other Life,* were published in *The New Yorker,* they were slyly categorized as "Fact and Fiction."

And since travel is, in a sense, about the conspiracy of perception and imagination, the two great travel writers, for me, to whom I constantly return, are Emerson and Thoreau (the one who famously advised that "traveling is a fool's paradise," and the other who "traveled a good deal in Concord"). Both of them insist on the fact that reality is our creation, and that we invent the places we see as much as we do the books that we read. What we find outside ourselves has to be inside ourselves for us to find it. Or, as Sir Thomas Browne sagely put it, "We carry within us the wonders we seek without us. There is Africa and her prodigies in us."

So, if more and more of us have to carry our sense of home inside us, we also—Emerson and Thoreau remind us—have to carry with us our sense of destination. The most valuable Pacifics we explore will always be the vast expanses within us, and the most important Northwest Crossings the thresholds we cross in the heart. The virtue of finding a gilded pavilion in Kyoto is that it allows you to take back a more lasting, private Golden Temple to your office in Rockefeller Center.

And even as the world seems to grow more exhausted, our travels do not, and some of the finest travel books in recent years have been those that undertake a parallel journey, matching the physical steps of a pilgrimage with the metaphysical steps of a questioning (as in Peter Matthiessen's great *Snow Leopard*), or chronicling a trip to the farthest reaches of human strangeness (as in Oliver Sacks's *The Island of the Colorblind,* which features a journey not just to a remote atoll in the Pacific, but to a realm where people actually see light differently). The most distant shores, we are constantly reminded, lie within the person asleep at our side.

So travel, at heart, is just a quick way of keeping our minds mobile and awake. As Santayana, the heir to Emerson and Thoreau, wrote, "There is wisdom in turning as often as possible from the familiar to the unfamiliar; it keeps the mind nimble; it kills prejudice, and it fosters humor." Romantic poets inaugurated an era of travel because they were the great apostles of open eyes. Buddhist monks are often vagabonds, in part because they believe in wakefulness. And if travel is like love, it is, in the end, mostly because it's a heightened state of awareness, in which we are mindful, receptive, undimmed by familiarity, and ready to be transformed. That is why the best trips, like the best love affairs, never really end.

Can You Say . . . "Hero"?
from Esquire

Once upon a time, a little boy loved a stuffed animal whose name was Old Rabbit. It was so old, in fact, that it was really an unstuffed animal; so old that even back then, with the little boy's brain still nice and fresh, he had no memory of it as "Young Rabbit," or even "Rabbit"; so old that Old Rabbit was barely a rabbit at all but rather a greasy hunk of skin without eyes and ears, with a single red stitch where its tongue used to be. The little boy didn't know why he loved Old Rabbit, he just did, and the night he threw it out the car window was the night he learned how to pray. He would grow up to become a great prayer, this little boy, but only intermittently, only fitfully, praying only when fear and desperation drove him to it, and the night he threw Old Rabbit into the darkness was the night that set the pattern, the night that taught him how. He prayed for Old Rabbit's safe return, and when, hours later, his mother and father came home with the filthy, precious strip of rabbity roadkill, he learned not only that prayers are sometimes answered but also the kind of severe effort they entail, the kind of endless frantic summoning. And so when he threw Old Rabbit out the car window the *next time,* it was gone for good.

You were a child once, too. That's what Mister Rogers said, that's what he wrote down, once upon a time, for the doctors. The doctors were ophthalmologists. An ophthalmologist is a doctor who takes care of the eyes. Sometimes, ophthalmologists have to take care of the eyes of children, and some children get very scared, because children know that their world disappears when their eyes close, and they can be afraid that the ophthalmologists will make their eyes close forever. The ophthalmologists did not want to scare children, so they asked Mister Rogers for help, and Mister Rogers agreed to write a chapter for a book the ophthalmologists were putting together—a chapter about what other ophthalmologists could do to calm the children who came to their offices. Because Mister Rogers is such a busy man, however, he could not write the chapter himself, and he asked a woman who worked for him to write it instead. She worked very hard at writing the chapter, until one day she showed what she had written to Mister Rogers, who read it and crossed it all out and wrote a sentence addressed directly to the doctors who would be reading it: "You were a child once, too."

And that's how the chapter began.

The old navy blue sports jacket comes off first, then the dress shoes, except that now there is not the famous sweater or the famous sneakers to replace them, and so after the shoes he's on to the dark socks, peeling them off and showing the blanched skin of his narrow feet. The tie is next, the scanty black batwing of a bow tie hand tied at his slender throat, and then the shirt, always white or light blue, whisked from his body button by button. He wears an undershirt, of course, but no matter—soon that's gone, too, as is the belt, as are the beige trousers, until his undershorts stand as the last impediment to his nakedness. They are boxers, egg colored, and to rid himself of them he bends at the waist, and stands on one leg, and hops, and lifts one knee toward his chest and then the other and then . . . Mister Rogers has no clothes on.

Nearly every morning of his life, Mister Rogers has gone swimming, and now, here he is, standing in a locker room, seventy years old and as white as the Easter Bunny, rimed with frost wherever he has hair, gnawed pink in the spots where his dry skin has gone to flaking, slightly wattled at the neck, slightly stooped at the shoulder, slightly sunken in the chest, slightly curvy at the hips, slightly pigeoned at the toes, slightly aswing at the fine bobbing nest of himself . . . and yet when he speaks, it is in *that* voice, *his* voice, the famous one, the unmistakable one, the televised one, the voice dressed in sweater and sneakers, the soft one, the reassuring one, the curious and expository one, the sly voice that sounds adult to the ears of children and childish to the ears of adults, and what he says, in the midst of all his bobbing nudity, is as understated as it is obvious: "Well, Tom, I guess you've already gotten a deeper glimpse into my daily routine than most people have."

Once upon a time, a long time ago, a man took off his jacket and put on a sweater. Then he took off his shoes and put on a pair of sneakers. His name was Fred Rogers. He was starting a television program, aimed at children, called *Mister Rogers' Neighborhood.* He had been on television before, but only as the voices and movements of puppets, on a program called *The Children's Corner.* Now he was stepping in front of the camera as Mister Rogers, and he wanted to do things right, and whatever he did right, he wanted to repeat. And so, once upon a time, Fred Rogers took off his jacket and put on a sweater his mother had made him, a cardigan with a zipper. Then he took off his shoes and put on a pair of navy blue canvas boating sneakers. He did the same thing the next day, and then the next . . . until he had done the same things, *those* things, 865 times, at the beginning of 865 television programs, over a span of thirty-one years. The first time I met Mister Rogers, he told me a story of how deeply his simple gestures had been felt, and received. He had just come back from visiting Koko, the gorilla who has learned—or who has been taught—American Sign

Language. Koko watches television. Koko watches *Mister Rogers' Neighborhood,* and when Mister Rogers, in his sweater and sneakers, entered the place where she lives, Koko immediately folded him in her long, black arms, as though he were a child, and then . . . "She took my *shoes* off, Tom," Mister Rogers said.

Koko was much bigger than Mister Rogers. She weighed 280 pounds, and Mister Rogers weighed 143. Koko weighed 280 pounds because she is a gorilla, and Mister Rogers weighed 143 pounds because he has weighed 143 pounds as long as he has been Mister Rogers, because once upon a time, around thirty-one years ago, Mister Rogers stepped on a scale, and the scale told him that Mister Rogers weighs 143 pounds. No, not that he *weighed* 143 pounds, but that he *weighs* 143 pounds. . . . And so, every day, Mister Rogers refuses to do anything that would make his weight change—he neither drinks, nor smokes, nor eats flesh of any kind, nor goes to bed late at night, nor sleeps late in the morning, nor even watches television—and every morning, when he swims, he steps on a scale in his bathing suit and his bathing cap and his goggles, and the scale tells him he weighs 143 pounds. This has happened so many times that Mister Rogers has come to see that number as a gift, as a destiny fulfilled, because, as he says, "the number 143 means 'I love you.' It takes one letter to say 'I' and four letters to say 'love' and three letters to say 'you.' One hundred and forty-three. 'I love you.' Isn't that wonderful?"

The first time I called Mister Rogers on the telephone, I woke him up from his nap. He takes a nap every day in the late afternoon—just as he wakes up every morning at five-thirty to read and study and write and pray for the legions who have requested his prayers; just as he goes to bed at nine-thirty at night and sleeps eight hours without interruption. On this afternoon, the end of a hot, yellow day in New York City, he was very tired, and when I asked if I could go to his apartment and see him, he paused for a moment and said shyly, "Well, Tom, I'm in my bathrobe, if you don't mind." I told him I didn't mind, and when, five minutes later, I took the elevator to his floor, well, sure enough, there was Mister Rogers, silver haired, standing in the golden door at the end of the hallway and wearing eyeglasses and suede moccasins with rawhide laces and a flimsy old blue and yellow bathrobe that revealed whatever part of his skinny white calves his dark blue dress socks didn't hide. "Welcome, Tom," he said with a slight bow, and bade me follow him inside, where he lay down—no, *stretched out,* as though he had known me all his life—on a couch upholstered with gold velveteen. He rested his head on a small pillow and kept his eyes closed while he explained that he had bought the apartment thirty years before for $11,000 and kept it for whenever he came to New York on business for the Neighborhood. I sat in an old armchair and looked around. The place was drab and dim, with the smell of stalled air and a stain of daguerreotype sunlight on its closed, slatted blinds, and Mister Rogers looked so at home in its gloomy familiarity that I thought he was going to fall back asleep when suddenly the phone rang, startling him. "Oh, hello, my dear," he said when he picked it up, and then he said that he had a visitor, someone who wanted to learn more about the Neighborhood. "Would you like to speak to him?" he asked, and then handed me the phone. "It's Joanne," he said. I took the phone and spoke to a woman—his wife, the mother of his two sons—whose voice was hearty and almost whooping in its forthrightness and who spoke to me as though she had known me for a long time and was making the effort to keep up the acquaintance. When I handed him back the phone, he said, "Bye, my dear," and hung up and curled on the couch like a cat, with his bare calves swirled underneath him and one of his hands gripping his ankle, so that he looked as languorous as an odalisque. There was an energy to him, however, a fearlessness, an unashamed insistence on intimacy, and though I tried to ask him questions about himself, he always turned the questions back on me, and when I finally got him to talk about the puppets that were the comfort of his lonely boyhood, he looked at me, his gray-blue eyes at once mild and steady, and asked, "What about you, Tom? Did you have any special friends growing up?"

"Special friends?"

"Yes," he said. "Maybe a puppet, or a special toy, or maybe just a stuffed animal you loved very much. Did you have a special friend like that, Tom?"

"Yes, Mister Rogers."

"Did your special friend have a name, Tom?"

"Yes, Mister Rogers. His name was Old Rabbit."

"Old Rabbit. Oh, and I'll bet the two of you were together since he was a very young rabbit. Would you like to tell me about Old Rabbit, Tom?"

And it was just about then, when I was spilling the beans about my special friend, that Mister Rogers rose from his corner of the couch and stood suddenly in front of me with a small black camera in hand. "Can I take your picture, Tom?" he asked. "I'd like to take your picture. I like to take pictures of all my new friends, so that I can show them to Joanne. . . ." And then, in the dark room, there was a wallop of white light, and Mister Rogers disappeared behind it.

Once upon a time, there was a boy who didn't like himself very much. It was not his fault. He was born with cerebral palsy. Cerebral palsy is something that happens to the brain. It means that you can think but sometimes can't walk, or even talk. This boy had a very bad case of cerebral palsy, and when he was still a little boy, some of the people entrusted to take care of him took advantage of him instead and did things to him that made him think that he was a very bad little boy, because only a bad little boy would have to live with the things he had to live with. In fact, when the little boy grew up to be a teenager, he would get so mad at himself that he would hit himself, hard, with his own fists and tell his mother, on the computer he used for a mouth, that he didn't want to live anymore, for he was sure that God didn't like what was inside him any more than he did. He had always loved Mister Rogers, though, and now, even when he was fourteen years old, he watched the Neighborhood whenever it was on, and the boy's mother sometimes thought that Mister Rogers was keeping her son alive. She and the boy lived together in a city in California, and although she wanted very much for her son to meet Mister Rogers, she knew that he was far too disabled to travel all the way to Pittsburgh, so she figured he would never meet his hero, until one day she learned through a special foundation designed to help children like her son that Mister Rogers was coming to California and that after he visited the gorilla named Koko, he was coming to meet her son.

At first, the boy was made very nervous by the thought that Mister Rogers was visiting him. He was so nervous, in fact, that when Mister Rogers did visit, he got mad at himself and began hating himself and hitting himself, and his mother had to take him to another room and talk to him. Mister Rogers didn't leave, though. He wanted something from the boy, and Mister Rogers never leaves when he wants something from somebody. He just waited patiently, and when the boy came back, Mister Rogers talked to him, and then he made his request. He said, "I would like you to do something for me. Would you do something for me?" On his computer, the boy answered yes, of course, he would do *anything* for Mister Rogers, so then Mister Rogers said, "I would like you to pray for me. Will you pray for me?" And now the boy didn't know how to respond. He was thunderstruck. Thunderstruck means that you can't talk, because something has happened that's as sudden and as miraculous and maybe as scary as a bolt of lightning, and all you can do is listen to the rumble. The boy was thunderstruck because nobody had ever *asked* him for something like that, ever. The boy had always been prayed *for.* The boy had always been the *object* of prayer, and now he was being asked to pray for Mister Rogers, and although at first he didn't know if he could do it, he said he would, he said he'd try, and ever since then he keeps Mister Rogers in his prayers and doesn't talk about wanting to die anymore, because he figures Mister Rogers is close to God, and if Mister Rogers likes him, that must mean God likes him, too.

As for Mister Rogers himself . . . well, he doesn't look at the story in the same way that the boy did or that I did. In fact, when Mister Rogers first told me the story, I complimented him on being so smart—for knowing that asking the boy for his prayers would make the boy feel better about himself—and Mister Rogers responded by looking at me at first with puzzlement and then with surprise. "Oh, heavens no, Tom! I didn't ask him for his prayers for *him;* I asked for *me.* I asked him because I think that anyone who has gone through challenges like that must be very close to God. I asked him because *I* wanted his *intercession.*"

On December 1, 1997—oh, heck, once upon a time—a boy, no longer little, told his friends to watch out, that he was going to do something "really big" the next day at school, and the next day at school he took his gun and his ammo and his earplugs and shot eight classmates who had clustered for a prayer meeting. Three died, and they were still children, almost. The shootings took place in West Paducah, Kentucky, and when Mister Rogers heard about them, he said, "Oh, wouldn't the world be a different place if he had said, 'I'm going to do something really *little* tomorrow,' " and he decided to dedicate a week of the Neighborhood to the theme "Little and Big." He wanted to tell children that what starts out little can sometimes *become* big, and so they could devote themselves to little dreams without feeling bad about them. But how could Mister Rogers *show* little becoming big, and vice versa? That was a challenge. He couldn't just say it, the way he could always just say to the children who watch his program that they are special to him, or even sing it, the way he could always just sing "It's You I Like" and "Everybody's Fancy" and "It's Such a Good Feeling" and "Many Ways to Say I Love You" and "Sometimes People Are Good." No, he had to show it, he had to demonstrate it, and that's how Mister Rogers and the people who work for him eventually got the idea of coming to New York City to visit a woman named Maya Lin.

Maya Lin is a famous architect. Architects are people who create big things from the little designs they draw on pieces of paper. Most famous architects are famous for creating big famous buildings, but Maya Lin is more famous for creating big fancy things for people to look at, and in fact, when Mister Rogers had gone to her studio the day before, he looked at the pictures she had drawn of the clock that is now on the ceiling of a place in New York called Penn Station. A clock is a machine that tells people what time it is, but as Mister Rogers sat in the backseat of an old station wagon hired to take him from his apartment to Penn Station, he worried that Maya Lin's clock might be *too* fancy and that the children who watch the Neighborhood might not understand it. Mister Rogers always worries about things like that, because he always worries about children, and when his station wagon stopped in traffic next to a bus stop, he read aloud the advertisement of an airline trying to push its international service. "Hmmm," Mister

Rogers said, "*that's* a strange ad. 'Most people think of us as a great domestic airline. We *hate* that.' Hmmm. *Hate* is such a strong word to use so lightly. If they can hate something like that, you wonder how easy it would be for them to hate something more important." He was with his producer, Margy Whitmer. He had makeup on his face and a dollop of black dye combed into his silver hair. He was wearing beige pants, a blue dress shirt, a tie, dark socks, a pair of dark blue boating sneakers, and a purple, zippered cardigan. He looked very little in the backseat of the car. Then the car stopped on Thirty-fourth Street, in front of the escalators leading down to the station, and when the doors opened—

"Holy shit! It's Mister Fucking Rogers!"

—he turned into Mister Fucking Rogers. This was not a bad thing, however, because he was in New York, and in New York it's not an insult to be called Mister Fucking Anything. In fact, it's an honorific. An honorific is what people call you when they respect you, and the moment Mister Rogers got out of the car, people wouldn't stay the fuck away from him, they respected him so much. Oh, Margy Whitmer tried to keep people away from him, tried to tell people that if they gave her their names and addresses, Mister Rogers would send them an autographed picture, but every time she turned around, there was Mister Rogers putting his arms around someone, or wiping the tears off someone's cheek, or passing around the picture of someone's child, or getting on his knees to talk to a child. Margy couldn't stop them, and she couldn't stop him. "Oh, Mister Rogers, thank you for my childhood." "Oh, Mister Rogers, you're the father I never had." "Oh, Mister Rogers, would you please just hug me?" After a while, Margy just rolled her eyes and gave up, because it's always like this with Mister Rogers, because the thing that people don't understand about him is that he's *greedy* for this—greedy for the grace that people offer him. What is grace? He doesn't even know. He can't define it. This is a man who loves the simplifying force of definitions, and yet all he knows of grace is how he *gets it;* all he knows is that he gets it from God, through man. And so in Penn Station, where he was surrounded by men and women and children, he had this *power,* like a comic book superhero who absorbs the energy of others until he bursts out of his shirt.

"If Mister Fucking Rogers can tell me how to read that fucking clock, I'll watch his show every day for a fucking *year*"—that's what someone in the crowd said while watching Mister Rogers and Maya Lin crane their necks at Maya Lin's big fancy clock, but it didn't even matter whether Mister Rogers could read the clock or not, because every time he looked at it, with the television cameras on him, he leaned back from his waist and opened his mouth wide with astonishment, like someone trying to catch a peanut he had tossed into the air, until it became clear that Mister Rogers could show that he was astonished all *day* if he had to, or even forever, because Mister Rogers lives in a *state* of astonishment, and the astonishment he showed when he looked at the clock was the same astonishment he showed when people—absolute strangers—walked up to him and fed his hungry ear with their whispers, and he turned to me, with an open, abashed mouth, and said, "Oh, Tom, if you could only hear the stories I hear!"

Once upon a time, Mister Rogers went to New York City and got caught in the rain. He didn't have an umbrella, and he couldn't find a taxi, either, so he ducked with a friend into the subway and got on one of the trains. It was late in the day, and the train was crowded with children who were going home from school. Though of all races, the schoolchildren were mostly black and Latino, and they didn't even approach Mister Rogers and ask him for his autograph. They just sang. They sang, all at once, all together, the song he sings at the start of his program, "Won't You Be My Neighbor?" and turned the clattering train into a single soft, runaway choir.

He finds me, of course, at Penn Station. He finds me, because that's what Mister Rogers *does*—he looks, and then he finds. I'm standing against a wall, listening to a bunch of mooks from Long Island discuss the strange word—χάριζ—he has written down on each of the autographs he gave them. First mook: "He says it's the Greek word for grace." Second mook: "Huh. That's cool. I'm glad I know that. Now, what the fuck is grace?" First mook: "Looks like you're gonna have to break down and buy a dictionary." Second mook: "Fuck that. What I'm buying is a ticket to the fucking *Lotto.* I just met Mister Rogers—this is *definitely* my lucky day." I'm listening to these guys when, from thirty feet away, I notice Mister Rogers looking around for someone and know, immediately, that he is looking for me. He is on one knee in front of a little girl who is hoarding, in her arms, a small stuffed animal, sky blue, a bunny.

"Remind you of anyone, Tom?" he says when I approach the two of them. He is not speaking of the little girl.

"Yes, Mister Rogers."

"Looks a little bit like . . . *Old Rabbit,* doesn't it, Tom?"

"Yes, Mister Rogers."

"I thought so." Then he turns back to the little girl. "This man's name is Tom. When he was your age, he had a rabbit, too, and he loved it very much. Its name was Old Rabbit. What is yours named?"

The little girl eyes me suspiciously, and then Mister Rogers. She goes a little knock-kneed, directs a thumb toward her mouth. "Bunny Wunny," she says.

"Oh, that's a *nice* name," Mister Rogers says, and then goes to the Thirty-fourth Street escalator to climb it one last time for the cameras. When he reaches the street, he looks right at the lens, as he always does, and says, speaking of the Neighborhood, "Let's go back to my place," and then makes a right turn toward Seventh

Avenue, except that this time he just *keeps going,* and suddenly
Margy Whitmer is saying, "Where is Fred? Where is Fred?" and
Fred, he's a hundred yards away, in his sneakers and his purple
sweater, and the only thing anyone sees of him is his gray head
bobbing up and down amid all the other heads, the hundreds of
them, the thousands, the millions, disappearing into the city and
its swelter.

Once upon a time, a little boy with a big sword went into battle
against Mister Rogers. Or maybe, if the truth be told, Mister
Rogers went into battle against a little boy with a big sword, for
Mister Rogers didn't *like* the big sword. It was one of those swords
that really isn't a sword at all; it was a big plastic contraption with
lights and sound effects, and it was the kind of sword used in de-
fense of the universe by the heroes of the television shows that the
little boy liked to watch. The little boy with the big sword did not
watch Mister Rogers. In fact, the little boy with the big sword
didn't know who Mister Rogers *was,* and so when Mister Rogers
knelt down in front of him, the little boy with the big sword
looked past him and through him, and when Mister Rogers said,
"Oh, my, that's a big sword you have," the boy didn't answer, and
finally his mother got embarrassed and said, "Oh, honey, c'mon,
that's *Mister Rogers,*" and felt his head for fever. Of course, she
knew who Mister Rogers was, because she had grown up with
him, and she knew that he was good for her son, and so now, with
her little boy zombie eyed under his blond bangs, she apologized,
saying to Mister Rogers that she knew he was in a rush and that
she knew he was here in Penn Station taping his program and that
her son usually wasn't *like* this, he was probably just tired. . . . Except that Mister Rogers wasn't going anywhere. Yes, sure, he was
taping, and right there, in Penn Station in New York City, were
rings of other children wiggling in wait for him, but right now his
patient gray eyes were fixed on the little boy with the big sword,

and so he stayed there, on one knee, until the little boy's eyes finally focused on Mister Rogers, and he said, "It's not a sword; it's a death ray." A death ray! Oh, honey, Mommy *knew* you could do it. . . . And so now, encouraged, Mommy said, "Do you want to give Mister Rogers a hug, honey?" But the boy was shaking his head no, and Mister Rogers was sneaking his face past the big sword and the armor of the little boy's eyes and whispering something in his ear—something that, while not changing his mind about the hug, made the little boy look at Mister Rogers in a new way, with the eyes of a child at last, and nod his head yes.

We were heading back to his apartment in a taxi when I asked him what he had said.

"Oh, I just knew that whenever you see a little boy carrying something like that, it means that he wants to show people that he's strong on the outside.

"I just wanted to let him know that he was strong on the inside, too.

"And so that's what I told him.

"I said, 'Do you know that you're strong on the inside, too?'

"Maybe it was something he needed to hear."

He was barely more than a boy himself when he learned what he would be fighting for, and fighting against, for the rest of his life. He was in college. He was a music major at a small school in Florida and planning to go to seminary upon graduation. His name was Fred Rogers. He came home to Latrobe, Pennsylvania, once upon a time, and his parents, because they were wealthy, had bought something new for the corner room of their big red brick house. It was a television. Fred turned it on, and, as he says now, with plaintive distaste, "there were people throwing *pies* at one another." He was the soft son of overprotective parents, but he believed, right then, that he was strong enough to enter into battle with *that*—that machine, that medium—and to wrestle with it until it yielded to him, until the ground touched by its blue shadow became hallowed and this thing called television came to be used "for the broadcasting of grace through the land." It would not be easy, no—for in order to win such a battle, he would have to forbid himself the privilege of *stopping,* and whatever he did right he would have to repeat, as though he were already living in eternity. And so it was that the puppets he employed on *The Children's Corner* would be the puppets he employed forty-four years later, and so it was that once he took off his jacket and his shoes . . . well, he was Mister Rogers for good. And even now, when he is producing only three weeks' worth of new programs a year, he still winds up agonizing—*agonizing*—about whether to announce his theme as "Little and Big" or "Big and Little" and still makes only two edits per televised minute, because he doesn't want his message to be determined by the cuts and splices in a piece of tape—to become, despite all his fierce coherence, "a message of fragmentation."

He is losing, of course. The revolution he started—a half hour a day, five days a week—it wasn't enough, it didn't *spread,* and so, forced to fight his battles alone, Mister Rogers is losing, as we all are losing. He is losing to it, to *our* twenty-four-hour-a-day pie fight, to the dizzying cut and the disorienting edit, to the message of fragmentation, to the flicker and pulse and shudder and strobe, to the constant, hivey drone of the electroculture . . . and yet still he fights, deathly afraid that the medium he chose is consuming the very things he tried to protect: childhood and silence. Yes, at seventy years old and 143 pounds, Mister Rogers still fights, and indeed, early this year, when television handed him its highest honor, he responded by telling television—gently, of course—to just *shut up* for once, and television listened. He had already won his third Daytime Emmy, and now he went onstage to accept Emmy's Lifetime Achievement Award, and there, in front of all the soap opera stars and talk show sinceratrons, in front of all the jutting man-tanned jaws and jutting saltwater bosoms, he made his small bow and said into the microphone, "All of us have special ones who have loved us into being. Would you just take, along with me, *ten seconds* to think of the people who have helped *you* become who you are. . . . Ten seconds of silence." And then he lifted his wrist, and looked at the audience, and looked at his watch, and said softly, "I'll watch the time," and there was, at first, a small whoop from the crowd, a giddy, strangled hiccup of laughter, as people realized that *he wasn't kidding,* that Mister Rogers was not some convenient eunuch but rather a *man,* an authority figure who actually expected them to do what he asked . . . and so they did. One second, two seconds, three seconds . . . and now the jaws clenched, and the bosoms heaved, and the mascara ran, and the tears fell upon the beglittered gathering like rain leaking down a crystal chandelier, and Mister Rogers finally looked up from his watch and said, "May God be with you" to all his vanquished children.

Once upon a time, there was a little boy born blind, and so, defenseless in the world, he suffered the abuses of the defenseless, and when he grew up and became a man, he looked back and realized that he'd had no childhood at all, and that if he were ever to have a childhood, he would have to start having it now, in his forties. So the first thing he did was rechristen himself "Joybubbles"; the second thing he did was declare himself five years old forever; and the third thing he did was make a pilgrimage to Pittsburgh, where the University of Pittsburgh's Information Sciences Library keeps a Mister Rogers archive. It has all 865 programs, in both color and black and white, and for two months this past spring, Joybubbles went to the library every day for ten hours and watched the Neighborhood's every episode, plus specials—or, since he is blind, *listened* to every episode, *imagined* every episode. Until one night, Mister Rogers came to him, in what he calls a visitation—"I was dreaming, but I was awake"—and offered to teach him how to pray.

"But Mister Rogers, I *can't* pray," Joybubbles said, "because every time I try to pray, I forget the words."

"I know that," Mister Rogers said, "and that's why the prayer I'm going to teach you has only three words."

"What prayer is that, Mister Rogers? What kind of prayer has only three words?"

"Thank you, God," Mister Rogers said.

The walls of Mister Rogers' Neighborhood are light blue and fleeced with clouds. They are tall—as tall as the cinder-block walls they are designed to hide—and they encompass the Neighborhood's entire stage set, from the flimsy yellow house where Mister Rogers comes to visit, to the closet where he finds his sweaters, to the Neighborhood of Make-Believe, where he goes to dream. The blue walls are the ends of the daylit universe he has made, and yet Mister Rogers can't *see* them—or at least can't know them—because he was born blind to color. He doesn't know the color of his walls, and one day, when I caught him looking toward his painted skies, I asked him to tell me what color they *are,* and he said, "I imagine they're *blue,* Tom." Then he looked at me and smiled. "I imagine they're blue."

He has spent thirty-one years imagining and reimagining those walls—the walls that have both penned him in and set him free. You would think it would be easy by now, being Mister Rogers; you would think that one morning he would wake up and think, Okay, all I have to do is be *nice* for my allotted half hour today, and then I'll just take the rest of the day off. . . . But no, Mister Rogers is a stubborn man, and so on the day I ask about the color

of his sky, he has already gotten up at five-thirty, already prayed
for those who have asked for his prayers, already read, already
written, already swum, already weighed himself, already sent out
cards for the birthdays he never forgets, already called any number
of people who depend on him for comfort, already cried when he
read the letter of a mother whose child was buried with a picture
of Mister Rogers in his casket, already played for twenty minutes
with an autistic boy who has come, with his father, all the way
from Boise, Idaho, to meet him. The boy had never spoken, until
one day he said, "X the Owl," which is the name of one of Mister
Rogers's puppets, and he had never looked his father in the eye
until one day his father had said, "Let's go to the Neighborhood of
Make-Believe," and now the boy is speaking and reading, and the
father has come to thank Mister Rogers for saving his son's
life. . . . And by this time, well, it's nine-thirty in the morning,
time for Mister Rogers to take off his jacket and his shoes and put
on his sweater and his sneakers and start taping another visit to
the Neighborhood. He writes all his own scripts, but on this day,
when he receives a visit from Mrs. McFeely and a springer spaniel,
she says that she has to bring the dog "back to his owner," and
Mister Rogers makes a face. The cameras stop, and he says, "I
don't like the word *owner* there. It's not a good word. Let's change
it to 'bring the dog *home.*'" And so the change is made, and the
taping resumes, and this is how it goes all day, a life unfolding
within a clasp of unfathomable governance, and once, when I lose
sight of him, I ask Margy Whitmer where he is, and she says,
"Right over your shoulder, where he always is," and when I turn
around, Mister Rogers is facing me, child-stealthy, with a small
black camera in his hand, to take another picture for the album
that he will give me when I take my leave of him.

Yes, it should be easy being Mister Rogers, but when four o'clock
rolls around, well, Mister Rogers is *tired,* and so he sneaks over to

the piano and starts playing, with dexterous, pale fingers, the music that used to end a 1940s newsreel and that has now become the music he plays to signal to the cast and crew that a day's taping has wrapped. On this day, however, he is premature by a considerable extent, and so Margy, who has been with Mister Rogers since 1983—because nobody who works for Mister Rogers ever *leaves* the Neighborhood—comes running over, papers in hand, and says, "Not so fast there, buster."

"Oh, please, sister," Mister Rogers says. "I'm done."

And now Margy comes up behind him and massages his shoulders. "No, you're not," she says. "*Roy* Rogers is done. *Mister* Rogers still has a ways to go."

He was a child once, too, and so one day I asked him if I could go with him back to Latrobe. He thought about it for a second, then said, by way of agreement, "Okay, then—tomorrow, Tom, I'll show you childhood." Not *his* childhood, mind you, or even *a* childhood—no, just "childhood." And so the next morning, we swam together, and then he put back on his boxer shorts and the dark socks, and the T-shirt, and the gray trousers, and the belt, and then the white dress shirt and the black bow tie and the gray suit jacket, and about two hours later we were pulling up to the big brick house on Weldon Street in Latrobe, and Mister Rogers was thinking about going inside.

There was nobody home. The doors were open, unlocked, because the house was undergoing a renovation of some kind, but the owners were away, and Mister Rogers's boyhood home was empty of everyone but workmen. "Do you think we can go in?" he asked Bill Isler, president of Family Communications, the company that produces *Mister Rogers' Neighborhood*. Bill had driven us there, and now, sitting behind the wheel of his red Grand Cherokee, he was full of remonstrance. "No!" he said. "Fred, they're *not home*. If we wanted to go into the house, we should have *called* first. Fred . . ." But Mister Rogers was out of the car, with his camera in his hand and his legs moving so fast that the material of his gray suit pants furled and unfurled around both of his skinny legs, like flags exploding in a breeze. And here, as he made his way through thickets of bewildered workmen—this skinny old man dressed in a gray suit and a bow tie, with his hands on his hips and his arms akimbo, like a dance instructor—there was some kind of wiggly jazz in his legs, and he went flying all around the outside of the house, pointing at windows, saying there was the room where he learned to play the piano, and there was the room where he saw the pie fight on a primitive television, and there was the room where his beloved father died . . . until finally we reached the front door. He put his hand on the knob; he cracked it open, but then, with Bill Isler calling caution from the car, he said, "Maybe we *shouldn't* go in. And all the people who made this house special to me are not here, anyway. They're all in heaven."

And so we went to the graveyard. We were heading there all along, because Mister Rogers *loves* graveyards, and so as we took the long, straight road out of sad, fading Latrobe, you could still feel the *speed* in him, the hurry, as he mustered up a sad anticipation, and when we passed through the cemetery gates, he smiled as he said to Bill Isler, "The plot's at the end of the yellow brick road." And so it was; the asphalt ended, and then we began bouncing over a road of old blond bricks, until even that road ended, and we were parked in front of the place where Mister Rogers is to be buried. He got out of the car, and, moving as quickly as he had moved to the door of his house, he stepped up a small hill to the door of a large gray mausoleum, a huge structure built for six, with a slightly peaked roof, and bronze doors, and angels living in the stained glass. He peeked in the window, and in the same voice he uses on television, *that* voice, at once so patient and so eager, he pointed out each crypt, saying, "There's my father, and there's my mother, and there, on the left, is my place, and right across will be Joanne. . . ." The window was of darkened glass, though, and so to see through it, we had to press our faces close against it, and where the glass had warped away from the frame of the door—where there was a finger-wide crack—Mister Rogers's voice leaked into his grave, and came back to us as a soft, hollow echo.

And then he was on the move again, happily, quickly, for he would not leave until he showed me all the places of all those who'd loved him into being. His grandfather, his grandmother, his uncles, his aunts, his father-in-law and mother-in-law, even his family's servants—he went to each grave, and spoke their names, and told their stories, until finally I headed back down to the Jeep and turned back around to see Mister Rogers standing high on a green dell, smiling among the stones. "And now if you don't mind," he said without a hint of shame or embarrassment, "I have to go find a place to relieve myself," and then off he went, this ecstatic ascetic, to take a proud piss in his corner of heaven.

Once upon a time, a man named Fred Rogers decided that he wanted to live in heaven. Heaven is the place where good people go when they die, but this man, Fred Rogers, didn't want to *go* to heaven; he wanted to *live* in heaven, here, now, in this world, and so one day, when he was talking about all the people he had loved in this life, he looked at me and said, "The connections we make in the course of a life—maybe that's what *heaven* is, Tom. We make so *many* connections here on earth. Look at us—I've just met you, but I'm invested in who you are and who you will be, and I can't help it."

The next afternoon, I went to his office in Pittsburgh. He was sitting on a couch, under a framed rendering of the Greek word for grace and a biblical phrase written in Hebrew that means "I am my beloved's, and my beloved is mine." A woman was with him, sitting in a big chair. Her name was Deb. She was very pretty. She had a long face and a dark blush to her skin. She had curls in her hair and stars at the centers of her eyes. She was a minister at Fred Rogers's church. She spent much of her time tending to the sick and the dying. Fred Rogers loved her very much, and so, out of nowhere, he smiled and put his hand over hers. "Will you be with me when I die?" he asked her, and when she said yes, he said, "Oh, thank you, my dear." Then, with his hand still over hers and his eyes looking straight into hers, he said, "Deb, do you know what a great prayer you are? Do you know that about yourself? Your prayers are just wonderful." Then he looked at me. I was sitting in a small chair by the door, and he said, "Tom, would you close the door, please?" I closed the door and sat back down. "Thanks, my dear," he said to me, then turned back to Deb. "Now, Deb, I'd like to ask you a favor," he said. "Would you lead us? Would you lead us in prayer?"

Deb stiffened for a second, and she let out a breath, and her color got deeper. "Oh, I don't know, Fred," she said. "I don't know if I want to put on a *performance.* . . ."

Fred never stopped looking at her or let go of her hand. "It's not a performance. It's just a meeting of friends," he said. He moved his hand from her wrist to her palm and extended his other hand to me. I took it, and then put my hand around her free hand. His hand was warm, hers was cool, and we bowed our heads, and closed our eyes, and I heard Deb's voice calling out for the grace of God. What is grace? I'm not certain; all I know is that my heart felt like a spike, and then, in that room, it opened and felt like an umbrella. I had never prayed like that before, ever. I had always been a great prayer, a powerful one, but only fitfully, only out of guilt, only when fear and desperation drove me to it . . . and it hit me, right then, with my eyes closed, that this was the moment Fred Rogers—Mister Rogers—had been leading me to from the moment he answered the door of his apartment in his bathrobe and asked me about Old Rabbit. Once upon a time, you see, I lost something, and prayed to get it back, but when I lost it the second time, I didn't, and now this was it, the missing word, the unuttered promise, the prayer I'd been waiting to say a very long time.

"Thank you, God," Mister Rogers said.

PHILIP LEVINE

After Leviticus
from Image

The seventeen metal huts across the way
from the great factory house seventeen
separate families. Because the slag heaps
burn all day and all night it's never dark,
so as you pick your way home at 2 A.M.
on a Saturday morning near the end
of a long winter you don't need to step
in the black mud even though you're not sober.

You're not drunk either. You're actually filled
with the same joy that comes to a great artist
who's just completed a seminal work,
though the work you've completed is "serf work"
(to use your words), a solid week's worth of it
in the chassis assembly plant number seven.
Even before you washed up and changed your shirt
Maryk invited you for a drink. You sat in the back,
Maryk and his black pal Williams in the front,
as the bottle of Seven Crown passed slowly
from hand to hand, eleven slow circuits
until it was empty and Maryk opened
the driver's side door and placed the dead soldier
carefully bottom-side down on the tarmac
of the parking lot and then drove you home

or as close to home as he could get
without getting his sedan stuck in the ruts.
Neither Maryk nor Williams had made a pass,
neither told a dirty joke or talked dirty.
The two, being serious drinkers, said
almost nothing though both smoked and both sighed
frequently, perhaps from weariness,
from a sense of defeat neither understands,
or more likely because their lungs are going
from bad air and cigarettes. You're nearly home
to number seven, where a single light burns
to welcome you back with your pay envelope
tucked in your shirt pocket, the blue, unironed
denim shirt your oldest, Walter, outgrew
eleven years ago. Bernadette Strempek,
let me enter your story now as you stand
motionless in the shadowy black burning
inhaling the first warm breeze that tells you
this endless winter is ending. Don't go in
just yet; instead gaze upwards toward the stars.
Those tiny diamonds, though almost undone,
have been watching over your house and your kids
while you've been away. Take another breath,
a deeper one and hold the air until you can't.
Do you taste it? You shake your head. It's God's
breath, a magical gift carried
all the dark way from Him to you on the wind
no one can see. Seventeen separate huts
hunkered down and soberly waiting, this night
three of you in a '47 Plymouth four-door
drinking Seven Crown for eleven circuits

until the work was done, one woman alone
beneath the blind sky, standing patiently
before number seven Mud Lane taking
into her blood one gasp after another
of the holy air: the numbers say it all.

BARRY LOPEZ

The Language of Animals
from Wild Earth

The steep riverine valley I live within, on the west slope of the Cascades in Oregon, has a particular human and natural history. Though I've been here for thirty years, I am able to convey almost none of it. It is not out of inattentiveness. I've wandered widely within the drainages of its eponymous river, the McKenzie; and I could offer you a reasonably complete sketch of its immigrant history, going back to the 1840s. Before then, Tsanchifin Kalapuya, a Penutian-speaking people, camped in these mountains, but they came up the sixty-mile-long valley apparently only in summer to pick berries and to trade with a people living on the far side of the Cascades, the Molala. In the fall, the Tsanchifin returned down valley to winter near present-day Eugene, Oregon, where the McKenzie joins the Willamette River. The Willamette flows a hundred miles north to the Columbia, the Columbia another hundred miles to the Pacific.

The history that preoccupies me, however, in this temperate rain forest is not human history, not even that of the highly integrated Tsanchifin. Native peoples seem to have left scant trace of their comings and goings in the McKenzie valley. Only rarely, as I hear it, does someone stumble upon an old, or very old, campsite, where glistening black flakes of a volcanic glass called obsidian, the debitage from tool-making work, turn up in soil scuffed by a boot heel.

I've lingered in such camps, in a respectful and deferential mood, as though the sites were shrines; but I'm drawn more to the woods in which they're found. These landscapes are occupied, still, by the wild animals who were these people's companions. These are the descendants of animals who coursed these woods during the era of the Tsanchifin.

When I travel in the McKenzie basin with visiting friends, my frame of mind is not that of the interpreter, of the cognoscente; I amble with an explorer's temperament. I am alert for the numinous event, for evidence of a world beyond the rational. Though it is presumptuous to say so, I seek a Tsanchifin grasp, the view of an indigene. And what draws me ahead is the possibility of revelation from other indigenes—the testimonies of wild animals.

The idea that animals can convey meaning, and thereby offer an attentive human being illumination, is a commonly held belief the world over. The view is disparaged and disputed only by modern cultures with an allegiance to science as the sole arbiter of truth. The price of this conceit, to my way of thinking, is enormous.

I grew up in a farming valley in southern California in the 1950s, around sheep, dogs, horses, and chickens. The first wild animals I encountered—coyotes, rattlesnakes, mountain lion, deer, and bear—I came upon in the surrounding mountains and deserts. These creatures seemed more vital than domestic animals. They seemed to tremble in the aura of their own light. (I caught a shadow of that magic occasionally in a certain dog, a particular horse, like a residue.) From such a distance it's impossible to recall precisely what riveted my imagination in these encounters, though I might guess. Wild animals are lean. They have no burden of possessions, no need for extra clothing, eating utensils, elaborate dwellings. They are so much more integrated into the landscape than human beings are, swooping its contours and bolting down its pathways with bewildering speed. They travel unerringly through the dark. Holding their gaze, I saw the intensity and clarity I associated with the presence of a soul.

In later years I benefited from a formal education at a Jesuit prep school in New York City, then at New York University and the universities of Notre Dame and Oregon. I encountered the full range of Western philosophy, including the philosophy of science, in those classrooms and studied the theological foundations of Christianity. I don't feel compelled now to repudiate that instruction. I regard it, though, as incomplete, and would say that nothing I read in those years fundamentally changed what I thought about animals. The more steeped I became in the biology and ecology of animals, the more I understood about migration, and the more I comprehended about the intricacy of their neural impulses and the subtlety of their endocrine systems, the deeper their other unexplored capacities appeared to me. Biochemistry and field studies enhanced rather than diminished my sense that, in Henry Beston's phrase, animals were other nations.

If formal education taught me how to learn something, if it provided me with reliable structures (e.g., *Moby-Dick,* approaching the limit in calculus, von Clausewitz's tactics) within which I could exercise a metaphorical imagination, if the Jesuits inculcated in me a respectful skepticism about authority, then that education gave me the sort of tools most necessary to an examination of the history of Western ideas, a concept fatally flawed by an assumption of progress. I could move on from Gilbert White's Selbourne to Thoreau's Walden. I could trace a thread from Aristotle through Newton to Schrödinger. Or grasp that in the development of symphonic expression, Bach gives way to Mozart who gives way to Beethoven. But this isn't progress. It's change, in a set of ideas that incubate well in our culture.

I left the university with two ideas strong in my mind. One was the belief that a person had to enter the world to know it, that it couldn't be got from a book. The other was that there were other epistemologies out there, as rigorous and valid as the ones I learned in school. Not convinced of the superiority of the latter, I felt ready to consider these other epistemologies, no matter how at odds.

When I moved into the McKenzie valley I saw myself beginning a kind of apprenticeship. Slowly I learned to identify indigenous plants and animals and birds migrating through. Slowly I began to expand the basis of my observations of their lives, to alter the nature of my assumptions. Slowly I began to recognize clusters of life in the valley as opposed to individual, isolated species. I was lucky to live in a place too steep for agriculture to have developed, too heavily wooded to be good for grazing, and too poor in commercial quantities of minerals for mining (though the evidence that all three occurred on a small scale is present). The only industrial-scale impact here has come from commercial logging—and the devastation in parts of the valley is as breathtaking a sight as the napalmed forests of the Vietnam highlands in the 1960s. Pressure is building locally now to develop retirement real estate—trailer parks, RV parks, condominiums; but, for the moment, it's still relatively easy to walk for hours across stretches of land that have never been farmed, logged, mined, grazed, or homesteaded. From where my house sits on a wooded bench above the McKenzie River, I can look across the water into a four- or five-hundred-year-old forest in which some of the Douglas firs are more than twenty feet around.

Two ways to "learn" this land are obvious: enter it repeatedly and attentively on your own; or give your attention instead—or alternately—to its occupants. The most trustworthy occupants, to my mind, are those with no commercial ties, beings whose

sense of ownership is guided not by profit but by responsible oc-
cupancy. For the valley in which I live, these occupants would theoretically be remnant Tsanchifin people and indigenous animals. To
my knowledge, the Tsanchifin are no longer a presence; and the
rational mind (to which many of us acquiesce) posits there is little
to be learned from animals unless we discover a common language
and can converse. This puts the emphasis, I think, in the wrong
place. The idea shouldn't be for us to converse, to enter into some
sort of Socratic dialogue with animals. It would be to listen to what
is already being communicated. To insist on a conversation with
the unknown is to demonstrate impatience, and it is to imply that
any such encounter must include your being heard.

To know a physical place you must become intimate with it.
You must open yourself to its textures, its colors in varying day
and night lights, its sonic dimensions. You must in some way become vulnerable to it. In the end, there's little difference between
growing into the love of a place and growing into the love of a
person. Love matures through intimacy and vulnerability, and it
grows most vigorously in an atmosphere of trust. You learn, with
regard to the land, the ways in which it is dependable. Where it
has no strength to offer you, you do not insist on its support.
When you yourself do not understand something, you trust the
land might, and you defer.

When I walk in the woods or along the creeks, I'm looking for
integration, not conversation. I want to be bound more deeply
into the place, to be included, even if only as a witness, in events
that animate the landscape. In tracking a mink, in picking a black
bear scat apart, in examining red alder trunks that deer have
scraped with their antlers, I get certain measures of the place where
I live. In listening to the songs and tones of Swainson's thrushes
and to winter wrens, to the bellows of elk, I get a dimension of the
valley I couldn't get on my own. In eating spring chinook, in burn-

ing big-leaf maple in the stove, in bathing in groundwater from the well, in collecting sorrel and miner's lettuce for a summer salad, I put my life more deeply into the life around me.

The eloquence of animals is in their behavior, not their speech. To see a mule deer stot across a river bar, a sharp-shinned hawk maneuver in dense timber, to watch a female chinook build her nest on clean gravel, to see a rufous hummingbird extracting nectar from foxglove blossoms, to come upon a rubber boa constricting a shrew, is to meet the world outside the self. It is to hear the indigenes.

We regard wild creatures as the most animated part of the landscape. We've believed for eons that we share a specific nature with them, different from the nature of wild berries or lightning or water. Our routine exchanges with them are most often simply a verification of this, reaffirmations that we're alive in a particular place together at a particular time.

Wild animals are like us, too, in that they have ancestors. When I see river otter sprawled mid-stream on a boulder in the noon sun, I know their ancestors were here before the fur trappers, before the Tsanchifin, before *Homo.* The same for the cormorant, the woolly bear caterpillar, the cutthroat. In all these histories, in the string of events in each life, the land is revealed. The tensile strength of the orb weaver's silk, the location of the salmon's redd, the shrew-moles' bones bound up in a spotted owl's cast, each makes a concise statement.

Over the years and on several continents I've seen indigenous people enter their landscapes. (I say *enter* because the landscape of a semipermanent camp or village, as I have come to understand it, is less intense, less numinous.) Certain aspects of this entry experience seem always to be in evidence. Human conversation usually trails off. People become more alert to what is around them, less intent on any goal—where to camp that night, say. People become more curious about animal life, looking at the evidence of what animals have been up to. People begin to look all around, especially behind them, instead of staring straight ahead with only an occasional look to the side. People halt to examine closely things that at first glance seemed innocuous. People hold up simply to put things together—the sky with a certain type of forest, a kind of rock outcropping, the sound of a creek, and, last, the droppings of a blue grouse under a thimbleberry bush. People heft rocks and put them back. They push their hands into river mud and perhaps leave patches of it on their skin. It's an ongoing intercourse with the place.

Learning one's place through attention to animals is not solely a matter of being open to "statements" they make about the physical, chemical, and biological realms we share. A more profound communication can take place. In this second sphere, animals have volition; they have intention and the power of influence; and they have the capacity to intervene in our lives. I've never known people who were entirely comfortable addressing such things. However we may define *consciousness* in the West, we regard it as a line of demarcation that separates human nature from animal nature. A shaman might cross back and forth, but animals, no.

In my experience indigenous people are most comfortable in asserting a spiritual nature for animals (including aspects of consciousness) only when the purpose of the conversation is to affirm a spirituality shared by both humans and animals. (They're more at ease talking about animals as exemplars of abstract ideals, as oracles and companions, and as metaphorical relations.) When someone relates something previously unheard of that they saw an animal do, something that demonstrates the degree of awareness we call consciousness, the person is saying the world still turns on the miraculous, it's still inventing itself, and that we're a part of this. These observations keep the idea alive that animals are engaged in the world at a deep level.

The fundamental reinforcement of a belief in the spiritual nature of animals' lives (i.e., in the spiritual nature of the landscape itself) comes from a numinous encounter with a wild creature. For many indigenous people (again, in my experience) such events make one feel more secure in the "real" world because their unfolding takes the event beyond the more readily apparent boundaries of existence. In a numinous encounter one's suspicion—profound, persistent, and ineluctable, that there is more to the world than appearances—is confirmed. For someone reared in the tradition of the cultural West, it is also a confirmation that Rationalism and the Enlightenment are not points on a continuum of progress but simply two species of wisdom.

Whenever I think of the numinous event, and how vulnerable it is to the pincers of the analytic mind, I recall a scene in a native village in Alaska. A well-meaning but rude young man, a graduate student in anthropology, had come to this village to study hunting. His ethnocentric interviewing technique was aggressive, his vocabulary academic, his manner to pester and interfere. Day after day he went after people, especially one older man he took to be the best hunter in the village. He hounded him relentlessly, asking him why he was the best hunter. The only way the man could be rid of the interviewer was to answer his question. He ended the assault by saying, "My ability to hunt is like a small bird in my mind. I don't think anyone should disturb it."

A central task facing modern Western cultures is to redefine human community in the wake of industrialization, colonialism, and, more recently, the forcing power of capitalism. In trying to solve some of the constellation of attendant problems here—keeping corporations out of secondary education, restoring the physical and spiritual shelter of the family group, preserving non-Western ways of knowing—it seems clear that by cutting ourselves off from Nature, by turning Nature into scenery and commodities, we may cut ourselves off from something vital. To repair this damage we can't any longer take what we call "Nature" for an object. We must merge it again with our own nature. We must reintegrate ourselves in specific geographic places, and to do that we need to learn those places at greater depth than any science, Eastern or Western, can take us. We have to incorporate them again in the moral universe we inhabit. We have to develop good relations with them, ones that will replace the exploitative relations that have become a defining characteristic of twentieth-century Western life, with its gargantuan oil spills and chemical accidents, its megalithic hydroelectric developments, its hideous weapons of war, and its conception of wealth that would lead a corporation to cut down a forest to pay the interest on a loan.

In daily conversation in many parts of the American West today, wild animals are given credit for conveying ideas to people, for "speaking." To some degree this is a result of the pervasive influence of Native American culture in certain parts of the West. It doesn't contradict the notion of human intelligence to believe, in these quarters, that wild animals represent repositories of knowledge we've abandoned in our efforts to build civilizations and support ideas like progress and improvement. To "hear" wild animals is not to leave the realm of the human; it's to expand this realm to include voices other than our own. It's a technique for the accomplishment of wisdom. To attend to the language of animals means to give yourself over to a more complicated, less analytic awareness of a place. It's to realize that some of the so-called equations of life are not meant to be solved, that it takes as much intelligence not to solve them as it does to find the putative answers.

A fundamental difference between early and late twentieth-century science in the cultural West has become apparent with the emergence of the phrase "I don't know" in scientific discourse. This admission is the heritage of quantum mechanics. It is heard eloquently today in the talk of cosmologists, plasma physicists, and, increasingly, among field biologists now working beyond the baleful and condescending stare of molecular biologists.

The Enlightenment ideals of an educated mind and just relations among differing people have become problematic in our era because the process of formal education in the West has consistently abjured or condemned non-Western ways of knowing, and because the quest for just relations still strains at the barriers of race, gender, and class. If we truly believe in the wisdom of Enlightenment thought and achievement—and certainly, like Bach's B Minor Mass, Goethe's theory of light, or Darwin's voyage, that philosophy is among the best we have to offer—then we should consider encouraging the educated mind to wander beyond the comfort of its own solipsisms, and we should extend the principle of justice to include everything that touches our lives.

I do not know how to achieve these things in the small valley where I live except through apprenticeship and the dismantling of assumptions I grew up with. The change, to a more gracious and courteous and wondrous awareness of the world, will not come in my lifetime, and knowing what I know of the modern plagues— loss of biodiversity, global warming, and the individual quest for material wealth—I am fearful. But I believe I have come to whatever I understand by listening to companions and by trying to erase the lines that establish hierarchies of knowledge among them. My sense is that the divine knowledge we yearn for is social; it is not in the province of a genius any more than it is in the province of a particular culture. It lies within our definition of community.

Our blessing, it seems to me, is not what we know, but that we know each other.

ANITA MATHIAS

The Holy Ground of Kalighat
from Notre Dame Magazine

Kalighat, the Home of the Dying Destitute, was the toughest assignment in the Missionaries of Charity convent, reputedly reserved for the mature. But I was greedy for challenge and kept asking for it until I got it. The place glowed in the light of literature, the poetic accounts of Malcolm Muggeridge, Desmond Doig, and Edward Le Joly; I *had* to work there.

We entered the quietness of Kalighat after a long Jeep trip through Calcutta's streets, raucous with the honking of buses and cars, the blare of radios, the shouts of vendors. We recited the rosary above the din around the Jeeps as the rule decreed we should, no matter how unpropitious our surroundings. Our voices growing hoarse and our throats parched, we trolled through the fifteen mysteries of the life of Christ.

This chanting was meant to serve as a barricade against distraction and doubt. Just as well perhaps. While we hurtled through the three-wheeled autos called "bone shakers" and snaked amid stray dogs I sometimes saw get run down (willfully? out of fathomable malice?), it was not easy to clasp simple verities: There is a God and God loves me as he loves every human on this crazy street. It was easier to believe in a "watchmaker God," who hurled the world into motion and then absconded, a notion I had heard denounced from the pulpit as atheistic absurdity.

Hail, Mary, full of grace; the Lord is with you. Blessed are you among women, and blessed is the fruit of your womb, Jesus, we chanted as our Jeep swerved through street children, trams, lorries, motorcycles, scooters, and dangerously lurching buses with youths leeching onto windows, railings, and roof. I usually kept my eyes closed. Calcutta was unnerving to a small-town girl. To open them was to contemplate the possibility that our driver would collide with rickshaws dragged by scrawny men and crammed with housewives and their purchases or hit a sacred cow or crush a child, and so cause an ugly communal riot for us to sort out. I remembered the time my father had to bail out a Jesuit professor, his colleague, who was nearly lynched when he hit a poor Hindu boy with his posh car.

Entering Kalighat is akin to entering a city church—or, for that matter, our chapel at Mother House in the center of Calcutta. You are stunned into stillness, into a guilty awareness of your racing pulse, your distracted mind. The silence shrouds you until you are aware that it is not silence, not really: There is the rustle of supplicants, the rattle of rosary beads, the breathing from bowed heads. So, in Kalighat, after your jangled spirit laps up the apparent silence, you hear soft sounds—low moaning, a tubercular cough, patients tossing in pain and restlessness.

Still, Kalighat felt like holy ground. I often sensed God in the dimness and hush of that place. *Bhogobaan ekane acche,* Mother Teresa whispered in Bengali as she went from bed to bed: *God is here.* Her creased face looked sad and sweet. This is *Bhogobaan ki badi,* God's house, the sisters tell new arrivals, believing that Kalighat is sanctified in its very stones by the thousands who have died peaceful deaths there. Perhaps the light created this aura. The light spilled from high windows through a filigreed lattice, spilled into the dim room with a stippled radiance that made working there an epiphany.

In this place Malcolm Muggeridge, curmudgeonly Catholic convert, experienced what he called "the first authentic photographic miracle" as he filmed a BBC documentary on Mother Teresa in 1969. The cameraman insisted that filming was impossible inside Kalighat—dimly lit by small windows high in the walls—but reluctantly tried it. In the processed film, the shots taken inside were bathed in "a soft, exceptionally lovely light," whereas the rest, taken in the outside courtyard as an insurance, was dim and confused. Muggeridge wrote: "I am absolutely convinced that this technically unaccountable light is Newman's 'Kindly Light.' The love in Kalighat is luminous like the halos artists have seen and made visible around the heads of saints. It is not at all surprising that this exquisite luminosity should register on a photographic film."

Perhaps Kalighat had that sense of being holy ground because it was an ancient Hindu pilgrimage site, the dormitory for pilgrims to Calcutta's famed Kali temple. I wondered whether the devotions of generations of Hindus, no less than Catholics, had hallowed the ground. Surely, I reasoned, all kinds of God-hunger are acceptable to Christ, who chose as his symbols bread and wine, who offered his flesh to eat, his blood to drink. Perhaps what happens in a pilgrimage spot is not that God descends to earth in a shower of radiance and the earth ever after exudes his fragrance. Perhaps it is we who make spots of earth sacred when we bring our weary spirits, our thwarted hopes, the whole human freight of grief, and pray—our eyes grown wide and trusting; our being, a concentrated yearning. Perhaps that yearning, that glimpse of better things, makes the spot sacred and lingers in the earth and air and water so that future pilgrims say, "God is here."

On our way to work, we frequently picked people off the pavements where they lay and transported them to Kalighat to die, in Mother Teresa's phrase, "within sight of a kind face." "Stop," we'd cry to the driver, who helped us carry them into the Jeep. Occasionally we picked up a drunk, who cursed us on his return to consciousness. Most people we picked up were as emaciated as famine victims; they lay limp on the pavements, a feeble hand outstretched for alms. And yet there was no famine in Calcutta; our prime minister protested that nobody, simply nobody, dies of starvation in India.

These people had probably worked all their lives. But in a land where it's not easy to find work that pays a living wage, to survive is enough. For an illiterate worker, saving money is a nearly impossible dream. "Naked they came into the world, naked they depart," as Job mourned. Many end their lives destitute on Calcutta's streets. They waste away as they grow too weak or sick to scavenge for themselves or root for food in the open garbage dumps.

For these people who are kicked aside, cursed, and ignored, Kalighat is an inexplicable miracle, a last-minute respite, a stepping stone into grace. In her speeches, Mother loved to quote the dying man she brought to Kalighat from Calcutta—"All my life I have lived like a dog, but now I die like an angel"—which was, perhaps, just what he said or, perhaps, a composite of many experiences.

Kalighat consists of two L-shaped wards accommodating about sixty men and women, with rows of low cots snuggled into every cranny. The Missionary Brothers of Charity, the male branch of the order, founded by Brother Andrew, an Australian ex-Jesuit, serve in the male ward; they sponge patients, change soiled clothes, hack off elongated and hardened toenails. When I entered the male ward to dispense medication, I would see these sweet, serious, humble, and hardworking men. Perhaps I perceived them in clichés since I never actually talked to them; a novice does not hobnob with men. We novices mainly worked in the female ward, an oblong room bathed in dim light from the beautiful white filigreed windows.

Iris, a tubercular Anglo-Indian patient, was Kalighat's presiding Fury. She hobbled all over the ward on her walking stick, which she thrashed around when enraged. Her puckered brown face was a maze of hate lines, and as she limped, she cursed: "Those bloody Muddses, I hate those swine. . . ."

"What's the matter, Iris?" people asked, mocking her—for everyone knew her story by heart and was fed up with it. And as if it were new every morning, she'd repeat her tale of the Muddses, her distant relatives who, in her old age, evicted her from her house and pushed her down the stairs, breaking her leg.

"Those bloody Muddses," she muttered, her rosary of hate. She was fond of me and would stroke me, telling me that I was nice, her smile surprisingly sweet. Everyone had to be very good to me when Iris was around, or she would brandish her stick at them, reprimanding, "No, this is a *nice* sister." Poor Iris, balladeer of old grievances, anger always at boiling point for old wrongs. Her grudges had driven her crazy, devastating her long past the original injury. I often talked to her, asking her about her childhood in pre-independence India, to try to divert her mind from the injustices over which it obsessively brooded. I realized how wise Mother Teresa was when she admonished, "Forgive. Never allow yourself to become bitter. Bitterness is like cancer; it feeds on itself. It grows and grows."

Sadness also grew in Kalighat. One round-faced old lady, too weak to feed herself, kept pushing away my hand that waited with the next spoonful of rice. While I tried vainly to feed her, we talked. Her son had deposited her on the streets from where the sisters had eventually picked her up. "I haven't seen my three sons in years," she cried.

I gave up on the rice and fed her the mango. She loved that. She fixed her eyes on the diminishing fruit, then asked for more. There was no more. So I folded the skin in two and drew it between her lips, again and again, until she had sucked the last drops of juice. Suddenly, her eyes lit up with love. Tears streamed down her face. She caught me, pulled me to her, and rocked me in an embrace, crying, "Ma. Ma. Ma," her mind reverting to childhood, her face grown baby sweet.

I hugged her back, not even trying to remember if she was tubercular, forgetting my mask and *Mycobacterium tuberculosis* spread by the respiratory route. During that insomniac night, I thought of her. The next evening, I sneaked out a mango from the convent kitchen and concealed it in my saree. I went straight to her bed. It was covered with a white sheet. She had died in the night.

Death was a constant in Kalighat, that home in the temple of the goddess of death. Only the ostensibly dying were admitted. About half recovered with rest, medication, and nourishing food. For the rest, this was the end. When we entered the ward, stark white sheets, the color of mourning in India, covered the beds of those who had died the previous night. In the face of death, its inevitability, how trivial much of life seemed. "Teach us to number our days," the psalmist cried, "that we may apply our hearts unto wisdom." I realized why the novice-mistresses preached detachment to us. *Guard your heart,* I admonished to myself, chary of emotional involvement with one who might soon be a corpse in the morgue or burnt to ashes on the shore of the River Ganges.

In a place like Kalighat, perspective is everything. My parents, on their monthly visits, complained that it was a grim place, daunting and unpleasant—and so it is until its strange charm, its eerie radiance, works on you. I loved Kalighat for its tiny miracles. An old, almost bald woman with a shriveled face occupied a bed in a corner. When she could sit up, she'd curse all within earshot. She spat gobs of yellow phlegm all over the floor, perversely ignoring her spittoon. Once, as I tried to feed her, she lost her temper and slapped me, sending my glasses flying across the ward.

Dealing with her was not a pleasure. So the other patients had often eaten their dinners and fallen asleep before she was brought her tray of gruel and boiled vegetables. One evening, chiding myself for my fastidiousness, I braced myself and took her tray to her. As I approached, she smiled, and her face glowed. No one had ever seen her smile. I hugged the memory to myself as a shaft of grace—though perhaps it was a trick of the light.

But I remembered Gerard Manley Hopkins, my favorite poet:

Christ plays in ten thousand places,
Lovely in limbs, and lovely in eyes not his
To the Father through the features of men's faces.

Most patients in Kalighat, too old or too weak to walk, crept around the ward or to the bathroom while squatting on their haunches, slowly moving one tired leg after the other. Since their diseases were highly infectious—cholera, typhoid, and, especially, tuberculosis—we had to be vigilant. Sister Luke, the stern-faced nurse who ran Kalighat, ordered us to use masks all the time we were in the ward. These we sewed ourselves, a double strip of thick cotton cloth that covered the nose and mouth. I often disobeyed orders and dispensed with my mask, partly because my smile helped in this difficult work with difficult people. (Months later at home, when I grew too weak to get out of bed and coughed blood, dread symptom, and X rays revealed a shadow on the lungs, first sign of TB, I looked back on those days of idiotic, uncalled-for faith with bemusement. I then had a sense of inviolability, common to children and puppies, a half-conscious sense that providence would protect the simple-hearted—and the foolish.)

The actual work dispelled any vestigial illusions of the glamour of being a Florence Nightingale of light and mercy. I often forced myself through the chores by sheer willpower. I reminded myself that I had decided to imitate Christ, and to be a saint in the tradition of Francis, Damien, Schweitzer, and Dooley, as I fought nausea and changed sheets fouled by the stools of those with cholera or dysentery.

Why do you do it? Monica, an intense, curly-headed, West German volunteer—an atheist—asked. No one assigned me this chore. (On the contrary, as one of the better-educated sisters, I was allotted the more "prestigious" jobs, which required some expertise: to give the patients their daily medications and injections, to set up and administer an intravenous drip when a patient was admitted delirious with typhoid or with the withered skin, sunken eyes, and icy hands of the cholera victim.) No, I chose. I was struck by the paradigm of Christ, "who, though he was rich, yet he became poor." Born amid a stable's dung, as literally as we cleaned feces; homeless during his ministry; dying naked on the cross. *Come follow me.* "One must go down, as low down as possible to find God," I reasoned with an eighteen-year-old's intensity. And to what did I equate God? Joy. Certainty. Peace.

The romance of the spiritual life, its pilgrim's progress through internal hills and valleys, shed a gleam on everyday chores—washing clothes and windows or scrubbing the stainless steel plates left pyramided on the courtyard floor after the patients' evening meal. We hoisted up our sarees (a rare glimpse of legs) and squatted on our haunches to scrub the endless pile of plates with a piece of coconut husk and our homemade detergent, ashes and soap shavings. Western volunteers helped, professing amazement at our primitive methods of washing clothes and dishes. "Mother Teresa has been offered dishwashers and washing machines many times and has refused. Mother says that we should live just like the poorest of the poor to be able to understand them." I'd parrot this explanation, smugly and self-righteously—repressing my annoyance at her rigidity on the many days that I was exhausted.

The new admission was brought in on a stretcher—a young girl with a prematurely haggard face, her hair an uncombed matted mass that I could see we'd have to cut off. How to unravel it? When I undressed her to bathe her, I saw that her thighs were bloodstained, her vulva a raw, feces-encrusted sore. I involuntarily moved back at the stench. A group of men had slashed her crotch with blades, she said.

"Why did they do that?" I asked, ignorant of perversion. I gathered from her faltering reply in Bengali that she had been forced into prostitution, and that there were all sorts. . . .

"How old are you?"

"Eighteen."

She was my age. I stood, staring at the raw flesh, wondering what to do first, when Sister Luke appeared. She pushed me aside, her long serious face grim. "Go away, child, go away," she growled, as she bent her lanky body down to the patient, sponging her down swiftly. Sister Luke later explained that the girl had venereal disease, something I'd never encountered before.

Sister Luke was good-hearted, but her volatile temper and gruff, no-nonsense manners scared patients, novices, and volunteers alike. My parents, visiting, were shocked and upset to hear her scream at the patients. Indeed, her manner was far from the ideal for workers in the Home of the Dying Destitute that Mother Teresa recommended in the Constitution: *We train ourselves to be extremely kind and gentle in touch of hand, tone of voice, and in our smile so as to make the mercy of God very real and to induce the dying person to turn to God with filial confidence.*

Since she perceived me as responsible, Sister Luke, a trained nurse, entrusted me with deciphering the doctor's scribbled prescriptions and doling out the evening medication. I also gave the injections and intravenous drips when I came on duty. In the absence of professionals, we picked up the elements of nursing from one another. I am sometimes appalled remembering our amateurishness, but then I recall that we looked after people we carried in from the streets, whom no one else cared about, and that we did alleviate their pain.

One evening, I balanced a tray of medicine—chloramphenicol, ampicillin, streptomycin, para-aminosalicyclic acid, isoniazid—sorted out in little cups, in one hand as I rushed from the office to begin my rounds. I tripped. Hundreds of pink, white, and parti-colored pills raced over the floor. Sister Luke had locked the medicine cupboard. Too terrified to ask her for a fresh dose for the 120 patients, I began to pick the pills off the floor, intending to use them anyway. The colored or unusually shaped pills were easy to separate. I slowed down at the homogenized mass of white pills, fond hope and guesswork intermingling as I sorted, when Nemesis descended.

"What *are* you doing?" Sister Luke stood over me, her hands on her hips.

I told her.

"You blessed child. You stupid child," she shrieked, throwing the tray into the trash, cups and all, tossing me her keys to get a fresh dose.

Sister Luke had probably sworn freely before she became a nun. Now, she ingeniously transmuted worldly expletives into heavenly ones. "Get the blessed bedpan to that blessed patient," she'd scream. Sister Luke was admired, almost hero worshiped, by all who worked in Kalighat—she was dedicated, efficient, and unpretentious—so "blessed" became a common expletive for all "Lukies."

For the first few weeks, I scrupulously followed the doctor's charts as I gave the patients their medication. But as the medicine and dosages grew familiar, I began to trust my memory. Teachers and friends had often commented on my "photographic memory," and I was proud of it. I made a point of smiling at Krishna, an emaciated, pale-skinned teenager with close-cropped hair, as I gave her medicine. ("Smile five times a day at people you do not feel like smiling at. Do it for world peace," Mother Teresa said. I'd cheat, though, selecting targets whom I liked, at least a little.)

Too frail to sit up, Krishna lay on propped-up pillows, a faint smile on her face, her eyes huge and haunted. She looked classically tubercular, like Severn's portrait of the dying Keats.

One evening, Krishna shivered feverishly, face flushed, eyes streaming. Her forehead burned. The thermometer read 106, the highest I'd ever recorded.

I went to Sister Luke. "Sister, the girl with TB has a very high temperature."

"Which girl?"

"Krishna."

"Krishna!" she laughed. "You know, Krishna was severely malnourished when she was brought to us. She looked as gaunt as a TB patient. We thought she was going to die. But she is recovering nicely. I think we will be able to discharge her soon. You say she is sick?"

Malnutrition! I flushed. Krishna was not sick. She had starved. And I had given her the dosage of isoniazid for a severely tubercular patient. Sister Luke had urged restraint with these potent drugs, cautioning us of the side effects.

"Krishna is feverish," I mumbled, and slunk away, stunned, too cowardly to tell her what I'd done. *If I have to confess, I will, but please, oh, God, oh, God, heal her.*

A Calcutta volunteer doctor was at work. I feigned jocularity. "So Doctor, what happens if you take drugs for TB when you don't have TB?"

"You want to kill yourself, Sister? You could pop off. That's potent stuff."

I had guessed that already; why did I ask? Miserable, remorseful about my hubris, I dashed to Krishna's bedside with paracetamol for her fever and laid my hands on the surprised girl's head. "Now, Krishna, listen. You are not feeling well, right? I'm going to pray for you. Right now." I prayed desperately, imploring for her life.

No result. I had other duties, but every few minutes I stole to Krishna's bedside, praying for her, for a miracle. Gradually Krishna's fever subsided.

I felt close to Krishna after all this. The severely malnourished girl had grown too weak to walk. And since she lay all day on her jute-strung cot, her legs atrophied. As she grew stronger, I helped her to walk again, walking beside her, her arms around my shoulders, or walking in front of her, holding her hands, until she regained balance and confidence and strength.

Krishna walked, shakily but unaided, before I left Mother Teresa's congregation. I saw her discharged, another Lazarus restored, another woman returned to Calcutta's Darwinian struggle for survival, but with an ounce of hope. Just one drop removed from the ocean of misery—but the ocean would be greater were it there.

WALT McDONALD

The Waltz We Were Born For

from First Things

Wind chimes ping and tangle on the patio.
In gusty winds this wild, sparrow hawks hover
and bob—always the crash of indigo
hosannas dangling on strings. My wife ties copper
to turquoise from deserts, and bits of steel
from engines I tear down. She strings them all
like laces of babies' shoes when the squeal
of their play made joyful noise in the hall.

Her voice is more modest than moonlight,
like pearl drops she wears in her lobes.
My hands find the face of my bride.
I stretch her skin smooth and see bone.
Our children bring children to bless her, her face
more weathered than mine. What matters
is timeless, dazzling devotion—not rain,
not Eden gardenias, but cactus in drought,
not just moons of deep sleep, not sunlight or stars,
not the blue, but the darkness beyond.

THOMAS MOORE

On Memory and Numbers
from Parabola

A few years ago I celebrated my fiftieth birthday. The fortieth had been easy and uneventful, and I expected the same for the fiftieth, but I was wrong. Not only did I feel the shaking of foundations in my person and in my world, but my life changed radically during that year. I was painfully torn away from old and familiar ways, places, and people, to begin an altogether new episode with a new family, a new home, and new work. Nothing has been the same since.

So what is in a number? Some would say that I went through a Saturn cycle, the seven-year crisis that reaches a peak at seven times seven, or forty-nine. I have no doubt that this astrological reckoning is valid. But I also have faith in zeroes, the ends of decades, and the midpoints of centuries.

For as long as I can remember, I have been, in spirit, a follower of Pythagoras, the ancient spiritual leader who based his philosophy on numbers. Several stories are told of how Pythagoras discovered the power of numbers through music, such as when he invented a single-stringed instrument and found that simple proportions of measurement made for consonant and pleasing sounds. The whole world, he concluded, must be numerically and harmonically constituted.

Perhaps it is the musician in me that appreciates the imminent end of a century and a millennium. We are deep into a cadence, a musical settling of harmonic and rhythmic tension, which is also usually a preparation for a new upswing of tempo and harmony, with new variations and maybe even a new idea.

Our culture, of course, has sucked the soul out of numbers, making them quantities void of inherent meaning. Numbers have succumbed to a modern form of nominalism, in which they simply point to quantities that we can now more effectively manipulate in the ones and zeroes of a computer. Great traditional meanings of numbers seem quaint and irrelevant today. What does it matter that St. Patrick's clover has three leaves, or that Augustine's twelve months are the product of the four directions times the three faces of God?

Thankfully, we still celebrate birthdays, which are simply twelve-month cycles, and we honor twenty-five and fifty years of marriage and the centennial anniversaries of a town's or institution's existence. We also remember the anniversaries of certain world events, such as the assassination of John F. Kennedy.

Besides their inherent value as symbols, numbers serve memory, and deep remembering is one of the chief activities of the human soul. If all we did every day was press on into the future, with no thought of the past, imagine what automatons we would be. Remembering the past keeps the psyche intact, educates us to the nature of human life, teaches us what is important, and keeps us tied to the dead and to our ancestors—all of which makes us human.

The turn of the century and the millennium will invite us powerfully to consider our past. These numbers, *centum* and *mille,* one hundred and one thousand, stir up reflection—and what could be more important for the development of wisdom and character? We wonder about the past, and the past has implications for the future. We may feel pride over what we have accomplished, and pride is of great importance in keeping the heart big and the spirit alive. We may feel remorse over gross mistakes—personal failures in courage and intelligence, as well as collective blunders that were true tragedies. Nothing carves out character and soul more effectively than remorse, an emotion of inestimable value for individuals and societies.

As we look over the past, we may also discover how much we have forgotten. Augustine devotes a large portion of his confessions to the subject of memory and to how, through remembering, we can find the very expanses of the soul. Unfortunately, the converse is also true: as we forget, we lose that substance, called "soul," that makes us human.

For a major portion of the past two thousand years, our ancestors directed much of their life and work, whether in cathedrals and temples, rites and sacred art, or volumes of literature, toward the eternal dimension—toward death and immortality, the eternal truths and archetypal images, the virtues and vices that measure a life, and the rituals that keep us in tune with the realities that are not passing and transient. Now we have forgotten many of these important activities, and we wonder why we have so much trouble keeping societies intact and finding life to be worth living. Forgetfulness quickly becomes neglect, and neglect makes for absence.

Today, biography means for the most part recalling the events of a life. For Augustine, however, his confessions were a remembering of the profound realizations that led a soul back to its immortal source. As the millennium draws near, we can choose either to recall facts or to examine our history as a story of the collective soul. We can argue about the causes of political and cultural events, or we can reflect deeply on the life we have been making for ourselves in the freedom of our creativity. This turning point can be an occasion for celebration or regret, or it can be the opportunity to consider seriously what we have become.

The *image* of evolution—not the theory or hypothesis—can blind us to the cyclic nature of time. We may arrive at a point where we believe that we have no control over history, no choice in our future. It's inevitable, people say, that our cities will be crowded by automobiles and our homes laced with electronics, that our very future will be measured by technology, and local life will be sucked up into international business and politics. A fatalistic evolutionism corrodes our sense of freedom and our creativity.

Remembering different ways of life that have been explored throughout the entire globe during these two thousand years, and not only in the major civilizations, we may discover what Augustine taught: that memory is a form of imagination. We may see that life can be lived fully and pleasurably without many things that we currently consider necessary. We may see that we have forgotten many things, because of the focus of our concerns, that could be brought back into our everyday lives. We may even notice that some of the developments we value are actually toxic in the deepest ways.

Memory is not only imagination, it is education. There is no doubt that we need to take a different course. Not that all our achievements are harmful—we have made beautiful things over the centuries, and we have expressed human life with unimaginable creativity. But looking at our world, it is clear that we are not as healthy and as beautiful as we could be. Personal and social tragedies are part of daily life; ignorance and self-serving corruption dominate.

It's fine to celebrate this millennial birthday, but it would also be appropriate to go on a collective retreat. We celebrate well, but we don't atone well. We have forgotten how to purify our hearts of their many kinds of pollution. Although we explain the past and resolve to do better, these are rationalistic responses. We could learn from our forebears to perform effective rites of passage that would cleanse us of past atrocities and lead us into a humane future.

Not the events and facts, but the unfolding of mysteries is what captivates me about my own fifty years of life and my culture's two thousand years of history. It's clear to me that fate or providence gives us raw material out of which to shape a life—the bedrock of our creativity. We don't have to do much except to respond with an open heart, courage, and imagination. Instead of manufacturing our lives or our culture, we can shape them, like Michelangelo revealing the forms he saw in raw marble, without effort and without excessive self-congratulation.

The end of a time cycle is a period of unusual vulnerability, when our sensitivities increase and our remorse bites at us with special severity, but it also contains the possibility of a turn toward the better. It is a *kairos,* a word used by the Greeks to refer to a crucial time of opportunity. Plato says that a worker must be able to seize the kairos, the right moment in which to be creative and productive. Paul Tillich used the word to refer to a suprahistorical moment that contains the opportunity for ultimate meaning: a time of promise and hope, requiring the achievement of justice, human dignity, and peace in the public sphere.

The brief span of our lives might also be seen as a kairos: a chance to exist in the moment and to feel the grace of vitality passing through us. To live in the kairos allows us simply to be, to become less absorbed in problem solving and inventing and more engrossed in life's deeper pleasures. The turning of the millennium is a special gift of time—time as a quality, not a quantity. At such a turning point, life makes itself available with unusual abundance and promise.

LOUISE RAFKIN

A Yen for Cleaning
from Tricycle

A friend had told me about Sho Ishikawa, who had grown up in Ittoen, a commune near Kyoto where toilet cleaning was considered a path to self-knowledge. Sho's parents had spent most of their lives in the commune. Indeed, his father was in some ways one of the present spiritual leaders.

Sho himself now lived in Manhattan and worked in public accounting. "It is difficult to imagine cleaning for your whole life," he warned me during the first of our phone conversations.

But perhaps I could. To augment my earnings as a writer, I had been cleaning professionally for six years.

Ittoen, "One Light" or "One-Lamp Garden," is a community inspired by the spiritual awakening, teachings, and life example of a man named Tenko Nishida (1872–1968). Not a religion in the sense of a creed with a specific object of worship or set of scriptures, Ittoen honored Tenko-san's "Oneness of Light" philosophy while embracing all spiritualities grounded in the ideal of humble service. Both Buddha and Christ lived the life of the homeless, I would be reminded later, and both washed the feet of others.

Tenko-san had first become disenchanted with capitalism in the late 1880s. Unwilling to struggle against others for his own survival, he challenged the assumption that one worked in order to live. Tenko-san's awakening came after three days of meditation: life was given freely to all by "the Light," or by God, and was not something that had to be worked for. Work was therefore a way of offering thanksgiving for the gift of life.

Renouncing his family, his status, and all possessions, Tenko-san began to serve others. He scrubbed, chopped wood, and cleaned privies. Declining all but the bare necessities, he connected with others through service. For him, this was enlightenment. Over the years, Tenko-san attracted followers, and in 1928, some land was donated for the establishment of a community. In the fifties and sixties, the commune had hundreds of members. Now, nearly thirty years after his death, only about one hundred and fifty remained.

I don't think Sho quite knew *why* I wanted to travel ten thousand miles to scrub toilets with a bunch of people I couldn't even talk to, and I wasn't sure myself. Nevertheless, after a succession of phone calls to Japan, a week-long visit was arranged that would culminate on the national Day of Labor, a day the entire community went cleaning. Sho's English teacher, a woman close to seventy who had lived over forty years in the commune, would be my official host.

The Ittoen compound is tucked into the hills east of Kyoto. Gorgeously kept grounds—maples and mossy, rolling hills—hug an odd array of buildings. Several older women were sweeping leaves with traditional bamboo brooms.

Outside the office, I met Sho's teacher, Ayako Isayama, a slight, short-haired woman in a black, karate-*gi*-like smock. She politely invited me to follow her to my room, then took off at such a clip that in order to keep up I was forced into a gallop.

I had imagined a small group of dedicated cleaners, living in spartan quarters, buckets and sponges always at hand. Instead, I found a highly organized group who run what is essentially a small town with its own complicated economy. I would soon learn

that although members own little personal property—all possessions are given up upon joining—the commune supports itself by
operating various businesses, including schools, a press, a theater
group, and a "theme park," dedicated to the ideal of peace, lo-
cated in a southern province.

The group also facilitates training sessions for young factory
workers and businesspeople, and as we approached the building
in which I was to stay, we encountered a line of gi-clad men and
women who looked, as they jogged past, to be in their early twenties. Though it was late afternoon and the fall air was crisp, they
wore their flip-flops barefoot, without *tabi,* the split-toed Japanese socks.

"Mr. Donut workers," Ayako explained. "Four days' training.
Humble toilet cleaning, door-to-door service."

Four thousand Mr. Donut workers spend time at Ittoen each
year; the training is meant to promote humility and facilitate
group dynamics. They are assigned specific houses in nearby towns
for toilet cleaning. And they seek out a variety of other tasks—
washing clothes, baby-sitting, weeding—wherever they are needed,
undertaking such service in the tradition of *takuhatsu,* the "beg-
ging-bowl rounds" practiced by Zen monks, who still visit house-
holds reciting sutras. The last day is set aside for the workers to
reflect on their training.

It's a stretch for me to imagine a group of American workers,
say from Dunkin' Donuts or Burger King, jogging door-to-door,
heads bowed, begging to clean toilets.

That night, Ayako made dinner in the quiet, dark kitchen of
our dormitory. We chatted in simple English. I asked if I might be
able to clean with the Mr. Donut trainees. Ayako, considering my
request, looked away from me. "Difficult, with no Japanese," she
short-handed. "May not be possible." She rose and began to wash

the dishes. "Saturday," she said. "You clean then, with the group." It was Monday. "Morning service at 5:30," she announced.

At dawn's light I followed Ayako down the dusky corridor of our ancient building, where she sped off towards the Spirit Hall. Inside the bare wood hall, both Buddhist and Christian images flanked the altar. At center position was a round window opening onto a view of the forest. Ittoen elders and Mr. Donut people were seated on both sides of the room, kneeling on tatami platforms, men on one side and women on the other. I took a seat behind Ayako. We began with a song recounting Ittoen history and then chanted a Buddhist sutra, the gist of which was nonattachment to worldly goods.

After the service, I raced behind Ayako back to our place for the daily morning cleaning. She offered me a choice of toilet brush or broom. I went with the brush and was handed a bucket and rag. Ayako set off to mop the entire building and was, of course, finished before me. Experience and a lifetime of cleaning, I told myself consolingly.

In the week that followed, I asked Ayako several times about going door-to-door, but each time she seemed evasive. Aside from our morning service, and helping her with some translating, my time was my own. Couldn't I take the initiative myself, even go into town on my own? The thought of knocking on a door without a translator was daunting. Would they invite me into their bathrooms?

One evening, I flipped through the pages of one of Ayako's many scrapbooks while she talked about her life. She spoke of her own spiritual awakening, which literally happened after cleaning a toilet.

"I swept the cobwebs and began to scrub. After about thirty minutes the grain of the floor came to be seen and the stool became white. Wiping my sweat, I looked behind me and saw the lady of the house chanting Buddha's name, her hands in prayer. It was a meeting of two persons, in prayer and in peace. I went outside and saw a tiny blue flower blooming by the roadside. I talked with the blue flower, just like I am talking to you."

I nodded, but never in my toilet-cleaning life had I ever come close to this kind of feeling, or spoken to a flower.

"In my heart I saw a big tree, with everything in its branches. You, me, air, birds, flowers. I knew everything was related. That was my realization after cleaning that toilet."

I flipped pages; the photos dated back decades. Many pictures documented *roto,* the "life of the homeless," and showed lines of uniformed disciples marching across the countryside or through small Japanese villages. In these, Ayako was often at the head of the group beside Tenko-san.

"Were you ever scared?" I asked. "Not knowing where you'd end up each night?" "Once," she said. "In America."

She pulled an album from the bottom of the stack. Inside, there were pictures of Ayako with American families, on a farm, one next to a Washington, D.C., apartment building. And there were newspaper clippings, circa mid-seventies, about a young Japanese "nun" who had volunteered to massage feet at several retirement homes. "For over one month I did humble service. I spent six dollars," she said. "Two dollars I gave to a church."

I drew out the whole story, beginning with Ayako's middle-of-the-night arrival at JFK Airport and the taxi driver who carted her to Manhattan for free at the end of his shift. At Penn Station, while waiting for a bus to rural New Jersey, she cleaned toilets and massaged the feet of a homeless woman.

It was in New Jersey, during a four-hour trek down a country road, that Ayako had felt afraid. She didn't know where she was going and felt so lonely she was almost crying. When she finally stumbled onto a family home, she explained her mission simply to the woman of the house. "I live in Japan. My work is to help people. May I work for you?" she asked, with her hands in prayer.

She stayed at this house almost a week, cleaning, cooking Japanese food, and working in the garden. "They asked me always to pray over their food," she said, translating the Ittoen grace: "True faithfulness consists of doing service for others and ignoring your own interests."

At 6:30 on Saturday morning, about seventy people gathered on the school grounds, each dressed in full Ittoen gear. Our destination was in Osaka, where, as a group, we were to clean a large Buddhist temple. After an official toilet-cleaning poem was recited, we marched out of the compound in a single line, while those staying behind bowed us on our way. With Ittoen flags flying and buckets looped over left arms, we snaked our way down to the nearby town where our buses waited.

Arriving in Osaka around eight, I was escorted with my team to a graveled area about the size of a football field. I was given a bamboo broom. At first look, the ground seemed clean, but closer inspection revealed tiny leaves, cigarette butts, and scraps of litter.

Sweep too hard and the gravel comes up, producing a mound of leaves, dirt, and trash, while leaving bald patches of ground. Sweep lightly and nothing moves. I watched as members of my team flicked their brooms expertly with the precise amount of oomph. In hopes of getting the "trick," I experimented with left-handed, right-handed, and back-handed techniques. After an hour, I had barely swept a quarter of the space completed by the others.

As we approached a particularly dirty and trash-laden area, I noticed a group of men sprawled on some stairs outside an abandoned building. Even at this early hour, most had been drinking. Red-faced and weary, they were watching us work. It made me nervous.

As we neared, several men got up and began throwing trash in the bins and stacking empty bottles. Then I remembered something Ayako had told me about Tenko-san. In his day, when down-and-outs came to Ittoen, as many did following the war's devastation, each was welcomed and given food and shelter. But after two days, they were required to join work groups or do *roto*. Tenko-san believed handouts would brew resentment and keep people disempowered. Work would reveal a heart of thanksgiving.

Over the course of the day, I had felt like my sweeping was improving, but at quitting time, I realized that someone from my group had always been working some distance behind me. I looked at the path that I'd cleared and then at the ground they had passed over. Shards of leaves and a tiny confetti of trash spotted my work. Where they had swept, the ground was pristine, a carpet of smooth, gray rock.

Suddenly, I was really tired.

On the bus ride back to Ittoen, the skyscrapers of Osaka disappearing behind me, I questioned if I were capable of selfless cleaning. The week's experience had set me face-to-face with my shortcomings and fears. In my cleaning world I got things—money, free time, acknowledgment. Here, cleaning was about giving everything up.

And yet, the complications of *my* life—what to do or be, where to live—fell away against the backdrop of this selfless community. Dust to dust? Who really believes it?

My last teatime with Ayako was brief. She offered tangerines, tart and juicy.

"How can others—how can I—live Ittoen principles out there? In America?"

Ayako's eyes were downcast. She carefully separated the sections of her fruit and didn't say anything for what seemed a long time, though this wasn't unusual during our talks.

"Live a simple life with an affluent spirit."

I sipped my tea and flipped again through my favorite photo album, the one with pictures of early Ittoen life. There were several photos of Ayako and Tenko-san cleaning together, which now, after my own cleaning experience, seemed truly beautiful. And another: Ayako with her headscarf tied behind her ears, barely visible over the right shoulder of an aged Tenko-san, he steadying himself with a staff, the misty Ittoen hillside in the background.

"Take whatever you wish," Ayako said.

"But these are originals. You must want them?" I asked. "Others must want them?"

"I'll die soon," Ayako said. "A few will be saved. The others will go with my body and with the ashes of others, with the ashes of Tenko-san."

I peeled several photos from the book.

"Take care of everything you have," she added. "Everything given to us is in trust from the Light."

I thought of the place I owned in the Bay Area. Eight years ago, when I had first quit my job and set off for a writer's colony, an adventure I thought might last a year, I had sublet the house. Since then, I had lived in at least seven cities, on several continents, snagged at least a dozen sublets myself, and begun my cleaning life.

I knew the basement of my house was now crammed full of other people's castoffs, and what had been a neatly tended garden was overgrown. The once-bountiful fruit trees were in desperate need of husbandry and no longer producing. A tenant had recently sent me pictures of my bedroom, post–1989 earthquake: cracks and hairline fractures crisscrossed the walls.

It was time to clean house.

PATTIANN ROGERS

Watching the Ancestral Prayers of Venerable Others

from DoubleTake

Lena Higgins, 92, breastless,
blind, chewing her gums by the window,
is old, but the Great Comet of 1843

is much older than that. Dry land
tortoises with their elephantine
feet are often very old, but giant

sequoias of the western Sierras
are generations older than that.
The first prayer rattle, made

on the savannah of seeds and bones
strung together, is old, but the first
winged cockroach to appear on earth

is hundreds of millions of years
older than that. A flowering plant
fossil or a mollusk fossil in limy

shale is old. Stony meteorites buried
beneath polar ice are older than that,
and death itself is very, very

ancient, but life is certainly older
than death. Shadows and silhouettes
created by primordial sea storms

erupting in crests high above
one another occurred eons ago,
but the sun and its flaring eruptions

existed long before they did. Light
from the most distant known quasar
seen at this moment tonight is old

(should light be said to exist
in time), but the moment witnessed
just previous is older than that.

The compact, pea-drop power
of the initial, beginning nothing
is surely oldest, but then the intention,

with its integrity, must have come
before and thus is obviously
older than that. Amen.

JONATHAN ROSEN

The Talmud and the Internet
from The American Scholar

Turn it and turn it for everything is in it.

Babylonian Talmud

Not long after my grandmother died, my computer crashed and I lost the journal I had kept of her dying. I'd made diskette copies of everything else on my computer—many drafts of a novel, scores of reviews and essays, and hundreds of articles—but I had not printed out, backed up, or copied the diary. No doubt this had to do with my ambivalence about writing and where it leads, for I was recording not only my feelings but also the concrete details of her death. How the tiny monitor taped to her index finger made it glow pink. How mist from the oxygen collar whispered through her hair. How her skin grew swollen *and* wrinkled, like the skin of a baked apple, and yet remained astonishingly soft to the touch. Her favorite songs—"Embraceable You" and "Our Love Is Here to Stay"—that she could no longer hear but that we sang to her anyway. The great gaps in her breathing. The moment when she was gone and the nurses came and bound her jaws together with white bandages.

I was ashamed of my need to translate into words the physical intimacy of her death, so while I was writing it, I took comfort in the fact that my journal did and did not exist. It lived in limbo, much as my grandmother had as she lay unconscious. My unacknowledged journal became, to my mind, what the rabbis in the Talmud call a *goses:* a body between life and death, neither of heaven nor of earth. But then my computer crashed and I wanted my words back. I mourned my journal alongside my grandmother. That secondary cyber loss brought back the first bodily loss and made it final. The details of her dying no longer lived in a safe interim computer sleep. My words were gone.

Or were they? Friends who knew about such things assured me that in the world of computers, nothing is ever really gone. If I cared enough about retrieving my journal, there were places I could send my ruined machine where the indelible imprint of my diary, along with everything else I had written, could be skimmed off the hard drive and saved. It would cost a fortune, but I could do it.

The idea that nothing is ever lost is something one hears a great deal when people speak of computers. "Anything you do with digital technology," my Internet handbook warns, "will leave automatically documented evidence for other people or computer systems to find." There is, of course, something ominous in that notion. But there is a sort of ancient comfort in it, too.

"All mankind is of one Author and is one volume," wrote John Donne in one of his most beautiful meditations. "When one man dies, one chapter is not torn out of the book, but translated into a better language; and every chapter must be so translated." I'd thought of that passage when my grandmother died and had tried to find it in my old college edition of Donne, but I couldn't, so I'd settled for the harsher comforts of Psalm 121—more appropriate for my grandmother in any case. Donne's passage, when I finally found it (about which more later) turned out to be as hauntingly beautiful as I had hoped. It continues:

God employs several translators; some pieces are translated by age, some by sickness, some by war, some by justice; but God's hand is in every translation, and his hand shall bind up all our scattered leaves again, for that Library where every book shall lie open to one another.

At the time I had only a dimly remembered impression of Donne's words, and I decided that as soon as I had the chance, I would find the passage on the Internet. I hadn't yet used the Internet much beyond e-mail, but I had somehow gathered that universities were all assembling vast computer-text libraries and that anyone with a modem could scan their contents. Though I had often expressed cynicism about the Internet, I secretly dreamed it would turn out to be a virtual analogue to John Donne's heaven.

There was another passage I wished to find—not on the Internet but in the Talmud, which, like the Internet, I also regard as a kind of terrestrial version of Donne's divine library, a place where everything exists, if only one knows how and where to look. I'd thought repeatedly about the Talmudic passage I alluded to earlier, the one that speaks of the *goses,* the soul that is neither dead nor alive. I suppose the decision to remove my grandmother from the respirator—despite her "living will" and the hopelessness of her situation—disturbed me, and I tried to recall the conversation the rabbis had about the ways one can and cannot allow a person headed toward death to die.

The Talmud tells a story about a great rabbi who is dying. He has become a *goses,* but he cannot die because outside his hut all his students are praying for him to live, and this is distracting to his soul. A woman climbs to the roof of the rabbi's hut and hurls a clay vessel to the ground. The sound diverts the students, who stop praying. In that moment, the rabbi dies and his soul goes to heaven. The woman, too, says the Talmud, will be guaranteed her place in the world to come.

This story, suggesting the virtue of letting the dead depart, was comforting to me, even though I know that the Talmud is ultimately inconclusive on end-of-life issues, offering, as it always does, a number of arguments and counter-arguments, stories and counter-stories. Not to mention that the Talmud was codified in the year A.D. 500, long before certain technological innovations complicated questions of life and death. Was I retelling the story in a way that offered me comfort but distorted the original intent? I am far from being an accomplished Talmud student and did not trust my skills or memory. But for all that, I took enormous consolation in recalling that the rabbis had in fact discussed the matter.

"Turn it and turn it for everything is in it," a Talmudic sage (who never said anything else the Talmud deemed worth recording) famously declared. The phrase, a sort of verbal Ouroboros, describes the Talmud and appears in the Talmud, a tail-swallowing observation that seems to bear out the truth of the sage's comment. The Talmud is a book and is not a book, and the rabbi's phrase flexibly found its way into it because, oral and written both, the Talmud reached out and drew into itself the world around it, even as it declared itself the unchanging word of God.

Though it may seem sacrilegious to say so, I can't help feeling that in certain respects the Internet has a lot in common with the Talmud. The rabbis referred to the Talmud as a *yam,* a sea—and though one is hardly intended to "surf" the Talmud, there is something more than oceanic metaphors that links the two verbal universes. Vastness, a protean structure, and an uncategorizable nature are in part what define them both. When Maimonides, the great medieval commentator, wanted to simplify the organization of the Talmud and reduce its peculiar blend of stories, folklore, legalistic arguments, anthropological asides, biblical exegesis, and intergenerational rabbinic wrangling into simplified categories and legal conclusions, he was denounced as a heretic for disrupting the very chaos that, in some sense, had come to represent a divine fecundity. Eventually, Maimonides was forgiven, and his work, the Mishnah Torah, is now one of the many sources cross-referenced on a printed page of Talmud. It has been absorbed by the very thing it sought to replace.

The Mishnah itself—the legalistic core of the Talmud—is divided into six broad Orders that reflect six vast categories of Jewish life, but those six categories are subdivided into numerous subcategories called tractates that range over a far more vast number of subjects that are often impossible to fathom from the name of the Order in which they appear. The Hebrew word for tractate is *masechet,* which means, literally, webbing. As with the World Wide Web, only the metaphor of the loom, ancient and inclusive, captures the reach and the randomness, the infinite interconnectedness of words.

I have often thought, contemplating a page of Talmud, that it bears a certain uncanny resemblance to a home page on the Internet, where nothing is whole in itself but where icons and text boxes are doorways through which visitors pass into an infinity of cross-referenced texts and conversations. Consider a page of Talmud. There are a few lines of Mishnah, the conversation the rabbis conducted (for some five hundred years before writing it down) about a broad range of legalistic questions stemming from the Bible but ranging into a host of other matters as well. Underneath those few lines begins the Gemarah, the conversation *later* rabbis had about the conversation *earlier* rabbis had in the Mishnah. Both the Mishnah and the Gemarah evolved orally over so many hundreds of years that even in a few lines of text, rabbis who lived generations apart give the appearance, both within those discrete passages as well as by juxtaposition on the page, of speaking directly to each other. The text includes not only legal disputes but fabulous stories, snippets of history and anthropology, and biblical interpretations. Running in a slender strip down the inside of the page is the commentary of Rashi, the medieval exegete, on the Mishnah, the Gemarah, and the biblical passages (also indexed elsewhere on the page) that inspired the original conversation. Underneath Rashi, and rising up on the other side of the Mishnah and the Gemarah, are the tosefists, Rashi's descendants and disciples, who comment on Rashi's work, as well as on everything Rashi commented on himself. The page is also cross-referenced to other passages of the Talmud, to various medieval codes of Jewish law (that of Maimonides, for example), and to the Shulkhan Arukh, the great sixteenth-century codification of Jewish law by Joseph Caro. And one should add to this mix the student himself, who participates in a conversation that began about fifteen hundred years ago.

Now all this is a far cry from the assault of recipes, news briefs, weather bulletins, library catalogues, pornographic pictures, Rembrandt reproductions, and assorted self-promotional verbiage that drifts untethered through cyberspace. The Talmud was produced by the moral imperative of Jewish law, the free play of great minds, the pressures of exile, the self-conscious need to keep a civilization together, and the driving desire to identify and follow the unfolding word of God. Nobody was trying to buy an airline ticket or meet a date. Moreover, the Talmud, after hundreds of years as an oral construct, was at last written down, shaped by (largely) unknown editors, masters of erudition and invention who float through its precincts offering anonymous, ghostly promptings—posing questions, proposing answers, offering refutations. One feels, for all the Talmud's multiplicities, an organizing intelligence at work.

And yet when I look at a page of Talmud and see all those texts tucked intimately and intrusively onto the same page, like immigrant children sharing a single bed, I do think of the interrupting, jumbled culture of the Internet. For hundreds of years, *responsa,* questions on virtually every aspect of Jewish life, winged back and forth between scattered Jews and various centers of Talmudic learning. The Internet is also a world of unbounded curiosity, of argument and information, where anyone with a modem can wander out of the wilderness for a while, ask a question, and receive an answer. I find solace in thinking that a modern technological medium echoes an ancient one.

For me, I suppose, the Internet makes actual a certain disjointed approach that I had already come to understand was part of the way I encounter both books and the world. I realized this forcefully when I went looking for the John Donne passage that comforted me after the death of my grandmother. I'd failed to find it in my Modern Library edition of Donne's *Complete Poetry and Selected Prose.* I knew the lines, I confess, not from a college course but from the movie version of *Eighty-Four, Charing Cross Road,* starring Anthony Hopkins and Anne Bancroft. The book, a 1970 best-seller, is a collection of letters exchanged over twenty years by an American woman and a British book clerk who sells her old leather-bound editions of Hazlitt and Lamb and Donne, presumably bought up cheap from the libraries of great houses whose owners are going broke after the war. I suppose the book itself is a comment on the death of a certain kind of print culture. The American woman loves literature, but she also writes for television, and at one point she buys Walter Savage Landor's *Imaginary Conversations* so she can adapt it for the radio.

In any event, I checked out *Eighty-Four, Charing Cross Road* from the library, hoping to find the Donne passage, but it wasn't

in the book. It's alluded to in the play that was adapted from the book (I found that too), but it isn't quoted. There's just a brief discussion of Donne's Sermon XV (of which the American woman complains she's been sent an abridged version; she likes her Donne sermons whole). So I rented the movie again, and there was the passage, read beautifully in voice-over by Anthony Hopkins, but without attribution, so there was no way to look it up. Unfortunately, the passage was also abridged, so when I finally turned to the Web, I found myself searching for the line "All mankind is of one volume" instead of "All mankind is of one Author and is one volume."

My Internet search was initially no more successful than my library search. I had thought that summoning books from the vast deep was a matter of a few keystrokes, but when I visited the Web site of the Yale Library, I discovered that most of its books do not yet exist as computer text. I'd somehow believed the whole world had grown digital, and though I'd long feared and even derided this notion, I now found how disappointed and frustrated I was that it hadn't happened. As a last-ditch effort, I searched the phrase "God employs many translators." And there it was! The passage I wanted finally came to me, as it turns out, not from the collection of a scholarly library but simply because someone who loves John Donne had posted it on his home page. (At the bottom of the passage was the charming sentence "This small thread has been spun by . . ." followed by the man's name and Internet address.) For one moment, there in dimensionless, chilly cyberspace, I felt close to my grandmother, close to John Donne, and close to some stranger who, as it happens, designs software for a living.

The lines I sought were from Meditation XVII in "Devotions upon Emergent Occasions," which happens to be the most famous thing Donne ever wrote, containing, as it does, the line "never send to know for whom the bell tolls; it tolls for thee." My

search had led me from a movie to a book to a play to a computer and back to a book. (The passage was, after all, in my Modern Library edition, but who could have guessed that it followed from "No man is an island"?) I had gone through all this to retrieve something that an educated person thirty years ago could probably have quoted by heart. Then again, these words may be as famous as they are only because Hemingway lifted them for his book title. Literature has been in a plundered, fragmented state for a long time.

Still, if the books had all been converted into computer text, and if Donne and Hemingway and *Eighty-Four, Charing Cross Road* had come up together and bumped into one another on my screen, I wouldn't have minded. Perhaps there is a spirit in books that lets them live beyond their actual bound bodies.

This is not to say that I do not fear the loss of the book as object, as body. Donne imagined people who die becoming like books, but what happens when books die? Are they reborn in some new ethereal form? Is it out of the ruined body of the book that the Internet is growing? This would account for another similarity I feel between the Internet and the Talmud, for the Talmud was also born partly out of loss.

The Talmud offered a virtual home for an uprooted culture, and it grew out of the Jews' need to pack civilization into words and wander out into the world. The Talmud became essential for Jewish survival once the Temple—God's pre-Talmud home—was destroyed, and the Temple practices, those bodily rituals of blood and fire and physical atonement, could no longer be performed. When the Jewish people lost their home (the land of Israel) and God lost his (the Temple), then a new way of being was devised, and Jews became the people of the book and not the people of the Temple or the land. They became the people of the book because

they had no place else to live. That bodily loss is frequently overlooked, but for me it lies at the heart of the Talmud, for all its plenitude. The Internet, which we are continually told binds us all together, nevertheless engenders in me a similar sense of Diaspora, a feeling of being everywhere and nowhere. Where else but in the middle of Diaspora do you *need* a home page?

The Talmud tells a story that captures this mysterious transformation from one kind of culture to another. It is the story of Yochanan ben Zakkai, the great sage of the first century, who found himself living in besieged Jerusalem on the eve of its destruction by Rome. Yochanan ben Zakkai understood that Jerusalem and the Temple were doomed, so he decided to appeal to the Romans for permission to found a yeshiva outside Jerusalem. In order to get him out of Jerusalem without being killed by the Zealots—the Jewish revolutionaries—Yochanan's students hid him in a coffin and carried him outside the city walls. They did this not to fool the Romans but to fool the Zealots, who were killing anyone who wasn't prepared to die with the city.

Yochanan wasn't prepared to die with the city. Once outside its walls, he went to see the Roman general Vespasian and requested permission to set up a yeshiva in Yavneh. Vespasian consented, and it is thus in Yavneh that the study of the oral law flourished, in Yavneh that the Mishnah took shape, and in Yavneh that Talmudic culture was saved while Temple culture died. In a sense, Yochanan's journey in his coffin is the symbolic enactment of the transformation Judaism underwent when it changed from a religion of embodiment to a religion of the mind and of the book. Jews died as a people of the body, of the land, of the Temple service of fire and blood, and then, in one of the greatest acts of translation in human history, they were reborn as the people of the book.

I think about Yochanan ben Zakkai in his coffin when I think about how we are passing, books and people both, through the doors of the computer age, and entering a new sort of global Diaspora in which we are everywhere—except home. But I suppose that writing, in any form, always has about it a ghostliness, an unsatisfactory, disembodied aspect, and it would be unfair to blame computers or the Internet for enhancing what has always been disappointing about words. Does anyone really want to be a book in John Donne's heaven?

A few weeks after my computer crashed, I gave in and sent it to a fancy place in Virginia, where—for more money than the original cost of the machine—technicians were in fact able to lift from the hard drive the ghostly impression of everything I had written on my computer during seven years of use. It was all sent to me on separate diskettes and on a single inclusive CD-ROM. I immediately found the diskette that contained my journal and, using my wife's computer, set about printing it out.

As it turns out, I'd written in my journal only six or seven times in the course of my grandmother's two-month illness. Somehow I'd imagined myself chronicling the whole ordeal in the minutest recoverable detail. Instead, I was astonished at how paltry, how sparse my entries really were. Where were the long hours holding her hand? The one-way conversations—what *had* I said? The slow, dreamlike afternoons with the rest of my family, eating and talking in the waiting area? Where, most of all, was my grandmother? I was glad to have my journal back, of course, and I'd have paid to retrieve it again in a second. But it was only when I had my own scant words before me at last that I realized how much I'd lost.

DAVID ROTHENBERG

The Necessary Note
from Parabola

You say that you want to find where ecstasy lies in music, and I tell you at once: don't try to describe it, just listen. Play, get lost, forget logic or the need to explain the pleasure that comes when you're carried away. Ah, but you tell me that you're a philosopher, and you love wisdom not because it makes you crazy but because you have been trained to ask the right questions, those best questions that can never have adequate answers. One question leads to another, and after just a few you are lost. That's the moment to start singing, I tell you—let out a piercing wail like the late Nusrat Fateh Ali Khan might have done, pushing your hands against the air as if to clear the sky for the ultimate lament, the total song where joy and sadness are conflated into one. For the best music is neither giddy nor portentous, major or minor, pathetic or glib. It inhabits pure pleasure, and forces oneness from those opposites that attract this world into being out of empty, deflecting forces.

These are my two personalities, tossing and turning upon each other: the musician and philosopher, one wailing, the other analyzing. Neither one is ever able to satisfy the other; they quarrel and resist each other's insights. But the ecstasy inside the art of sound is not so much pure pleasure as an escape from these divisions into an essential oneness with the unspeakable meaning of the world. This celebration may seem like a language, but it is not. Why? Because you can love it and participate in it even if you have no idea what is going on.

The real musician must exude love and passion with every single note. The tones must appear inevitable, such that no other sound could possibly do at that moment, in that place and at that time. Because music is the art that leaves as soon as it arrives, it always comes to us *suddenly*, and it departs the same way. It stays with us only if its power is so pure and strong that it binds artist and audience with a message deeper than any language. Pure music speaks of nothing beyond itself, standing for no emotion, no story outside its ways of rhythm and timbre. It cannot be doubted, and it can't be explained. Its passion can only be talked around, never represented or recounted . . . and yet it concerns itself with everything as much as nothing.

You don't need to understand in order to know it or to love it. When music works it speaks to people of many worlds, as well as to animals, plants, the gods, and even the earth. The best of all musics have this emphatic and spiritual side. The music must seem indispensable, impossible not to play or to hear. Seeking it brings you comfort as much as adventure.

Gently turning dervishes lifting feet softly above the ground, quivering Balinese monkey chanters shaking their hands toward the circle's pulsing center, Hasidic *nigunim* whose melodies can never resolve—ecstasy is not only found in spiritual musics, but it's there in all those that gather our usually diffuse energy and draw it toward a single point. From that point bursts forth the shout or the song, the concentrated melody, the tune that seems not merely pleasant but *necessary*, so present that it is impossible to refute.

Sometimes there are elaborate reasons for the existence of such music, and stories that explain why what we hear or perform can matter so much. Take this one of Reb Nachman's original Hasidic tales:

At one end of the world there is a mountain; on the top of the mountain, there is a fountain from which water springs forth without ceasing. At the other end of the world lies the heart of the world, and although all things have a heart, the heart of the world is more worthy than any human heart. So at one end of the world is the fountain that gushes from the summit crags, and at the other end is the heart of the earth.

Now the heart is stuck at its end, and the fountain is way at the other. But the heart is in love with the mountain spring: it is filled with an unutterable, endless longing for that distant geyser of water spraying straight from the faraway peak. The heart cannot move, it lies scorched by the sun, but it stares at the mountain so far away, and, barely visible, it sees the gushing water. Since the waters roar only at the summit, they can always be seen, even from thousands of miles away. If the heart were to lose sight of the spring for even one instant, it would cease to live, and if the heart would die, then all the world would die, for the life of the world is contained within the life of its heart.

Once the heart tried to get closer to the fountain, but when it moved just a bit nearer the water fell out of view, so it could not proceed, as it needs to be able to see the water to remain alive.

So what happens at night, you ask? The heart becomes dark with grief, for as the sun falls the water stops glistening in the distance. The earth's heart knows that it will die of longing, and when the heart is dead all the earth and all creatures on this earth will die. As the day draws to a close, therefore, the heart begins to sing farewell to the mountain waters, singing its grief in a wild, astonishing melody, while the mountain spring sings farewell to the heart. Their songs are filled with endless love and longing.

Why does everything continue? Why isn't the world long dead and gone if even one night brings with it such impossible sadness? That's why we are here. The true and attentive human being keeps watch over the situation. In that last moment before the day is done, and the spring is gone, and the heart dead, and the world over, a good person comes and gives a new day to the heart, and the heart gives the new day to the spring, and so they live again.

When the day returns, it too returns with melody, and with strange and beautiful words that contain all wisdom. Each day comes with its own song, a song that no one has ever seen or heard before. And for as long as there are good people, true musicians, on this earth, each new day will not be the last.

Love is about the search, the longing, the striving for the pure sound you will never quite find. Yet ecstasy is not the same as love. It is the deep pleasure that actually arrives, that is there for the taking. For example, I find it is impossible to doubt music while actually playing it. Even as the rest of my life seems overpopulated with questions and uncertainties about why one thing should be done instead of another, in the midst of the playing, dancing around silence and space with the presence of notes, the music always seems to matter.

Mattering in itself is not enough, though. I still want to reach for those notes that *must* be played, that are right because they are essential melodies, unavoidable tones, songs that cannot be defied. This music is silent even when it sings because it does not speak—it cannot be reduced by explanation. Musical mystics are often smiling, laughing, crying with joy into the world with songs that spread the human spirit not above the world but out into it, mingling with the arena of colors, species, and winds. You must make these notes matter almost too much, such that you can't imagine the sound ever stopping and an instant of it lasts an eternity of pleasure.

The best music is both certain and ambiguous at once. You don't know why it matters so; you don't know what it's for. It falls between cracks of genre and purpose, being neither popular nor ascetic, earthy or mannered, raw or refined, but in between all categories and rules, transcending all boundaries critics wish to place it in. You need not know anything about it to love it; you will feel it grab hold of you and not want to turn it off or down, yet not know that it is manipulating you or stealing away your soul. For perfection may be a dream, but ecstasy is never beyond our reach. It's right there in the accessible realm of rough delight.

I write music not for instruments but for people. It doesn't matter what horns they play, but who they are and how they can fill in a situation with as little advance knowledge as possible. This is not to encourage a free-for-all but to enjoy the possibilities that chance may suggest. Improvisation may lead to ecstasy when it catches you off guard, when you are surprised into instant pleasure by forces you never knew were there. This is not to deny the reality of the long predictable pursuit, but to remind us that there is always something accidental about happiness as well.

I think of the time I lived above the Ear Inn, a remote Manhattan hangout way downtown, nearly at the edge of the Hudson River. Legendary clarinet master Perry Robinson had a band that would start playing at midnight on a Monday night. Always one of my heroes, the only friend who would ever call me "Maestro!," he sometimes let me join in. One night, the man on the squeeze-box leans near the microphone and starts crooning the tale of the mysterious Buddy Bolden, the first jazz musician, who went ga-ga holding out an ultimate high note on the cornet and then lived thirty more years unnoticed at the Alabama State Mental Institution. What happened to him, I wonder . . . what was he thinking about all those years? What did that one note do to him? He needed to play it; he needed to get lost. There was no other way.

Perry turns to me and calls me up—"Now do it, your turn, *play like Buddy, like this is the last note you will ever let loose*"—and then

I know just where the history of jazz began and where it went wrong: how that first note let loose the madness of our century's sudden music. I'm up there—it's 2 A.M.—and I'm privileged to stand by the master as he leads me into a Russian folk tune he first recorded in the sixties. These impossible memories are the ultimate refrain. The sound and the stories, the memory and the moment, the master and the student—all sounds are Buddha's voice: all one, all none. Our cries are longing for a goal that will never be attained, although it is always right here. For an instant, question no more. Far away from this city lie the fountain and the heart, the mountain and the desert of the world. I taste the wet song with my dry, parched tongue.

LUCI SHAW

Some mornings she simply cannot

Some mornings she simply cannot
bring herself to pray. Even so, a prayer
will at times break through her clenched lips,
announcing the slow drain at her heart.
She will raise her face from its cage of fingers
and gape at the fog that has lain itself down
over the field behind her house like
a dream of erasure. Even the green trees have
lost color. No air breathes. Not a wing of sound
flies back from the highway behind the hill.

And then some midnight, when faith
has quite emptied itself, a familiar loneliness
makes itself at home under her ribs.
A ghost of God? An inkling? She holds
her breath, listens as a small draught
weathers its way through the eaves,
into her ears. The next moment she hears her child
stir in the room down the hall, calling
her name, as if he names her longing and in
that naming, names a kind of answer.

ELIEZER SHORE

A Single Glance: A Retelling
from Bas Ayin

The first thing young Moshe Yitzchak did upon arriving in Vienna was to change his name; the second was to enroll in an academy of secular studies. Neither step would have pleased his parents, but it would be a long time before they found out. Moshe Yitzchak had been traveling for several years now, and his contact with them during that time had been minimal. Of course he still loved them, and had many fond memories of his childhood, but life had carried him to a place where they could not go.

Moshe Yitzchak had grown up in the small Polish town of Linden. He had received a traditional Jewish education, and his father had tried hard to instill in him an appreciation for his religious heritage. But young Moshe's heart was drawn to something else— to a wider world, to new ways of thinking and acting. The ghetto walls were collapsing, and new possibilities were opening themselves to the Jews. Moshe read avidly and was drawn to philosophy and science. As soon as he was old enough, he left Linden and began to travel. Slowly, his outer appearance adapted to the new world in which he found himself, and likewise did his beliefs. How archaic were the superstitions of his parents, how unsuited to the modern world in which he now lived.

Finally, Moshe Yitzchak arrived in Vienna. He changed his name to Moses and enrolled in a conservatory. Because he was bright, he quickly made up for years of lost studies. And as he progressed, he took on more and more of the local customs. It was not long before he lost all semblance of a small-town Jewish boy. On finishing his studies, he decided to pursue a career in medicine. He enrolled in university and quickly rose in prominence. After receiving his degree, he began to work as a surgeon in the Central Vienna Hospital. He was admired for his skill and expertise; his Jewishness was never an issue.

Rabbi Yehoshua Rokeach, the Grand-Rabbi of Belz, was one of the leaders of European Jewry. From his Chassidic court in Galicia, his influence spread throughout Europe. In 1855, at the age of thirty, he had inherited his father's place as rebbe, and for nearly forty years he led his flock with wisdom and insight. He was not only a scholar of Torah, but a man of the world, engaged in politics and every area of communal activity. Like his father, he was a fierce antagonist of the *Haskalah,* the "Enlightenment" movement that was stealing so many European Jews away from their heritage.

Now, at only sixty-nine years of age, he was showing serious signs of weakness. A strange illness gripped his body, and though outwardly he remained positive and encouraging, inwardly he suffered terribly. He had visited nearly every doctor in Galicia, but none could offer him a cure. His chassidim were even more concerned, for the rebbe had hinted to them that soon, his guiding presence would no longer be available to lead them through the world.

When his condition deteriorated further, his followers pressed him to travel to Vienna for treatment by Europe's finest doctors. The trip from Galicia was difficult, and the rebbe arrived weak and depleted. At the Central Vienna Hospital, the experts assessed his condition—he would need a major operation as soon as possible, and even then the chances of his recovery were slim. The operation was scheduled for one o'clock the following afternoon. The chassidim spent that entire morning fasting and praying for their leader's welfare.

At about a quarter to one, the rebbe was brought into the operating room. Before separating from his chassidim, he spoke to them privately. He told them not to fear, that G-d would not abandon them, that they needed only to follow in the path he set to speed the final redemption. Then, as the attendant wheeled him away, the rebbe closed his eyes and went deep inside himself. His face was still, his lips were uttering a silent prayer.

The doctors in the operating room were all ready. They were only waiting for the anesthesiologist. Moses stood among them, towards the back. When the rebbe was wheeled in, Moses was struck by his beauty—such a love and gentleness radiated from his pale face. The room was quiet; the rebbe was in another place.

Suddenly, the rebbe opened his eyes and began to survey the doctors who surrounded him. It was as though he was looking for something familiar that he sensed in the room. Finally, he noticed the young doctor standing beside the wall.

"Doctor, what is your name?" he asked. Moses was taken aback by the sudden, personal call.

"Moses Wilner," he answered.

"Moses, are you Jewish?" the rebbe asked gently.

Moses coughed. He nodded his head in acknowledgment.

The rebbe continued. "Moses, do you believe in the Creator and Ruler of the world?"

Moses' face went red. What a question! He wanted to leave the room, to avoid the stares of his colleagues—but the operation was about to begin. He paused a moment. "Yes, Rebbe, I do," he answered.

The other doctors in the room were bewildered. They looked on in amazement as a strange dialogue began to unfold between patient and doctor. The rebbe, however, paid them no attention. All his concentration was focused upon the young Jewish doctor who had turned his back on his faith.

"And in our righteous Moshiach, who is ready to come at any moment and redeem his people from exile, do you believe in him too, Moses?"

Moses was dead still. There was no place to hide. He closed his eyes from the rebbe's enquiring gaze and tried to formulate an answer. The words came out slowly.

"Ah, hmm, you see, Rebbe, I believe in the historical process, that mankind is gradually progressing. One day, there will come a time of world peace, and then our people will experience their redemption and find a place among the nations of the world. But I do not believe that this will come about through the influence of one man, the Moshiach, who will somehow transform all of humanity. That strikes me as completely impossible."

The rebbe of Belz was silent. Then, suddenly, he turned his whole head to face the young doctor. His glance was penetrating.

For the first time, Moses looked directly into his eyes—they were so deep, so full of wisdom; kind but strong, gentle but intense. Moses was transfixed. He felt himself being drawn into the rebbe's gaze, as though it contained some profound secret. Then, in his own mind, hidden chambers of memory slowly began to open. Memories of a forgotten past, of his childhood and his parents' home, beautiful memories—and disturbing ones. Powerful emotions surged through him: elation, ecstasy, fear, longing. The rebbe's eyes grabbed him, they were touching his soul. Enough! He had to look away. Too much was being revealed, emotions that he could not face.

He tried to avert his gaze, but he could not. He tried to turn his head, but it was impossible. It was as though he was gripped by the rebbe's gaze. Moses' face became white, then red, then white again. The veins on his neck began to protrude. His body started to shake, his hands to tremble.

The other doctors stared on in amazement. A storm was raging inside their colleague, though they could not perceive its source. Moses gasped for air. All his efforts to calm himself failed, which only increased his panic. The rebbe held him firmly with his eyes; they penetrated to his depths. The young doctor began to softly cry.

Another moment passed, and then the rebbe removed his gaze from him. Moses felt his composition slowly returning. Afterward, the rebbe looked at him once more. This time his eyes were gentle, comforting.

"Moses, now do you believe that one person can influence another with a single glance alone? That is exactly how it will be when the Moshiach comes. G-d has chosen him to lead the world to perfection. He will return all people from their erroneous ways."

Moses lowered his eyes and nodded in submission. "The rebbe is right, and I was mistaken," he said in a whisper.

The anesthesiologist had already arrived, and in a few moments the rebbe was asleep. The operation lasted several hours and was a success. Throughout Europe, chassidim rejoiced.

Two weeks passed, and the rebbe recuperated in the hospital. During that time, an air of sanctity and peace rested upon the building. Finally, he left Vienna to return home. On the train ride back to Galicia, Rabbi Yehoshua Rokeach, the Grand-Rabbi of Belz, passed away. He was surrounded by a small group of chassidim at the time. Among them was a young doctor named Moshe Yitzchak Wilner, who was returning home to recover a treasure he had long ago left behind.

LOUIS SIMPSON

A God in Darkness: Literature and Belief
from Image

A god in darkness often walks obscured.

Gérard de Nerval

It's four o'clock, past the heat of midday, and a sea breeze has sprung up. Trees are rustling, the hollow trunks of bamboo in the lane are knocking together and talking, and our mother is telling about her childhood in Russia.

There was snow and freezing cold. She was terribly afraid of rats because they ran across the floor of the cellar where she slept. Rats brought the fever, typhus, of which her sister Lisa died. She was sick too—if a kind-hearted neighbor had not nursed her she would have died. When she regained consciousness she looked in the mirror. They had cut off all her hair and burned her doll, the only one she had, made of rags and a stick.

She told of coming on a ship to New York, bringing the two youngest children with her. She herself was only twelve years old. She worked in the garment district, sewing tucks in shirts, then became a movie actress, a "supernumerary" as they were called in those days. She traveled to Jamaica as one of Annette Kellerman's Bathing Beauties to make a movie. There she met my father and they were married. "And lived happily ever after," my brother Herbert said. He was five years older and went to a boarding school in the country. He was home for the holidays.

Our father's side of the family was from Scotland. An old lady named Aunt Annie drove up to the house in a black buggy. She had come for tea, and she sang us a Scottish song, "Annie Laurie." Sometimes Herbert and I would stay with our father's relatives. One of his sisters was married to the postmaster general. They were Methodists, and Sabbath was to be a day of rest. We were not allowed to do anything that might be construed as not resting. Playing was strictly prohibited. I was not to run about in the yard with the chickens and turkeys and pretend that a drifting feather was an aeroplane. I could not play a board game such as snakes-and-ladders with my cousin Sybil. My aunts and cousins took me with them to church at Easter. The scent of flowers and the heat were stifling. It seemed that the hymns and prayers would never end. The sun was dazzling.

Sundays at our house were different. Our father was a lawyer and a "free thinker." One day when I explored a closet I came across a sword and a case containing some regalia, including medals and ribbons—he was a Freemason. On the weekend he might be on a trip in the country, bird shooting with a friend, or he would work at fixing or making something in his "carpenter's shop." Then he joined the Yacht Club, bought a motorboat, and spent Sunday mornings boating in the harbor.

Though our mother told stories about her Russian childhood she did not say anything about being Jewish. When she was living in New York and came home from the factory there would be people in outlandish clothes, black coats and hats, who stared at her and made comments to her mother in Yiddish. She was glad to escape from this atmosphere. In Jamaica she joined the golf club and served tea at four o'clock. She admired the English with their fine manners and way of speaking.

One day she disappeared. No one told us why. Our father had been having an affair with his stenographer, and our mother had found out—but there were things it was better for children not to know. Such was the wisdom of Jamaicans of the "better class"—they were still living in the age of Queen Victoria. All that my brother and I were told was that our mother had gone to America.

There would be no more stories about Russia. I turned to the garden boy and pestered him to tell me a story while he was cooking his lunch in a can suspended over a circle of stones. The stories he told had come all the way from Africa. The hero was Br'er Nancy, the long-legged spider who was full of cunning and tricks. There were Br'er John Crow, Br'er Alligator, Br'er Tiger. How could there be a tiger in a story that came from Africa?

I read or looked at the books in my father's study. There was a set of books for young people called *Journeys Through Bookland.* The first volume had nursery rhymes with pictures. The reading progressed in difficulty until, in the last volume, you would be reading a story by Edgar Allan Poe, an essay on self-help, or a humorous piece in dialect. I didn't keep to the order of reading but jumped ahead, so that I landed in a picture of a skeleton in armor that scared the daylights out of me. I kept returning to it, turning the pages with a fascination mixed with fear, the way a tongue returns to a cavity.

There was the London *Times History of the Great War.* There were books with heavy covers lettered in gold, about travel in South America, India, or Africa. The pages were decorated with drawings of jaguars, pythons, and other wild animals. These belonged to my father; there was a bookplate saying that the book had been awarded to Aston Simpson as a prize by his school.

There was a copy of *Tales from Shakespeare.* It had a drawing of Banquo's ghost—this too gave me a turn. In those days people weren't careful about protecting young people from reading that was beyond them. Perhaps its being beyond them was why they found it interesting.

Our father had been a fan of Rudyard Kipling. There were pocket editions of *Barrack Room Ballads* and *Plain Tales from the Hills*. And—these may have been our mother's—novels, the best-sellers of the twenties, works by such writers as Elinor Glyn and Warwick Deeping. All these books were mixed higgledy-piggledy on the shelves—the best arrangement, I think, for it leads you into making discoveries and broadens the mind.

From time to time our mother in America would send us books with brightly colored jackets: *Gulliver's Travels, Tom Sawyer, Tarzan and the Golden Lion, Penrod and Sam*, and, when I was older, *Traveller's Library*, edited by Somerset Maugham. I still have the book and recall the excitement with which I read Joseph Conrad's *Youth*. The tubby volume held whole novels and an assortment of stories, essays, and poems by English authors.

But I am getting ahead of myself. When I was nine I was sent to a boarding school in the country. My brother had preceded me by a few years. Munro College was a hundred miles from home, and we were taught to be just like boys in England. Masters had been brought from England to teach us—with a few exceptions: the French master who came from Alsace-Lorraine, and a teacher of mathematics who was a Jamaican and had a dusky complexion. A fine time he must have had in the common room where the masters hung out to smoke between classes!

On my first evening at Munro, when we prepared our lessons, I was given a Latin verb to memorize. Latin was the basis of a British public school education. It taught you to think just like the boy sitting next to you. One day if you should find yourself at some far-flung outpost of the empire you could take comfort in the thought that a fellow at an outpost six thousand miles away knew the same passage by Virgil. Or if standing in a trench with cold water up to your knees, you could remember Horace: "*Dulce et decorum est pro patria mori.*" The exams we would take in order to leave school would be graded in England, and a few of us would stay an extra two years and be awarded the Cambridge Higher Schools Certificate, equivalent to two years' attendance at Cambridge.

There was the usual required reading—Shakespeare's *Julius Caesar* was a perennial. But most of my reading was done in books from the school library: stories of adventure by writers such as "Sapper," Baroness Orczy, and Rafael Sabatini, comical stories by W. W. Jacobs. There were magazines, the *Gem* and *Magnet,* with stories about schoolboys in England. They made school seem like great fun. The French master was funny with his fractured English. The fat boy, Billy Bunter, was always eating pies and jam, and was often whacked on the bottom with a "fives bat," whatever that was, by one of the big boys. How Billy would howl, "Yaroo!" Tom Merry and his friends were cheerful and good at games. A few boys were bullies and liars. They went sneaking around but were always found out.

One day I discovered literature, that some books are more interesting because they are better written. The crucial event was reading *Vanity Fair.* I was fascinated with the battle of Waterloo and read that Thackeray wrote about it in *Vanity Fair,* so I sent away to England for the book, out of my pocket money. There was no battle, Thackeray tiptoed around it, but I was enthralled by his voice. It was vivacious, yet there lurked behind it an enormous grief. I would read lying beneath the willows that lined the drive from the gate to the chapel. At about the same time I discovered the poems of A. E. Housman. He too was sad and enchanting. I had many of his lines by heart, about lost love, or being hanged, or going off to war never to return.

In class we read poems by twentieth-century English poets of the Georgian school: Walter de la Mare, John Masefield, W. H. Davies, and a dozen others. Much of it was about nature. Or the poet might express a wish to be in some exotic, faraway Eastern place—Samarkand, wherever that was. The wish to be there was understandable if you lived in the English drizzle. There were patriotic poems such as the sonnet by Rupert Brooke saying that if he died in some foreign field the dust where he was buried would be richer because it was "forever England."

I have remembered one of the Georgian poems because it was remarkably obtuse. Many people think that poetry is written without thought, and this certainly was. It was titled "To a Lady Seen from a Train." The woman was walking in a field. The poet found her ridiculous because she was wearing gloves and she was fat. You could hear him telling it as an amusing anecdote at the table.

O why do you walk through the fields in gloves,
Missing so much and so much?
O fat white woman whom nobody loves?

The poet thought the woman insensitive because she was not touching the flowers with her bare hands. It did not occur to him that she was at least walking in a field while he was sitting in a railway carriage smelling cigars and coal smoke. Why was being fat so contemptible? And how did he know that nobody loved her? The poet was one of those people who think themselves superior but are actually quite foolish. They take what I. A. Richards calls their stock responses to be their guide.

Public school boys had a whole set of stock responses. Above all, we believed in the empire on which the sun never set. Heroes had won the British empire from the cruel Spaniards and vainglorious French and defended it against the beastly Germans. We believed that England was the finest place on earth. When I was fourteen I wrote an essay in celebration of the coronation of George VI that won a first prize and was published in the *Daily*

Gleaner. It was a paean to the royal family and the glory of empire.

We also had a religion. We went to the Anglican chapel every morning and evening, and on Sunday we dressed in blue suits and attended a long service. We were exposed to religion in this way for most months of the year, and this lasted until, at the age of seventeen or eighteen, we left school. But in fact very few of the boys took their chapel-going to heart. When I was a small boy the services were presided over by the headmaster. He also taught Latin to the upper forms. He taught it with a cane in his hand with which he would beat a boy who was slow to learn. He was feared and detested by the boys. And this was the man who preached to us on Sunday.

If we could we avoided the long Sunday service—we hid out in the woods. One Sunday a number of boys had the same idea. Too many unfortunately—the gaps in the ranks were plainly visible. We were found out and called up to the headmaster's study. We expected to be flogged near to death, but instead he told us to memorize the psalms of David. When we had memorized a psalm we were to climb the stairs to his study, stand before him, and repeat it. We were to do this for the rest of the term.

When this man died there was another, better headmaster who came from Canada and was a marvel of civilization by comparison. But in neither case did we see a reason to believe what we were being taught about religion. It played no part in our lives. The parables and miracles we heard about from the pulpit did not help with math or science or with football, cricket, track, gymnastics, or boxing. As for the Sunday morning Prep when we sat and read scripture or drew, once again, a map of the valley of the Euphrates, what did this have to do with us who lived thousands of years and as many miles away?

We lived every day with human nature. Some of the boys were innocent, the kind mothers dote on. Others were knowing and cunning, and a few were positively evil. There were big boys who liked to beat and kick small boys. We were exposed to human behavior in most of its varieties, with one big exception. There were no women at the school except the school nurse and the old woman who supervised the laundry. There were black or brown women who made our beds, emptied the chamber pots under our beds, and scrubbed the floor. I am sorry to say that we did not regard them as women. They were servants.

When I was fifteen I had a teacher, H. J. Andrews, who came from Scotland. He taught us Shakespeare. His teaching of *Macbeth* opened my eyes—the play was life concentrated and intensified. The hair rose on the back of my neck. When we read *The Tempest* I was filled with a sense of beauty and wonder.

In my last years at school I was reading modern authors such as D. H. Lawrence and T. S. Eliot. The writer considered most avant-garde in the late 1930s was Aldous Huxley. He wrote about science as one who was informed, and about sex as though he knew all about that too. Then I came across the so-called Oxford poets, W. H. Auden, Stephen Spender, C. Day Lewis, and Louis MacNeice. Their poems were published by Penguin Books in a series called New Writing. They wrote scathingly of the bourgeoisie, how beastly it was, and looked forward to a workers' state.

When I left school I fell in with some young men in Kingston who wrote for a publication called *Public Opinion.* The opinions were to the Left. In the late 1930s there was social unrest. The men who worked in the cane fields and banana plantations wanted a fair share of the profits. There was a movement by Jamaicans to break with the Mother Country and take the government in their own hands. I published a few pieces in *Public Opinion:* a book review, a short story, and two or three poems, and thought of myself as politically sophisticated.

Our father died suddenly. Our stepmother inherited almost all the estate, and my brother and I had to find lodgings in town. When my mother wrote asking if I would like to visit her in New York, I did not hesitate. My father had not left me enough money to go to a university—I might win a scholarship to Oxford, but the chances were slim. My brother would stay in Jamaica to continue his study of law, but what would I do? I sailed for America. The journey would last all my life.

In the fall of 1940 I entered Columbia College. There was a course in great books, Humanities, that all Columbia freshmen had to take. One week I agreed with the Greek writer of tragedy that it was better not to have been born. The next, I was persuaded to think like Socrates that the world was a reflection and distortion of perfect forms. I visualized them as hovering in the sky. When I came to the end of the freshman year with Freud and Kafka, I did not know what to think.

Halfway through my studies at Columbia I was drafted into the American army. I saw active service in Europe with the 101st Airborne Division. We were trained to land by parachute or glider behind the enemy, wreak havoc, and hold till the main body caught up with us. I served with the 101st in Normandy, Holland, Belgium, and Germany.

At Bastogne the division was surrounded by the Germans. It was freezing and we were hungry. On Christmas Eve a man came from the rear to tell us that a religious service was being held for those who wanted to go. I trudged with some others through the snow to Bastogne and heard the chaplain deliver a short sermon. He said that we might be wondering why we were here—we were defending our way of life. We said some prayers, sang a hymn, trudged back to our foxholes, and waited for the next German attack.

Those scenes have passed like a dream. I returned to the United States and was discharged from the army. I went back to Columbia to finish my degree, and it seems that I forgot to eat or sleep and spent hours writing short stories and trying to write a novel. I had a breakdown—what then was called combat fatigue and now is called post-traumatic stress syndrome—and was sent to a hospital on Long Island.

It seems that before my breakdown I was much concerned about God. I have no recollection of this but was told so by a psychologist, one I had to see after leaving the hospital. He asked me if I was still thinking about Jesus. I said that I wasn't and he nodded approval. He said that it was all nonsense.

In the novel by Nathanael West, *Miss Lonelyhearts,* the protagonist thinks obsessively about Jesus. At the same time he is looking at things like a surrealist. It seems that in the months preceding my collapse I was like Miss Lonelyhearts: I saw symbols in store window displays, and words had a hidden significance.

My mind was disordered. I set about putting it in order. In the years that followed I had nothing to do with religion unless it were to go to a wedding. I studied, wrote, and published poems and literary criticism. The poems were about my experiences in the war, about love, and about America, for there was much about my adopted country that I found strange. Common things held more meaning for me than they did for those who were accustomed to them. I supported myself by working in a publishing house. Then I went back to Columbia, obtained a Ph.D., and in due course became a professor of English.

In the 1960s I was teaching English at the University of California at Berkeley. The professors then most admired were epigones of the New Criticism and trained to explain the use of figures of speech, symbols, and so on. Literature was to be examined objectively as a text and not another thing. There were fallacies to be avoided by the good critic—for instance, the intentional fallacy. What the author thought he was doing was irrelevant.

I wasn't much good at analyzing texts—it killed the pleasure of reading. My way of teaching was to concentrate on the ideas in the work. But this kind of teaching too was unsatisfactory. It was all very well to enthuse over the ideas in a novel or poem or play, but one book was not like another. It was like ordering in a Chinese restaurant, one dish from column A, another from B, and so on. There was no connection, no meaning to the whole.

The university gave me a grant so that I could get some of my own writing done, and I traveled with my wife and children to New York. A man I had known at Columbia was now a leading psychoanalyst. I asked him to arrange for me to take a beginner's course in psychoanalysis at Presbyterian Hospital. He obliged, and I sat alongside men and women who were training to be analysts.

I came away from the course thinking that Freudian psychology might cure the neuroses but threw no light on the urge to create. Dostoevsky was epileptic, and he was said to have molested a child. Other men have had epilepsy and have molested a child, but they have not written a work comparable to *The Brothers Karamazov*. Why do we write? And in one form rather than another?

Some years later I was given another grant, this time by the Guggenheim Foundation, and took my family to London. It happened that in London there was a teacher of Buddhism, Christmas Humphreys. The poet Gary Snyder had learned about Buddhism in Japan, and people in San Francisco had adopted an Asian way of life—streets in Haight-Ashbury shimmered with beads and tinkled with bells. I introduced myself to Christmas

Humphreys and for several months attended sessions in meditation. With half a dozen others I learned to sit on the floor with my
legs crossed, hold an upright position, and concentrate on . . .
nothing. I was to keep my mind from wandering, following a
sound or thought. This was an exercise of considerable difficulty.
To be conscious and not to think is almost impossible—I was able
to do this for only a few seconds. At such moments I felt that my
breathing was merging with a rhythm in space. I could almost feel
and hear it. I was becoming *It*. But a car would go by on the street,
and I was back with my thoughts and myself.

However, these exercises did make a difference. The essence of
Buddhism is concentration on what is actually there—reality is in
the present moment. The thing is to rid the mind of distractions.
This suited my taste in literature and my practice as a writer. I did
not like fanciful writing—I much preferred realism. There were
writers who were lavish with metaphors: a thing was not what it
appeared to be, but another thing. I found this an unwelcome in-
trusion of the author's personality. I subscribed to Whitman's idea
of writing: "I will not have in my writing any elegance of effect or
originality to hang in the way between me and the rest like curtains. . . . What I tell I tell for precisely what it is."

Mark Twain in *Huckleberry Finn* had written magnificent passages of clear prose that made you feel you were actually at the
scene. Hemingway perfected a transparent style in his short stories and *The Sun Also Rises*. So did William Carlos Williams in poems such as the one about an old woman eating plums out of a
paper bag. This was the kind of writing I liked. My exercises in
meditation encouraged me to think that I was on the right track.

But when I returned to the States I gave up meditating. It
seemed unnecessary. When I was absorbed in writing, forgetful of
self, I was as close to reality as I ever wished to be. On two other
occasions, however, I meditated again. The first time was in the

company of a poet and his female companion. A remarkable thing happened. I felt that I was being filled with waves of energy. This built until my body felt like iron. At the same time it seemed that I was about to rise and float in the air. These feelings became so strong that I had to clap my hands and break off. I resumed meditating, and the same thing happened again as though I were connected to a dynamo. The poet, who was knowledgeable about such matters, told me that I had entered an advanced stage of meditation, something to do with my spine and a snake.

The other occasion was not so exciting. I was in Hawaii and thought I would visit a group of Americans who practiced Buddhism. I sat in a circle of people who chanted meaningless sounds. It struck me as ridiculous. In any case, neither the Zen Buddhism I had been learning about in London nor this other, ritual kind was the answer I was seeking. But what was I seeking? If I knew that I would have found it.

I must step back once more to find the thread. As I have said, my parents separated when I was a child and my mother went back to America. My brother was away at school in the country. There were days when I had no one to talk to but my dog. Then I too went off to boarding school where I had no time to feel lonely. The vacations, however, would find me once more alone with my thoughts.

Our father married his typist and we moved to a house at Bournemouth, on the sea. My brother was studying law and left every morning for the office. In the vacations I had plenty of time on my hands. I would read a book from the library in Kingston and go bicycling or swimming. I had a friend who lived on the same street, and we swam together or played table tennis. But I spent many days alone. I would walk along the shore or bicycle to the foothills above Kingston. I had time to commune with nature. At such times I felt a connection between myself and the scene I was looking at. It wasn't just waves or trees—the scene held an intelligence that was communicating with me in some fashion.

The sense of this can be strong. Here is a poem on the subject by the French poet Gérard de Nerval. It is titled "Lines in Gold." Above the poem Nerval quotes a saying by Pythagoras: "Why not! Everything feels!"

Man, do you think yours is the only soul?
Look around you. Everything that you see
Quivers with being. Though your thoughts are free,
One thing you do not think about, the whole.

Beasts have a mind. Respect it. Flowers too.
Look at one. Nature brought forth each petal.
There is a mystery that sleeps in metal.
"Everything feels!" and has power over you.

Be careful. The blind wall is spying on us.
All matter is connected to a word . . .
Do not make it serve some unholy purpose.

A god in darkness often walks obscured.
As eyelids of a new-born infant open
A spirit wakes and gazes in the stone.

It is not uncommon to feel that there is a god concealed in darkness, and it is only a short step from this to the feeling that the "god in darkness" is not one of a multitude of gods, but one. Looking back, I think that I have taken that short step many times in my life, but not consecutively. In between I would not think about it.

I cannot say that I was religious. And I didn't have much faith in principles—what Conrad's Marlow calls "acquisitions, clothes, pretty rags—rags that would fly off at the first good shake." And I had not managed to acquire what Marlow says you need, a "deliberate belief." I wasn't yet experienced enough in the ways of the world to have one.

Some years ago I traveled to Australia as writer-in-residence at a college in their New England, sheep and cattle raising country. I have written a poem about what happened there. It tells how I would go outside at night and, with the aid of a map, try to find the positions of the southern constellations. One day I was invited by a friend to travel with him and his girlfriend to a party. We were to stay the night. The poem continues:

We arrived. I was introduced,
and they made up a bed for me
on the porch at the back.
Then the party began to arrive:
Australians, lean and athletic.
They put a tape on the stereo,
turned it up full blast,
and danced or stood and shouted

to each other above the noise.

I danced with two or three women
and tried shouting. Then I went
and sat on the bed on the porch.
There was nowhere to go, no door
I could close to shut out the noise.

So I went for a walk
in the dark, away from the sound.
There were gum trees, wind rustling
the leaves. Or was it snakes?

There are several venomous kinds.
The taipan. There's a story
about a child who was sitting
on a log and fell backward
onto a taipan. It struck him
twenty-three times.
There's the tiger snake and the brown.
When they have finished telling you
about snakes, they start on spiders.
You don't need these—you have only to walk
into the bush. There are stories
about campers who did, and were lost
and never seen again.

All this was on my mind.
I stepped carefully, keeping the lights
of the house behind me in sight.
And when I saw a clearing
in the trees, I walked to it.

                    *

I stood in the middle of the clearing
looking at the sky. It was glittering
with unknown constellations.
Everything I had ever known
seemed to have disappeared.

And who was I, standing there
in the middle of Australia
at night? I had ceased to exist.
There was only whatever it was
that was looking at the sky
and listening to the wind.

After a while I broke away
and went back to the lights and the party.
A month later I left Australia.
But ever since, to this day,
there has been a place in my mind,
a clearing in the shadows,
and above it, stars and constellations
so bright and thick they seem to rustle.
And beyond them . . . infinite space,
eternity, you name it.

There's nothing that stands between me
and it, whatever it is.

I have said that it is a short step from this kind of feeling to believing in God. But it isn't an easy step to take. How does the It
become a You? For many people who have had the kind of feeling
I have described, who have stepped outside and looked at the
night sky, the next step is not necessary. They do not take it. Jean-
Jacques Rousseau believed that nature was good and did not take
the next step. Wordsworth wrote poems about communing with
nature, but not until he was well on in years did he take the step
from saying that there was a power that worked through nature to
calling this power God. Other poets and writers in the nineteenth
century would turn away from nature but not to a belief in God.

They rejected the faith the church represented. Instead they made a goddess of Beauty and a god of Art.

Why not be satisfied to remain with nature? Why not be like the chemist Homais in Flaubert's novel *Madame Bovary*, who sums up the spirit of the Age of Reason? Why not believe with Monsieur Homais in nature and science?

> "I have got a God, a religion—my own religion," the chemist answered. "In fact I've got more than the lot of them, with all their mumbo-jumbo.—I worship God! I believe in the Supreme Being; a Creator, no matter who he be, who has placed us here below to do our duty as citizens and fathers. . . . But I don't need to go and kiss a lot of silver plate in a church. . . . You can praise God just as well in the woods and the fields, or by gazing up into the vault of heaven, like the ancients. My God is the God of Socrates, of Franklin, of Voltaire and Béranger! . . . And I cannot worship an old fogey of a God who walks round his garden with a stick in his hand, lodges his friends in the bellies of whales, dies with a cry on his lips and comes to life again three days later: all of which is intrinsically absurd and utterly opposed, moreover, to all physical laws. . . ."

There you have it, the Enlightenment in a nutshell. Why not take your stand with Monsieur Homais and stay gazing up at the vault of an empty heaven?

The authors I admire, whom I keep in mind when I write, whom I try to please, hold certain ideas in common: ideas about kindness, about love, about justice. They detest cruelty and injustice. Under this broad description I include authors as far removed in space and time as Shakespeare and Chekhov. Like members of a family, these authors may quarrel, but there is something that binds them together. They are not bound by principles—as Marlow said, principles fly off at the first good shake.

But love binds and moves in a certain direction. Being moved isn't fun . . . love may move you in a direction that is hard and painful to take.

In Chekhov's play *Uncle Vanya,* Vanya suffers a great deal. When Professor Serebryakov urges selling the estate that he, Vanya, has worked so hard to preserve, Vanya tries to shoot him, but luckily he misses. At the end of the play Vanya's niece, Sonia, speaks:

> *Well, what can we do? We must go on living! We shall go on living, Uncle Vanya. We shall live through a long, long succession of days and tedious evenings. We shall patiently suffer the trials which Fate imposes on us; we shall work for others, now and in our old age, and we shall have no rest. When our time comes we shall die submissively, and over there, beyond the grave, we shall say that we've suffered, that we've wept, that we've had a bitter life, and God will take pity on us. And then, Uncle dear, we shall both begin to know a life that is bright and beautiful and lovely. We shall rejoice and look back at these troubles of ours with tender feelings, with a smile—and we shall have rest. I believe it, Uncle, I believe it fervently, passionately. . . . We shall have rest!*

Sonia continues to speak . . . of a heaven covered with stars like diamonds, of seeing all earthly evil and suffering swept away by a grace that will fill the whole world, and a life that will be peaceful and sweet as a caress. "I believe it," she says, "I believe it."

Did Chekhov share the belief he is expressing? Any literary critic could point out that Sonia is only a character in a play and that the feelings a character expresses are not to be taken to be those of the author. But surely if Chekhov does not share Sonia's belief he understands it. Nothing can come of nothing, and something—words that move us like this—must come of something.

When I think of what the authors I have loved agree on, there appears not a mist, not the vault of heaven, but a palpable living being with flesh and blood—the figure of a man who died two thousand years ago on a hill outside Jerusalem. There is nothing this man said that I do not believe.

But was he God? Can I bring myself to believe this? Could a man have risen from the dead? To believe this is to take a truly giant step—as the chemist Homais said, it is against all physical laws. But there have been wonderful changes in physical laws since Homais spoke. Besides, it seems impossible that I am alive, here, writing this. And yet I am.

CODA

Literature is concerned with the life of the world, belief with the life of the spirit and takes the form of religion, set prayers and rituals. I have wondered if my belief is going to change my writing. I would not want this to happen—I cannot imagine myself writing in any other way. To change would mean giving up writing altogether.

But what is new is not belief. Some years ago I said, in the preface to a book of poems, "I have always felt that there is a power and intelligence in things. I felt it as a boy when I watched the sun setting from the top of a mountain, when I rode a bicycle in the lanes of Kingston or walked along the shore listening to the sea. I felt that power when I first saw Manhattan rise out of the Atlantic, the towers a poet describes as 'moody water-loving giants.' During the war I felt there was an intelligence watching and listening." I said that in my poems I drew disparate experiences together and attempted to bring order out of chaos.

My brief exercises in Buddhism were helpful; they taught me to concentrate on the thing before me and to understand that reality, eternity, is here and now. But I could not lose myself in contemplation of an impersonal universe.

The change is not in what I believe, but in me—now I know that I believe. But if this will not change my writing, what difference has it made? The difference is in me—I am a great deal easier in my mind for knowing why I think as I do.

Others will do different things—there is one thing I can do, and since I can I must. I shall continue to write as I have, about real events, in language that can be understood. I have always found the abstract and vague writing that some people think of as poetry to be pointless and boring. Baudelaire said it: the life we see around us is a "transitory and fugitive element," but we do not have the right to hold it in contempt or pass it by. "In suppressing it you must necessarily fall into the void of an abstract and indefinable beauty."

The author of the parables spoke to men and women in words they could understand and illustrated his teaching with stories from common life. He did not give lectures but pointed to the lilies of the field. He is an author—dramatist, story-teller, and poet.

Bible Studies
from Poetry

1

Outside Kroger, the prophet rages,
There is none righteous, no, not one!
holding the book aloft, the chosen pages
memorized. The parking lot is biblical
in this heat; he's working hard. My wife smiles
at him after strapping on the harness
and settling our newborn close against her chest,
happy with the weight of the small body
fragile as belief in God.

No, there is none righteous, no, not one.

2

Inside, the other shoppers stop their carts
and offer their clichés. "She's so good,
just a little angel." "They're such miracles
aren't they?" I nod and give the smile
expected. But really I want to say, "No,
I think you've got the simile wrong.
Parenthood is a land of signs, where

without speech she lets her will be known.
She's more like God. The world needs repair,
and we rush to do her bidding."

3

While God nurses there is relief
for the first time this hour. I gather
cloths, drops, close the hamper. Together
my wife and I think, *Dear Lord, forgive us our unbelief.*

4

Today is Passover,
but I'm a Christian, not a Jew.
The question, What to do?
since not only first-born sons need cover.

Dear God, I will do anything—
paint the door a color the neighbors
will comment on, seed the lawn with ragweed,
goldenrod—to keep the Angel at bay.

Help us through this afternoon, this night,
that will last the rest of our lives.
Help us take faith in the darkening quiet
each evening when it passes over our hearts.

BARBARA BROWN TAYLOR

The Day We Were Left Behind
from Christianity Today

> *When Jesus had said this, as they were watching,*
> *he was lifted up, and a cloud took him out of*
> *their sight.*
>
> Acts 1:9 NRSV

On Sunday mornings, a great division takes place among American people as some go to church and most stay home. Those who stay home are not taking a week off; church is simply not part of their lives. As far as they are concerned, houses of worship are little more than pretty antiques, fussed over by wishful thinkers who do not know when to admit they are wrong and go home. It is one of the most peculiar things twentieth-century human beings can do—to come together week after week with no intention of being useful or productive, but only of facing an ornate wall to declare things they cannot prove about a God they cannot see.

Our word for it is *worship*, and it is hard to justify in this day and age; but those of us who do it over and over again begin to count on it. This is how we learn where we fit. This is how we locate ourselves between the past and the future, between our hopes and our fears, between the earth and the stars. This is how we learn who we are and what we are supposed to be doing: by coming together to sing and to pray, to be silent and to be still, by peering into the darkness together and telling each other what we see when we do.

We may baffle our unbelieving friends and neighbors, but it cannot be helped. Half the time we baffle ourselves, proclaiming good news when the news is so bad, trusting the light when the sky is so dark, continuing to wait on the Savior in our midst when all the evidence suggests that he packed up and left a long, long time ago.

To be theologically correct, we have been waiting on the Savior ever since the first Ascension Day, when Jesus led his disciples to a mount called Olivet just outside of Jerusalem, spoke to them for the last time, and disappeared inside a cloud for good. You can read in Acts 1:6–11 how one moment he was there with them and the next moment he was gone, his well-known hand raised in final blessing, his face grown bright and indistinct, his familiar shape vanishing into the fog like the end of a dream too good to be true—all of it slipping out of their reach until he was no longer there for them, no longer present but past, a memory that would haunt them to the end of their days.

Where he went was to heaven—which may not be up, exactly, as much as it is beyond—and what he went there to do was to finish what he had begun with us. It was not enough that through him God was born into the body of the world; that was just his Christmas gift to us. His ascension gift was that through him the body of the world was borne back to God. By presenting his own ruined, risen body to be seated at the right hand of God, Jesus imported flesh and blood into those holy precincts for the first time. He paved the way for us, so that when we arrive there later everyone will not be quite so shocked by us. He restored the goodness of creation, and ours in particular. By ascending bodily into heaven, he showed us that flesh and blood are good, not bad; that they are good enough for Jesus, good enough for heaven, good enough for God. By putting them on and keeping them on, Jesus has not only brought God to us; he has also brought us to God.

I tried all of that out on a friend last week. "Isn't that incredible?" I said. "Doesn't that make the Ascension come alive for you?"

"Interesting," he said, "but not compelling."

What he meant, I think, is that it is still an abstract idea—an explanation that has very little to do with our day-to-day experience. Almost everything else that happened to Jesus makes sense in terms of my own life. He was born to a human mother; so was I. He ate and drank and slept at night; so do I. He loved people and got angry with people and forgave people; so have I. He wept; me too. He died; I will die too. He rose from the dead; I even know something about that. I have had some Easterlike mornings of my own—joy found in the midst of sorrow, life in the midst of death.

But ascending into heaven to be seated at the right hand of God? That is where Jesus and I part company. That is where he leaves me in the dust. My only experience of the Ascension is from the ground, my neck cranked back as far as it will go, my mouth wide open, my face shielded from the sun by the cloud that is bearing my Lord away.

Luke ends his gospel by telling us that the disciples returned to Jerusalem with great joy. But you have to remember that it had just happened for them, that they had just been with him, and the memory was fresh. They were still running on adrenaline; you can see it in the pictures. Almost every church with stained-glass windows has an ascension window tucked away somewhere. In it, Christ generally hovers in the air, his hands upraised in blessing, while the disciples look up at him with something between awe and delight. But he is there with them—he is in the window—and if they went away joyful, then I cannot help thinking that it was because they thought he would be back in a day or two, next week at the latest.

Two thousand years later, we tend to see the whole thing a little differently. We need a new window to describe our own situation: a window with just us in it—no angels, no Jesus, no heavenly light—just us, still waiting, still watching the sky, our faces turned up like empty cups that only one presence can fill. But he is not present anymore, not the way he used to be.

Ascension Day is the day the present Lord became absent, which may be why it is the most forgotten feast day of the church year. Who wants to celebrate being left behind? Who wants to mark the day that Jesus went out of this world, never to be seen again? Hungry as we are for the presence of God, the one thing we do not need is a day to remind us of God's absence.

Or is that really the one reason, underneath all the other reasons, we are here? Because we have sensed God's absence—in our hollow nights, our pounding hearts, our unanswered prayers—and because those things have not discouraged us from coming here but have in fact brought us here, to seek the presence we have been missing?

Sometimes I think absence is underrated. It is not nothing, after all. It is something: a heightened awareness, a sharpened appetite, a finer perception. When someone important to me is absent from me, it becomes clearer than ever what that person means to me. Details that got lost in our togetherness are recalled in our apartness, and their sudden clarity has the power to pry my heart right open. I see the virtues I have overlooked, the opportunities I have missed. The quirks that drove me crazy at close range become endearing at a distance. From that enlarged perspective, I can see that they are the very things that make my someone *someone* and not just anyone.

There is something else that happens during an absence. If the relationship is strong and true, the absent one has a way of becoming present—if not in body, then in mind and spirit.

My husband, Edward, is devoted to hawks and especially to the golden eagles that are coming back to our part of Georgia. Driving down the highway with him can become a test of nerve as he cranes over the steering wheel to peer at the wing feathers of a particularly large bird. Is it an eagle? Or just a turkey vulture? He has to know, even if it means weaving down the road for a while, or running off it from time to time.

"Keep your eyes on the road!" I yell at him. "Who cares what it is? I'll buy you a bird book; I'll buy you a bird. Just watch where you're going." Then a couple of summers ago we spent two months apart and I thought I would get a break from hawks, but instead I began to see them everywhere—looping through the air, spiraling in rising thermals, hunkered down in the tops of trees. Seeing them, really seeing them for the first time in my life, I understood that I was not seeing them with my own eyes but with Edward's eyes. He was not there, so I was seeing them for him. He was absent—or was he? He was present in me.

One thing is for sure: there is no sense of absence where there has been no sense of presence. What makes absence hurt, what makes it ache, is the memory of what used to be there but is no longer. Absence is the arm flung across the bed in the middle of the night, the empty space where a beloved sleeper once lay. Absence is the child's room now empty and hung with silence and dust. Absence is the overgrown lot where the old house once stood, the house in which people laughed and thought their happiness would last forever.

You cannot miss what you have never known, which makes our sense of absence—and especially our sense of God's absence—the very best proof that we knew God once, and that we may know God again. There is loss in absence, but there is also hope, because what happened once can happen again, and only an empty cup can be filled. It is only when we pull that cup out of hiding, when we own up to the emptiness, the absence, the longing inside—it is only then that things can begin to change.

It is our sense of God's absence, after all, that brings us to church in search of God's presence. Like a band of forlorn disciples, we return to this hillside again and again. It is the place we lost track of him; it is the last place we saw him, so of course it is the first place anybody thinks to look for him to come again. We have been coming here a long time now, but even in his absence it is a good place to remember him—to recall best moments and argue about the details, to swap all the old stories until they begin to revive again, the life flowing back into them like feeling into a numb limb. It hurts at first, but then it is fine, and the joy of remembering makes the pain seem a small price to pay.

"Men of Galilee, why do you stand looking up toward heaven?" That is what the two men in white robes said to the disciples on the mount called Olivet just outside of Jerusalem. Luke calls them men in white robes, anyway, so as not to scare anyone, but you can bet your last nickel that they were angels—angels sent to remind God's friends that if they wanted to see him again, it was no use looking up. Better they should look around instead, at each other, at the world, at the ordinary people in their ordinary lives, because that was where they were most likely to find him—not the way they used to know him, but the new way, not in his own body but in their bodies, the risen, the ascended Lord who was no longer anywhere on earth so that he could be everywhere instead.

No one standing around watching them that day could have guessed what an astounding thing happened when they all stopped looking into the sky and looked at each other instead. On the surface, it was not a great moment: eleven abandoned disciples with nothing to show for all their following. But in the days and years to come it would become very apparent what had happened to them. With nothing but a promise and a prayer, those eleven people consented to become the church, and nothing was ever the same again, beginning with them.

The followers became leaders, the listeners became preachers, the converts became missionaries, the healed became healers. The disciples became apostles, witnesses of the risen Lord by the power of the Holy Spirit, and nothing was ever the same again.

That probably was not the way they would have planned it. If they had had it their way, they would probably have tied Jesus up so that he could not have gotten away from them, so that they would have known where to find him and rely on him forever. Only that is not how it happened. He went away—he was taken away—and they stood looking up toward heaven. Then they stopped looking up toward heaven, looked at each other instead, and got on with the business of being the church.

And once they did that, surprising things began to happen. They began to say things that sounded like him, and they began to do things they had never seen anyone but him do before. They became brave and capable and wise.

Whenever two or three of them got together it was always as if there were someone else in the room with them whom they could not see—the strong, abiding presence of the absent one, as available to them as bread and wine, as familiar to them as each other's faces. It was almost as if he had not ascended but exploded, so that all the holiness that was once concentrated in him alone flew everywhere, flew far and wide, so that the seeds of heaven were sown in all the fields of the earth.

We go to church to worship, to acknowledge the Lord's absence and to seek the Lord's presence, to sing and to pray, to be silent and to be still, to hold out the empty cups of our hands and to be filled with bread, with wine, with the abiding presence of the absent Lord until he comes again. Do you miss him sometimes? Do you long for assurance that you have not been left behind? Then why do you stand looking up toward heaven? Look around you, look around.

PTOLEMY TOMPKINS

Lao Tzu's Water, Chuang Tzu's Mud

A SMALL WHITE BOOK ON THE WAY OF LIFE

> *There was something undefined and complete, coming into existence before heaven and earth. How still it was and formless, standing alone, and undergoing no change, reaching everywhere and in no danger of being exhausted! It may be regarded as the mother of all things. I do not know its name, and I give it the designation of the Tao. Making an effort further to give it a name, I call it The Great.*
>
> *Tao Te Ching*

Before everything, there was the Tao. Subtle and silent, void of all form or extension and yet at the same time immeasurably vast, it held the noise and pandemonium of the entire universe within itself, like a mother awaiting term. It was from deep within the boundless watery hush of the Tao that the world and all the things within it were born, and once it had given birth to them, these things became like objects moving downstream in a giant river. In this great drift, nothing stays as it is for long. Trees, animals, entire civilizations: all of this material is like the scrim of twigs and litter you see on the surface of the water on a day after there has been a lot of rain. Sometimes bobbing at the surface, sometimes sinking out of sight, drifting and bumping and turning in the dark, downward-moving water, all things flow in the Tao without knowing it. Beyond all thought and action, beyond both life and death, the Tao is the one constant, the sole aspect of all the universe that is entirely beyond change. It is the ultimate source, the ultimate support, and the ultimate destination of everything there is.

I first learned about the great Tao in the summer of 1979, when I was seventeen. I was on a canoe trip in the woods of northern Canada and spending a good deal of my time amid the flowing water that plays such a big part in Taoist writings. I had signed on for this trip because it had seemed like it might satisfy a yearning that had been building in me recently: a desire to go on a journey that would help me make sense of who I was and what I was doing in the world. This particular journey, however, turned out to be a far more labor-intensive affair than I had expected, and I almost immediately found myself wishing that I was back home in my room, reading about adventures rather than actually being stuck on one. Books, and the time to read them, were luxury items on this trip. As the days wore on and my fellow campers and I slogged through mile after mile of muskeg and moss and paddled our canoes through one endless lake or river after another, sometimes even paddling *up* rivers for days on end, the moments I would have to myself, to think or read among the small collection of books I had brought with me, took on greater and greater importance.

As I struggled to find short moments of psychic sustenance within their covers, I soon realized that the selection of books I had made was not an ideal one. Awakening every day around five-thirty—this is only a guess, as the hard-driving nature purists in charge of the adventure had asked that all timepieces be left behind—and traveling until the sun was touching the tops of the trees, I found myself placing a great burden of expectation on whatever I happened to be reading during the few stray minutes when I was both comfortable and awake enough to do so at all. What I needed was the literary equivalent of pemmican or beef jerky—something concentrated, pithy, and powerful—and the titles I had brought along weren't doing the trick.

Growing ever more frustrated with my own little stack of paperbacks, I began to eye the collection of one of my fellow campers.

Like everyone else on the trip, this fellow was some years older than I, but I saw that more than everyone else he had a certain eye for literature. Central to his collection was a small, white, wafer-thin volume with a large Chinese character printed on the cover, and the words *The Way of Life* beneath. Tired, uncomfortable, itching from countless mosquito and black fly bites, and irritated at the outrageous amount of work that my wilderness adventure was demanding of me, I found the look of this little volume increasingly appealing. So there was an entire strategy for living that could fit into such a slim package? If there was, I wanted to know about it.

Back in civilization at the end of the summer, I hunted around in bookstores until I found a copy of the thin white volume and bought it. *The Way of Life According to Lao Tzu, An American Version by Witter Bynner.* I took the book home and commenced to study it in earnest. Thus did my quest for a life recipe, a set of genuinely workable instructions on how to move through the world as if it were a river that one is riding smoothly downstream rather than paddling arduously up it, begin. It was a long quest, and rockier than I ever bargained for.

The Disaster of Adulthood

> *There is nothing in the world more soft and weak than water, and yet for attacking things that are firm and strong there is nothing that can take precedence of it.*
>
> Tao Te Ching

On Saturday afternoons when I was a child, I often turned to a show called *The Wide World of Sports.* I had no great interest in the show itself, but the title sequence was irresistible to me. Each week, as a montage of assorted athletic events flashed across the screen, an announcer's voice repeated the same words. "Bringing you the entire world of sports in all its variety, from the thrill of victory . . . to the agony of defeat." As the announcer spoke the last part of this sentence—the "agony of defeat" part—a clip would run of a skier on a jump. Down the skier would whiz. Then, just as he got to the end of the jump and flew off into space, something went badly wrong. Instead of jetting gracefully up into the air, the skier was transformed by some invisible error—some tiny miscalculation known, perhaps, only to him—into a hurtling ball of limbs. Crashing headlong through the barricades and banners, knocking person after person down and refusing to stop no matter how many people and things he ran into, the unknown hero of this tragedy became a weekly reminder of just how wrong things could go in life if you weren't careful—and perhaps even if you were.

The agony of defeat was a topic I devoted quite a bit of thought to throughout my childhood, and by the time I was seventeen I had arrived at certain conclusions about it. From my perspective at this age, the real defeat to watch out for—the botched jump of all botched jumps and disaster of all disasters—was nothing less than the condition of adulthood itself. Like countless teenagers before and after me, I realized that simply becoming a grown-up was likely the most distilled and overshadowing species of failure to be had in life. Was there not—didn't there simply have to be—a way out of it?

That was where the Tao came in. Go to a bookstore or library today, and you will find any number of Taos. The Tao of Business. The Tao of Tennis. The Tao of Pooh. The word *Tao* is both so inescapable and so threadbare these days that it is easy to forget that, just a few decades ago, it was a new—and extraordinary—addition to the American cultural vocabulary. A teenager in 1949, 1959, and probably even 1969, would most likely not have had the slightest idea about the Tao—neither that you pronounced it with a *D* and not a *T* sound, nor that an understanding of it was the antidote to the hectic and contorted world of twentieth-century existence and all the ills that went along with it.

For a certain sort of teenager—and in 1979 I was definitely this sort myself—learning about the Tao was like reinstating a missing vitamin into my diet—a vitamin that no one had told me I needed before but whose absence had secretly created all sorts of discomforts and deficiencies. Thanks to the Tao—and specifically, Lao Tzu's little book outlining what it was all about—I was given a genuinely useful tool for making sense of the countless yeses and nos, the endless arbitrary goods and bads, of which my life, like most teenagers' lives, was full. SATs, B-pluses, C-minuses, physics, chemistry, biology, biochemistry, college placement, wisdom teeth, sexual frustration, driving school. . . . In the midst of all this garbage, the Tao descended upon my imaginative life like a magic lens, allowing me for the first time to see all the mass of confusing details that competed endlessly for my attention for the nonsense that it was. For the Tao was, quite simply, bigger than all this stuff. Bigger, and yet at the same time so subtle and simple that when you tried to describe it, to imprison it in some sort of categorical box or other, you ended up with nothing.

From the beginning of time, translator Bynner assured me, the Tao had possessed this marvelous simplicity. And likewise from the beginning, people had been out to mess with it—to dress the Tao up as something it wasn't and spoil all the good that came from just allowing it to take its mysterious course without getting in the way. The history of the Tao was, in fact, little more than a list of the endless attempts by confounders and complicators of one sort or another to distort the words of the ancient masters who had lived in effortless harmony with it. The great project for someone like me, then, who had not yet calcified into one of these

Tao-obstructing adults, was to somehow learn how to get in line with the Tao before that happened.

The question was how to do it. According to legend, old Lao Tzu himself—if he had in fact ever existed, for this was open to question—ultimately got so fed up with his fellow humans' inability to follow the Tao that he had only scribbled down the eighty-one chapters of the *Tao Te Ching* at the behest of a gatekeeper whom he passed while leaving civilization once and for all on the back of a water buffalo. Even in the mists of China two thousand and some years ago, the chances of growing into one of these supple, Tao-attuned adults was slim. What chance would I have, marooned in the suburbs of late-twentieth-century America?

THE ADULT-UNLIKE-OTHER-ADULTS

> *The multitude of men look satisfied and pleased. . . . I alone seem listless and still, my desires having as yet given no indication of their presence. I am like an infant which has not yet smiled.*
>
> *Tao Te Ching*

The *Tao Te Ching* is in many ways the original wisdom book, by the original adult-unlike-other-adults. The figure of Lao Tzu, or The Old Boy, as this name is often translated, has a basic vagueness to it that is profoundly satisfying, and the fact that Lao Tzu might not have existed at all only furthers his charm. Lao Tzu exists at such a distance from us that he serves as an ideal canvas—rough, bright, absorbent—for the wild brush strokes of our creative projections of the perfect adult. The same holds for his little book on the Way of Life, which legend tells us Lao Tzu knocked off in three days after that gatekeeper he passed on his way into the mists of history requested it from him. The *Tao Te*

Ching's text is so relentlessly ambiguous that some scholars have argued that not a single statement within it can be interpreted in one way only. This Rorschach quality has made the *Tao Te Ching* perhaps the most durable wisdom book around.

Tao literally means "path" or "way," and from Lao Tzu, hovering at the flickering fringes of existence and legend, comes one of the very first recorded emphases on the image of a path or way that one deliberately walks through life, as well as the notion that this path is set distinctly apart from the one the majority of humans are trudging. Also from Lao Tzu comes one of the first statements of the basic wisdom book idea that most people, deny it though they might, aren't really happy. An ingredient that nobody talks about but that everybody, at some level of their mind, is thinking about all the same, is missing from their lives. Since the *Tao Te Ching* first pointed out this news, people have never tired of hearing it.

Upon completing my grueling and inconclusive wilderness adventure, I returned to my room on the second floor of my sister and brother-in-law's house in the suburbs of Virginia just outside Washington. I had moved from my parents' to my sister's house the previous year—ostensibly because she lived closer to the Washington high school I was now attending, but also to take a vacation of sorts from my parents. Unlike my bohemian father and mother, my sister and brother-in-law were "normal," and this quality of theirs had come as a great relief when I joined their household.

Not that I wanted to *be* like my sister or my brother-in-law—admirable folk as they were in many ways—any more than I wanted to end up like my parents. The fact of the matter was that I didn't want to be like any of the adults I knew, and the reason for this was very simple: regardless of their various good qualities, all of these adults inevitably fell into one of two basic categories. Either they worked diligently and modestly in offices, schools, and other such places, like my brother-in-law; or else they were "rebels" like my father, shaking their fist at the Establishment, avoiding offices and schools, and making certain that the world was aware of their existence at all times.

Normalcy and rebellion: to me at seventeen, both looked like two sides of the same useless coin. The trick, as I saw it, was to become one of that magical third group, whose members neither railed against the regular world around them nor made up a part of it. These were the invisible ones: the ones who drifted through life somewhere far above the rest, in the pull of a larger, more meaningful current. The men of the Tao.

MUD

> *The skillful masters of the Tao in old times, with a subtle*
> *and exquisite penetration, comprehended its mysteries. . . .*
> *Evanescent like ice that is melting away; unpretentious like*
> *wood that has not been fashioned into anything; vacant*
> *like a valley, and dull like muddy water.*
>
> *Tao Te Ching*

Anticipating the chaos theorists who now tell us more or less the same thing in different terms, the Taoists maintained that the entire universe was characterized by flux. Everything is in a constant state of destruction and change, with one thing transforming into another, one thing devouring another, in an endless orgy of ingestion, defecation, combustion, disintegration, and procreation.

Rather than recoiling in horror at the sight of this universe where nothing sits still and nothing is safe from ultimate destruction—as the Buddha and his followers were to do over in India—the early Taoists claimed to be completely at home in it. Wandering here and there in the pull of the great Tao, changing their habits along with the seasons, these men lived out their lives to the fullest; and when it came time to die, they did that well too. "These great Taoists," one scholar writes, "were so thrilled by the fact that they were inalienably a part of this mighty cosmos that the incident of death seemed quite insignificant." When the time came to die, we are told, they fell apart like gingerbread men, smiling to the last.

So enthusiastic were the ancient Taoists about the transformations and destructions taking place in the universe around them that dirt and mud—the symbols par excellence of the final destination of all things, no matter how ordered and lofty—is rivaled only by water as the natural substance they call upon to illustrate their view of life. In the *Chuang Tzu,* the celebrated book of Chinese wisdom that is second only to the *Tao Te Ching* as a source of Taoist ideas, the universe itself is called the "Great Clod" or, in another translation, the "Mighty Mudball."

The Taoist concept that brings out this mudlike aspect of the universe more than any other is *Hun Tun*—a word sometimes translated as "dark essence" or simply, "chaos." All things, at heart, are Hun Tun, and all things are destined, ultimately, to return to it. Like so much of Taoism, Hun Tun is not really susceptible to any single definition, but most of its translations hint at the idea of a certain ungraspable mixed-up-ness that lies at the heart of all phenomenal existence. As one of Taoism's most respected scholars has described it, Hun Tun means "an amorphous state where nothing is clearly delineated, nothing is clearly distinguishable, but which is far from being sheer non-being; it is, on the contrary, an extremely obscure 'presence' in which the existence of something—or some things, still undifferentiated—is vaguely and dimly sensed."

In the seventh chapter of the *Chuang Tzu,* the story is told of a certain emperor of a shadowy land lying between the North Sea, ruled by the Emperor Hu, and the South Sea, ruled by the Emperor Shu. This emperor's name was Hun Tun. Hu and Shu once paid a visit to the domain of Hun Tun, who was distinguished by having none of the seven bodily openings normally present in human beings. At the end of their stay, Hu and Shu were so impressed with their host's hospitality that they resolved to do him a favor. Taking hold of Hun Tun, they carefully drilled seven holes where body openings would have been on an ordinary human. They drilled a new opening each day "until the seventh day," when, as the text of the *Chuang Tzu* laconically states, "Hun Tun died."

Just because all things belong at their core to the chaos of Hun Tun does not mean that it is open to inspection or manipulation. This, it has been argued, is the meaning of Chuang Tzu's story of Hu and Shu and their ill-fated visit with the emperor. The minute you try to lay a finger on it, the story suggests—the minute you try to bring Hun Tun into the light for all to see and understand—this magical, shadowy chaos will die on you, and you will be no wiser than when you began.

Hun Tun is dark and heavy. It holds all things in potentiality, but when you try to grab it, to change it, or to settle on a particular shape or form for it, it slips through your fingers and is gone.

It's a lot like mud.

VOICES OF HUN TUN

Move as I will, I manifest the ancient Tao.

Hsiang-yen

As the weeks passed, the influence of Lao Tzu's words upon me, and those of other writers on the Tao that I started to come across, grew and grew. Like a river in flood season overflowing its banks and obscuring the lines of the countryside around it, the great

Tao, and the books I read about it, slowly but surely swallowed up all my other interests and concerns. History, science, English: like houses shuddering on their foundations, their basements filling up with roiling brown water until their walls finally gave way and drifted off downstream, all rival concerns ultimately surrendered to the Tao's relentless pull.

Perhaps it was only appropriate that I should have ended up enlisting the sponsorship of the Tao as enthusiastically as I did, for the Tao's and my histories were intertwined from the very beginning. I was born in 1962, right around the time when the Tao as a going concern was getting its first real foothold in America. In California in 1962 Eastern mysticism was much on people's minds and had been increasingly ever since the May morning nine years earlier when Aldous Huxley had flushed out the doors of his perception with a glass of water and dissolved mescaline powder and written about the experiences that followed. Huxley and his circle had been popularizing Indian mysticism with increasing effect down in the Los Angeles area, and in the northern part of the state the same thing was happening with the Chinese and Japanese varieties. The chief voice on behalf of these latter traditions was that of another British émigré—a recently defrocked Episcopal priest named Alan Watts. In the early fifties, following a messy dismissal from a clergy post at the University of Chicago, the captivating, eloquent, and personable Watts had set up shop in the San Francisco area—and it was he who really got the word out on what Americans, and especially young Americans, could learn from Taoism, Zen Buddhism, and other Far Eastern traditions.

Watts was the great master of pop mystical rhetoric, the most energetic and influential among the creators of that whole body of what-to-do-about-life literature that started to appear in force in America in the early sixties. If you went looking for news of the Tao in the seventies, Watts was still the first, and the friendliest, voice you were likely to come across. I discovered Watts early on in my Taoistic investigations and did my best to put his prescriptions for becoming one with the Tao (or rather for realizing my inherent unity with it, for the first thing you learned from Watts was that there was no getting away from the Tao even if you wanted to) into action.

Watts's great desire was to undermine Western civilization's infatuation with structure—to get people away from Hu and Shu and back into the far more satisfactory domain of Emperor Hun Tun. According to Watts, the universe was a squiggly and structure-free place: a vast, playful arena where distinctions of up and down, right and left, and even good and evil ultimately meant nothing. From acne to Auschwitz, the negative stuff that life had to offer only seemed to possess a solid ontological core. Worrying too much about categories like Good and Bad was, Watts told me, like making "comparisons between right and wrong stars, . . . between well and badly arranged constellations." From the perspective of one who sees things from the *inside* of the Tao—rather than the outside, where most poor saps were stuck—life unfolds "beyond anxiety."

"If we live, we live," said Watts, apparently speaking to me direct from the very heart of Hun Tun's domain. "If we die, we die; if we suffer, we suffer; if we are terrified, we are terrified. There is no problem about it."

Watts was also very interested in dispossessing his readers of their mistaken notions of self. "The ego," he assured me, "is neither a spiritual, psychological, or biological reality but a social institution of the same order as the monogamous family, the calendar, the clock, the metric system, and the agreement to drive on the right side of the road." With a little effort on my part—or rather the right kind of noneffort from my self that was in truth a nonself— I would, Watts told me, find my way into a condition where that problematic, embarrassing, anxiety-prone fiction I called *me* would be mercifully left behind. In its place there would appear "a continuous, self-moving stream of experiencing, without the sense either of an active subject who controls it or of a passive subject who suffers it. The thinker would be seen to be no more than the series of thoughts, and the feeler no more than the feelings." In other words, I would become the Tao and the Tao would become me.

SINKING INTO THE MUD

> *The true men of old knew nothing of the love of life or the hatred of death. Entrance into life occasioned them no joy; exit from it awakened no resistance.*
>
> Chuang Tzu

It doesn't take a confirmed Taoist to understand that life is confusing. Everything is mixed up with everything else, to the point where distinguishing one aspect from another with any consistency is all but impossible. Good people act bad at some times, bad people act good at others. It's a mess. The people who write wisdom books know this, of course, and tend to counter this problem by dividing up their work into nice clean compartments. Once again, the *Tao Te Ching* sets the pace. Life may have been a chaotic stew of endless transformation and destruction for the ancient Taoists, but open any of the dozens of English translations of the *Tao Te Ching* that have appeared in this century, and your eyes will fall upon pure order and clarity. Eighty-one chapters, all full of calm, clean, declarative sentences like "Those who know do not say," and "The way to do is to be."

To read the *Tao Te Ching,* like all really effective wisdom books, is to be pulled away for a moment from the swamp of ordinary events and into a wonderful new domain where things actually do seem to be making more sense than usual. "Maybe now," most people can't help thinking when encountering this book for the first time, "I'm going to get to the bottom of things at last."

Yet for all their reassuring beauty on the page, there is something about the proclamations of these mighty mudball masters have a quality that is challenging, and even slightly chilling, to the reader who tries to take them seriously. I encountered this chilly aspect to the Taoist project early on in my investigations and for a long time didn't know how to make my peace with it.

Part of my nagging reservations about fully plunging into Lao Tzu's water and Chuang Tzu's mud no doubt had to do with my particular, personal associations with the latter of these two substances. As a child I lived near a large lake that in summertime functioned as a public swimming area. Two plain wooden platforms, held up by a series of metal drums, floated at anchor out in the lake's center, while a pair of docks stuck out from the grassy shore with a stretch of trucked-in white sand lying between them. The lake was shallow and swampy in parts, and swimmers tended to stay in the deep water right around where the two platforms floated. Children were encouraged to keep to the sandy area and not step into the water on the far side of either dock, for if you did your foot sank into a layer of black, ultrafine mud that a few inches down turned into a thick bed of clay. The mud and the clay sucked and dragged at your feet, making walking difficult and uncomfortable.

One day when I was ten or so I watched a boy about my age march out into this muddy area on the far side of one of the docks. Taking one step after another, he left a rich black trail in the water behind him. After several of these bold, deep steps, the boy stopped short, uttered a little bark of surprise, and limped back out onto dry land. One of the adults on hand came over and held his foot up to examine it. A slick of blood, bright like enamel model paint, flowed from the upheld foot and blended with the mud and clay that coated the pale skin of the boy's leg. Apparently he had made contact with a buried edge of some sort—a broken bottle or the torn lip of a tin can—and it had cut deep into his big toe. All that blood mixing with the mud and clay had a shiny, voluptuous look to it, and I could imagine what it must have felt like as the hidden object had cut into the toe—so fast and clean and decisive that at first the boy would not have known that something had broken the skin at all.

For me at age seventeen, groping my way into the curiously tranquil teachings of my new Taoist masters, there was still a lingering suspicion that the mighty mudball of the world held a little more in it than they said it did: something alienating and sinister and not so easy to love as all that. It was one thing, it seemed to me, to happily contemplate one's disintegration into a universe composed solely of floating clouds, flowing rivers, and whispering trees, such as Lao Tzu, Chuang Tzu, and their associates had presumably made their home in. But what about the universe I had been born into—the one of napalm, lead-based paint, child molesters, and fifteen-car pile-ups? Was sinking into the mud of Hun Tun really as viable a business in my day as it had been for the Taoists in theirs?

Mind at Large

> In recent years we have witnessed the growing interest in mysticism and Eastern religion, which . . . has introduced powerful new ideas into the currents of Western thought; chief among them, perhaps, is the idea of the states of human consciousness and the suggestion that the whole of our lives, individually and collectively, proceeds in a diminished state of consciousness, far from the capacities that would be possible were we to live at the level of consciousness that is natural to us.
>
> Jacob Needleman

Despite these initial doubts and perplexities, my researches into the alternate life my new wisdom masters had alerted me to continued to move forward. From Watts's assured proclamations on how to make oneself at home with the disorder of the universe, I soon made my way to Huxley and found that he was full of no less heady and promising stuff. The edition of *The Doors of Perception* I purchased at one of the local shopping malls that fall cost me ninety-five cents plus tax and weighed in at an astonishing sixty-seven pages. The book was no fatter than my copy of the *Tao Te Ching*, and in that very smallness I read portent: clearly, another crucial manual for living had come my way. A scant six or seven pages in, Huxley, having drunk his famous half-glass of mescaline-laced water, was telling me about "seeing what Adam had seen on the morning of his creation . . . a bunch of flowers shining with their own inner light and all but quivering under the pressure of the significance with which they were charged." This significance, in turn, was made up of "nothing more, and nothing less, than what they were—a transience that was yet eternal life, a perpetual perishing that was at the same time pure Being, a bundle of minute, unique particulars in which, by some unspeakable and yet self-evident paradox, was to be seen the divine source of all existence."

For page after page, as Huxley wandered back and forth between his living room and garden, looking at pictures of paintings in books, listening to music, and staring for minutes on end at a garden chair or his pants leg, I followed along as if my life depended on it. *The Doors of Perception* was less a book than a telegram, sent from the high peaks of essential insight down into the foggy flatlands of ordinary consciousness where I was for the moment—but only for the moment—stuck.

According to Huxley, the mind had what he called a "reducing valve"—the product of its evolution in the harsh realities of day-to-day survival—and this valve acted automatically to filter out all the fabulous, superluminescent suchness of the world as it truly was, leaving instead the bleached, boring, and all-too-ordinary one that I was more than used to. It was this reducing valve that accounted for the readily observable fact that so many of the adults around me appeared to be having such a dull time in life. If turning into an adult was exactly the disaster I had started to suspect it to be, Huxley was actually giving me some genuine, nuts-and-bolts hints on how to avoid this fate myself.

The blast of clarity Huxley had attained with his half-glass of mescaline was, I was happy to read, potentially available to anyone—with drugs but preferably without. Mescaline was nothing magical or mystical in itself. It simply had the effect of reducing the supply of sugar fed to the brain, thus allowing what Huxley tantalizingly referred to as "Mind at Large" to flow past the gates of the ordinarily circumscribed ego (the same ego that, thanks to Watts, I already knew didn't really exist anyhow). The basic trouble in life was that ordinary adults had been conditioned by the necessities of the workaday world to shut themselves off from this domain. Caught up in the struggle for survival, we had all trained ourselves to say no to the greater reality, even though the splendors of Mind at Large were all around, just waiting for us to take notice of them.

"For the artist as for the mescaline taker," Huxley confided to me as I lay in my bed on the second floor of my sister's house late one night, "draperies are living hieroglyphs that stand in some peculiarly expressive way for the unfathomable mystery of pure being." Looking up from the book, I could see that the draperies hanging there in *my* room certainly weren't any of these things—but that was all right for the moment because now I at least knew they could be.

Patterns of Organic Energy

*Is the life of man indeed enveloped in such darkness? Is it
I alone to whom it appears so?*

Chuang Tzu

By the time I got to them that fall of 1979, the proclamations
of Huxley and Watts on the Tao, Hun Tun, mescaline, enlightenment, Mind at Large, and related matters were no longer hot from
the oven but cool and crusty with age. Both men were dead by this
point, and over the last decade and a half or so, legions of other
disgruntled seventeen-year-olds had already seized upon their
books as road maps to a different and better sort of life. But I didn't
know this at the time and might not have cared if I did. After all,
if others before me had had the maps but failed to find the treasure, that was not necessarily the fault of the maps.

So I read on. Like a child wandering along the beach after a
great storm, picking up interesting pieces of flotsam that the waters
have blown up onto the sand, I went from paperback to paperback, from voice to confident, reassuring, visionary voice, growing more convinced with each one I discovered that a genuine
plan of action could be found: a way out of the disappointingly
ordinary—or in the case of my father, obnoxiously extraordinary—
adulthood that I knew was coming and that I was determined,
one way or another, to avoid.

My knowledge of the Tao grew ever more eclectic. Huxley's
mescaline narratives and Watts's sermons on Hun Tun were soon
joined by the explicators of the mesons, gluons, quarks, and sub-
quarks of the new physics. Zipping in and out of existence, transforming into one another, moving forward and backward in time,
these likable subatomic entities, it turned out, actually made up
the stuff of the entire world around me. More than one writer informed me that the very table I was reading at was something in

the area of 99.999999 percent empty space. Not only that, but the less than 0.000001 percent of the table that was "matter" was itself nothing more than a temporary knot of energy. And energy, my authors were quick to mention, was at bottom just a particularly congealed and intractable form of consciousness itself. I was the table, and the table was me.

My vocabulary grew along with my reading list. I learned about *Wu-Wei*, or doing-nondoing, the mysterious method of active nonaction that the Taoist masters of old had employed on those rare occasions when they actually needed to get something done in the world. I learned as well about *Wu Li*, or "patterns of organic energy"—a term that described all the random-yet-intelligent shapes that appear in nature, from the formations made by migrating birds to the tracings left by breaking waves along a beach to the routes—both forward and backward in time—followed by the subatomic particles in the table I was reading at. And I tried, in my haphazard teenage manner, to apply the whole mass of this material to my daily life. During study period at school, I practiced "sitting in oblivion," the ancient Taoist practice of allowing one's mind to become empty so that only the pure white static of the universe would flow through it, like the snow on a television screen after all the programs have left the air. Doing the dishes after dinner with my sister and brother-in-law, I would ponder again and again Watts's admonitions, borrowed from the masters of old and slightly reformulated, to *be* the dishes—to surrender to the revolutionary assertion that, at bottom, dish and self were not different but one and the same.

Sometime before Christmas vacation, the select company of oriental sages and nuclear physicists lining the little bookshelf by my bed was joined by the works of another great figure of the teenage transformatory wisdom manual: Carlos Castaneda. Don Juan, the squinty-eyed hero of Castaneda's celebrated odyssey in the deserts of the American Southwest, dumped a whole new glossary of terms into my head. These all sounded strange at first, but before long they became as pleasantly familiar as *Wu-Wei, Wu Li,* and *Yin-Yang.* Following along behind the wise and wiry Don Juan and the bumbling, hopelessly empirical Carlos, I journeyed into the otherworldly sands of the Sonora Desert in search of the separate reality of the sorcerer's understanding. Along with thousands of other gratefully mystified teenagers hidden away in their own bedrooms across America, I learned about the luminous egg that humans look like to the eyes of a sorcerer, about getting spun by the Ally, about the difference between *seeing* and mere looking, and about making friends with my death. I learned that most human beings were stuck in the *tonal*—Castaneda's term for the ordinary, everyday world and the ordinary, everyday sort of consciousness that went along with it. And I nodded with satisfaction as Don Juan explained to Carlos that this ordinary world, which seemed to be all and everything, was really only a little island, at the shores of which lapped the uncanny waters of the *nagual*— the place where draperies glowed like living hieroglyphs, flower vases became pulsating matrices of Buddhalike suchness, anthropology students flew like crows, and people turned into the giant luminous eggs that they had, in fact, been all along.

With varying degrees of success, I tried to synthesize Carlos and Don Juan's chilly, neo-Gnostic calisthenics out in the Sonora Desert with what Alan and Aldous had told me about the nonexistence of my ego and my identity with the cosmos; and when I had these materials balanced together in my head for a moment, I threw in what I now knew about Bell's Theorem, Planck's Constant, and Heisenberg's Uncertainty Principle.

And on better days, when all this material did actually balance itself in my head for a moment or two, I felt what I had been so hoping to feel: that the Taoists and the Buddhists and the physicists and Don Juan the Yaqui sorcerer were all talking about the same thing: a whole alternate universe, far more interesting than

the one I was being groomed to inhabit by "consensusculture."
Out beyond the shores of the *tonal,* the *nagual*—or the great Tao,
or Mind at Large, or whatever you wanted to call it—lay, just
waiting for me to plunge in.

Leaving the House

> *When we renounce learning we have no troubles.*
>
> Tao Te Ching

Wisdom books come in two basic varieties: those with plots
and those without. Wisdom books without plots tend to be, like
the *Tao Te Ching,* simple instruction books: recipes for living.
Wisdom books with plots offer recipes for living too, but these are
folded into story lines, and these story lines tend to run in a very
similar manner. There is the period of wandering, during which
the hero seems to be drifting at the mercy of blind chance. Then,
out of nowhere, there is the meeting with the master, the adult-
unlike-other-adults, who after initially denying his role of teacher,
submits the hero to a period of apprenticeship. During this period, the hero undergoes a series of trials, temptations, and confusions that are generally unpleasant but that have the effect of
gradually jolting him into higher levels of awareness. Finally, the
moment arrives when enlightenment is reached, and the hero sets
off happily on his own. He no longer needs contact with the master because he possesses the secret to life himself now and is ready
to engage the world with the same ease, assurance, and power that
the master had so impressively exhibited to him.

If wisdom books came in two varieties, it seemed possible that
lives might come in these two varieties as well. If so, which one
was I to shoot for?

No matter how good my prospects could start to look during
my late-night reading, out in the left-brain, Newtonian world I

was still a high school senior, and as a result of this my attention was dragged away from my extracurricular studies with annoying regularity. Was I to go to college? If so, which one? Thanks to all my reading on the Tao and its obfuscators, these questions tended to put me on the defensive. What could I expect to learn in an institution of higher learning that was going to take me anywhere but further away from that mysterious, neither-this-nor-that condition that constituted the true state of a man of the Tao? Even if I did go to college, what on earth would I study there? I could just imagine what Eastern Religion 105 would be like. Textbooks on the Tao! A total sacrilege.

Likewise, if I were to pursue an education in my own cultural legacy, the prospects were even uglier. The *Iliad,* the *Odyssey, Moby-Dick, Hamlet:* much of the basic meat and potatoes of Western literature—material that I had successfully eluded so far—loomed before me like a great gray cloud of knockout dust. What did all these books amount to, really, but a long and ugly footnote to that initial subject-object dualism that, my new masters told me, had been initiated by the Greco-Roman, Judeo-Christian worldview some twenty-five hundred years ago? As for the science courses with which I would no doubt be threatened, these would only poison my understanding further.

Who needed any of it? Why not avoid contamination by this sort of thinking as much as possible and hang out, instead, with my select library of Taoists, Zen masters, and Yaqui metaphysicians? How was *Moby-Dick* ever going to help me do those blasted dishes with the right attitude? For when all was said and done, it was precisely things like the dishes—and all the other ordinary, inexplicable little chores and obligations that filled my life—that were the real problem. How was I to steer between the Scylla of an ordinary life and the Charybdis of an extraordinary one? How was I to stick to the true path and become the Taoist Nobody that I really aspired to being?

As the year ground on, I sat through the majority of my school classes with the attitude of a miner forced by an uncaring coal company to work a defunct vein. As soon as possible, I was going to toss all the straw of Western learning aside once and for all and take a big bite of Huxleyan visionary bread. I needed to figure out how to open up the flow nozzle of Mind at Large, to shift from a habitual into a nonhabitual mode of perception, to subvert the tyranny of the known and recover the incalculably greater realities of the hidden-yet-unhidden Tao. From here on out, I knew, it would just be a matter of time until I did so.

A Vision of Mickey

It was inexpressibly wonderful, wonderful to the point, almost, of being terrifying. And suddenly I had an inkling of what it must feel like to be mad.

Aldous Huxley, *The Doors of Perception*

The next fall found me in college, but not for long, as I soon lost patience with all the unmagical teachers I encountered there and the distressingly mundane lectures and formulas they expected me to listen to. After just one semester, I left school and all its irritating Western dualisms behind and embarked upon a full-time study of the chorus of reassuring, disembodied voices who spoke to me from the pages of my wisdom manuals. After several months I determined that, for all my attempts to do and think—or not-do and not-think—as these manuals told me to, I was still missing out on some key part of the enlightenment process. To right this situation, I borrowed my mother's Pontiac Sunbird and my father's credit card and embarked on a road trip—a journey into the heart of the country along the lines of the ones that a number of my new wisdom heroes had practiced to good effect.

It was during this earnest and boneheaded odyssey, deep in the desert of New Mexico, that I had one of the defining experiences of this period of my life. Tired of waiting for enlightenment to arrive of its own and seeking to jump-start the process, I fasted for three days, took a triple dose of hallucinogenic mushrooms, and tramped off alone into the wastes of what I had been assured was an Indian burial ground on the night of a full moon to await a vision.

I got one, too—though not the sort that my authors had prepared me for. The vision I received out there in the desert—dark, portentous, nightmarishly real—was of Mickey Mouse. Some seven feet tall, dressed in his *Fantasia* sorcerer's robes, and staring at me with an unaccountably malevolent, two-dimensional grin, this apparition struck me at the time as a terrible—and terrifying—disappointment: a miserable anticlimax to the many months that I had spent in the company of all those wise books that had promised so convincingly to take me into the secret, visionary center of things. After taking Huxley's tasteful encounters with Botticelli paintings and radiant flower vases and Castaneda's didactic initiations in the softly glowing cactuslands of the Sonora so seriously, I found it both humiliating and frightening to discover that the hidden levels of my own psyche seemed to be populated with nothing more than mean-spirited cartoons.

THE REAL MAGICIAN

In our society . . . the elders are missing.

Louise Carus Mahdi

At the time, I wrote my mushroom-induced vision of Mickey off as meaningless. Once my psilocybin-befuddled brain had reassembled itself sufficiently for me to figure out where I was, I got up, dusted myself off, and headed out of that blasted Indian burial ground wishing I'd never entered it in the first place. Later, however—years later—I came to realize that my vision of Mickey that night wasn't really as off the mark as I had first thought it was. In fact, it was about as appropriate a summation of my situation at the time as any other that my poor, besieged, blown-open subconscious might have thrown my way. Even now, searching for a single image to stand for that whole period of my life and all the odd concerns that had filled it, I can't think of a better one than Mickey in his role of Sorcerer's Apprentice: the enthusiastic but ill-prepared youth who tries desperately to be like the wise but absent adult he so admires and botches the job completely.

This is a Sorcerer's Apprentice kind of time we are living in—a time when much magic is available, but not nearly enough genuine, flesh-and-blood magicians are around to dispense proper advice and directions on what to do with it. A great many of my own masters, I also discovered over time, had feet of clay and should never have been listened to with anything like the near-desperate earnestness that I once gave them. Watts, the man of the Eternal Now, turned out to have been a person whose own life was far more complex and tormented than his breezily written prescriptions for living suggested. Meanwhile Castaneda, the steely-eyed walker of the sorcerer's path, turned out to have been an inspired hoaxer and wise old Don Juan most likely a pure product of his imagination. Others among my early masters—Huxley for one—survived the test of time in better shape, but their general legacy remains ambiguous. America's taste in prescriptive wisdom literature continues to grow ever more insatiable but at the same time becomes ever more simpleminded, with a new cast of Celestine Prophets and Mutant Messengers spinning tales for a new generation of Sorcerer's Apprentices—who have about as much chance of bungling their way into Enlightenment as I had out on that Indian burial ground.

Real wisdom—the genuine, no-nonsense variety that in times past held entire cultures together and helped the individual members of those cultures toward an understanding of who and what they really were—remains as hard to approach successfully today as it was back in Lao Tzu's day. Emperor Hun Tun is now, as ever, a tough person to get ahold of—and once found, all too easy to kill.

JANWILLEM VAN DE WETERING

Seeing into Your Nature and Other Pastimes

While living at Daitoku-ji monastery in Japan I noticed a lot of activity having to do with the spiritual development of the monks, which, in Zen parlance, was called "seeing into their nature." They weren't just sitting quietly in the zendo or working in silence in the gardens, they were talking a lot to one another. Not having any language to speak of (with) yet, I didn't have much idea of what was going on, but gradually, as I picked up words, I began to catch on. Up till then Japanese had been an exotic language to me. I thought that most everything that was said in Kyoto had a deeper meaning. Kyoto is the spiritual heart of Japan or, as other local experts told me, a projection of "true Japanese nature." Any day I was out of the sodo I saw senior citizens, brought in by the busload from all over the country, being guided along the neighborhood of temples, halls, palaces, and living museums of religious folklore. The old folks seemed somewhat in a hurry to learn to "see into their nature," before, back in their hometowns, priests chanted their funeral rites. Dressed in formal kimonos, immaculate black for the men with their shaved skulls and white wispy beards, purple and gray for the women who were often bent double with osteoporosis, the seekers for final insight stopped at every shrine. They bowed and clapped their hands to summon Buddha, the bodhisattvas, Shinto deities, even the spirit of a long-dead emperor when they faced the former Imperial Palace. They all looked serious and devout.

The first time I was aware of emotions of a lower level was when Han-san, my English-speaking monk-friend, and I overheard a conversation of two giggling old ladies who were bowing to the Temple of the Thousand Buddhas. Han-san pointed discreetly and whispered. "Second Buddha on the third row, the one with the movie mustache, the ladies were saying that he looks like a lover they shared fifty years ago." As I learned Japanese I began to understand overheard conversations, in a streetcar or a bathhouse. None of them had anything to do with "looking into their nature"; it was like home, all gossip, complaints, showing off, exchange of trivial information, or, in the case of young males, rough talk. It was a disappointment to know that, in this heavenly temple town, I was definitely not in heaven. However, as the president of a Dutch Buddhist club was to say to me many years later, when she heard that a speaker canceled a lecture she had planned: "I have suffered so much in this life already, this can be added, it won't increase the pain."

I should have known better anyway. I had gotten used to a lack of esoteric meaning in Japanese everyday conversation on the French cargo/passenger vessel that took me from Saigon to Kobe, the last lap on my liberation journey in 1957. Two young Japanese engineers were returning from the Vietnamese jungle, where they had overseen local laborers collecting scrap metal (the war with the French colonial government hadn't been over that long and the American army hadn't arrived yet). The engineers liked the French apple brandy the *Anna Marie*'s bar was stocked with. They would show one another (and, what the hell, me too) photographs of tall blonde nude women they had bought in Saigon and shouted *"yosh"* (okay) and *"tai-hen"* (very) as they pointed out the models' dimensions. Didn't I think so? Sure, I thought so. They shouted *"kampai"* (bottoms up) when they raised freshly filled glasses, but with me the toast was invariably *"Bussho"* (Buddha nature). I never had the impression that they were making fun of me. They had asked me why I was going to Japan, and I had told them I was looking to "realize my Buddha nature." They didn't understand me at first, but I copied out the characters for "Buddha nature" from a footnote in a D. T. Suzuki Zen book and showed it to them at the bar. They nodded. *Bussho* was *yosh* (okay) too. The pictures of the naked blondes were put away for the moment. They showed me photos of elephants pulling disabled French tanks from under palm trees. "See, that's me sitting on Big Jumbo." They told me that Kobe steel, cooked from the dead French tanks traveling in the holds of the *Anna Marie,* would be shipped to the States, where new Vietnam-bound tanks were being built now. They saw much profitable business coming their way. "Kampai!" "Kampai," I said. "Bussho!" "Bussho," I said. They banged on the bar. "Monsieur Steward? Another apple brandy for Looking into His Own Nature here."

I felt like a character in *The Razor's Edge II.* The first version, by Somerset Maugham, had made an impression on me. A young man, heir to a fortune, sets out on a spiritual mission and recognizes, after some meditation and soul-searching exercises prescribed by a guru, his true nature in a hermitage in the Himalayas. A new man, he goes home to Chicago, gives up his upper-class status, and becomes a cab driver "to help the other people out," but the book doesn't say how he aims to do that. The hero just wanders off the last page, looking insightful and happy. I wouldn't, I thought while drinking applejack with Japanese tank recyclers, mind helping the other people out either, but I'd need to get to know something first—something to help out with. My true nature presumably. It all seemed very tricky, especially when the other people only wanted to look at naked blonds and help build better killing machines. Maybe there weren't any other people in need of being helped out spiritually, which would suit me fine; I would just take off for bliss in the void.

The monks of Daitoku-ji seemed to be getting results in this field of investigation "into their own nature" by solving koans at great speed. Han-san, from time to time, would show me his list for getting there, or getting "nowhere," which, as a true Buddhist, he preferred to call it. The list showed koan titles on the left side, tick-off marks on the right side. He also studied poetry-puzzle books. Roshi, in sanzen, would indicate part of a poem in one book, and Han-san would have to find a matching piece in another book. Han-san said he was good at it. Completing a holy poem usually took just a few days of reading and rumination. He said he was gifted in literature. He had noticed I liked to read too and got me translations of novels by the Japanese genius Tanizaki. I really liked Tanizaki's writing, the way things twisted into one another, the long monologues, the descriptions of moods, the aberrations of human behavior minutely described, with a comforting but hopeless undertone, and always little touches of nature: a bird sings, a cloud passes. But there was no way out; the intelligent reader knows all this will end in terminal madness.

"Of course you like Tanizaki," Han-san said. "The man is totally neurotic." He bowed enthusiastically to express his admiration. "Try Kawabata next. Very sad, and his tales go nowhere too. He and Tanizaki both have the same nature."

I didn't like this. Why would I like neurotic natures?

"Because you are crazy." Han-san laughed. "What are you blundering about here for? What good will all this agonizing do you? Do you have any pleasant goal in sight? I am going to be a priest at a temple in a happy town somewhere, not part of a training ground like this business here. There'll be no sweat in my temple, no stink, no boiled cabbage, no lukewarm bath once every nine days. Flush toilets instead of holes in the floor, home to bird-sized flies waiting for the holy ass. I'll be eating sushi for dinner week-days and delicacies the good folks bring in during weekends. There'll be a car! You had all that. You gave it up because you were *curious,* you say?"

"You have no curiosity?" I asked furiously. I pointed at the sky. "The creation doesn't make you wonder? What does it all mean, man?"

Han-san playfully punched my stomach. "Doesn't mean shit, man-san." He punched me harder and made an angry face. "Form is emptiness. The ego is empty on all five levels. There is no suffer-ing because only the ego is suffering; once the ego pops, pain pops with it." Han-san was getting himself all worked up, dancing around me on his clackety-clack geta, punching me every time he got close enough. "You chant the Heart Sutra with us every morn-ing, singing '*mu* this *mu* that' in your creaky voice, making us laugh, making the head monk yell at us afterward. Chanting the Heart Sutra, with all the percussion going on, the drum droning, the gong clanging, is supposed to make you look into your true nature by hypnosis." He pointed at his list of solved koans. "They all say the same thing. *There is nothing there.* You still don't get it? That everything is empty? That there's nothing to carry around? That all we have to do is enjoy our nonselves? I'm going to drive an empty car and eat empty sushi once I graduate from here. Maybe meet some empty women while I'm at it. What kind of emptiness are you going to do?"

I hit him too to make him stop hitting me, maybe too hard, for he ran off.

Some company arrived at the temple, two American graduate students, fluent in Japanese, who wanted to add Zen Buddhism to their collection of credits. They came with impressive recommen-dations, and Roshi had accepted them as temporary students provided they would attend some arduous meditation weeks and see him in sanzen a hundred times or so. Future Ph.D.'s at first-class American universities, Adam and Trevor told me they would like to solve some koans and get Roshi to give them a certificate at the end of their stay in beautiful Kyoto. They bought motorcycles and rented comfortable quarters in a private house halfway between the sodo and the willow quarter. They were friendly fellows. "What koan are you on, Jan?"

I was on Mu.

They had done a lot of homework. They knew about Mu. There was, Adam said, nothing to Mu. The story is obvious. Of course the puppy dog has Buddha nature, the monk knows it, the teacher knows it, the question is silly. Everything has Buddha nature. The universe is, in essence, divine. The monk is testing the teacher. That's what happens in a lot of koans. Monks challenge masters. Right? Right. Now then, why is the Mu koan so important? Why is it called a "gate koan"? Why does it offer an opening out of the maze where we, developed human souls (undeveloped souls don't even know there is a maze), are looking for real answers? Because the teacher strikes the monk down with this great shout of "Mu." The teacher's answer goes infinitely beyond the question of the puppy dog (a lesser creature, the teacher is Chinese, Chinese eat dogs, the dog could be a pig here or a louse or the little simple life form that causes syphilis) being as holy as anything else. Mu means the valueless void, the absolute nonexistence of anything. It is empty space with the idea "space" taken out; it is zero with the ring removed. Mu takes the Mickey out of all monkish questions.

Trevor knew about Mu too. The answer to the koan is "Mu." The monk shouts "Mu" at the teacher. The void is filled with the void. No more room for questions. Right?

"Tell Roshi," I said.

They told him, seven times a day during the first week of December, which is the toughest week in Zen training, the week where students keep seeing the teacher in between lengthened meditations and very short meals and naps. "I am a cow," Trevor told Adam during a break. "I shout 'Mu' so much that's what I am now, a fucking cow, man." He held his hands behind his ears, stuck his face into Adam's face and bellowed *"Muuuuu."*

Adam asked me whether I was making any progress. I had been there for some time now. What kind of answer was I giving at sanzen? I said I wasn't getting anywhere but that Roshi had told me, in case I was moving without me being aware of it, not to count any passing milestones. Just keep going, and, sure, I was still saying "mu" too, sometimes. Mostly I said nothing. Roshi would ring his bell. I would leave, be back a few hours later, say nothing, Roshi would ring his bell again.

"What pisses me off," said Adam, "is these monks making progress. They are only here for their careers or because their parents threw them out. This Han-san guy showed me his list of solved koans. He says he will be a priest next year. He'll wear a white robe under his gray robe. Different socks. Some kind of colored shawl. He'll be asked to join other priests in another temple for ceremonies, with chanting and dancing. He won't be before the mast any more, he'll be sailing his own temple. But will he know anything?"

Adam complained that Han-san didn't have the right motivation to solve koans, while he, Adam, had. He was a genuine student of Asiatic advanced thinking, so was Trevor, and even I, although they thought I was there to get therapy for troubles caused by a trauma picked up in World War II, could perhaps be classified as a genuine seeker. So how come Roshi wouldn't let us in on the Mu koan, which we obviously, all three of us, understood? Any practically unlettered farmer's son coming in from the country passed it in a few months or so. Why not us? Did Roshi not like foreigners perhaps? Did he believe in Japanese superiority, to the point where he denied the possibility of insight in a *gai-jin,* an outsider?

Trevor mentioned Roshi saying he had been in Manchuria during the war, as a soldier in the Imperial Army. Roshi was a monk when the war broke out, but monks had to be soldiers too; if they refused for religious reasons the *Kempetai,* the Japanese military police, would arrest, jail, and eventually kill them. Not being a warrior, Roshi had volunteered for guard duty, which was granted because of his poor health. He had meditated while standing still, holding on to his rifle. "The enemy could have come driving tanks at me, and I probably wouldn't have noticed." "Interesting," said Trevor, "but what was he guarding? Manchuria was where the heavy war industry was, run by an enslaved population, but there were also facilities where Chinese POWs were used in terminal experiments. There were biological weapon factories, all sorts of bad stuff to be guarded there." He wobbled his eyebrows. "You know?"

We stubbed our cigarettes in an empty beer can hidden behind a stone overgrown with moss that marked the grave of a famous Zen saint and went back to the zendo for another three hours of meditation. Well, so what. I preferred to appreciate Roshi on his present level rather than worrying about his war past. I thought there was karma there, unavoidable circumstances, determining the where and when of a human birth. Roshi's birth as a Japanese around 1900 would irrevocably lead to him being a soldier, a guard—at a mustard gas factory, perhaps. (He could have been guarding sake bottles, who knows? I certainly never asked him.) Because of different unavoidable karma Trevor and Adam happened to be born as good Americans, to live splendid lives that nobody would ever be able to find fault with. By chance I was born as the son to an anti-Nazi middle-class Dutch couple, which, according to current values (1940–1945, when Germany occupied Holland), made me a good guy too. My karma made me feel good but soon led to doubts too. What on earth is "good"? Two boys at the school in Rotterdam that I attended were identical twins, blond and blue eyed. They were fifteen years old, I was nine. I fell in a moat once, and they got me out. Once the hated occupation started my heroes became German citizens. Their parents had been German but had left Germany before the war for some business reason. Once settled in Holland, they became Dutch nationals. New laws made by the Occupation Authority reversed that choice. The boys were conscripted by the Nazi bureaucracy and came to school one day in Hitler Youth uniforms on a motorcycle and sidecart, part of the propaganda that was heating up at that time. What fifteen-year-old boys will refuse to show off a motorcycle and sidecart? Their jealous anti-Nazi classmates ganged up on *Humpty & Dumpty Heil Hitler,* as we called Heinz and Hans since we discovered they had been relabeled. We regular Dutch boys (I stood back, but I didn't help them either) were going to kill these hateful outsiders by banging bricks on their heads, but a teacher broke up the melee and told the victims to go home and change into civilian clothes, quoting a fictitious school rule that forbade wearing of uniforms in class. Heinz and Hans went back to Germany later in the war and died in the firebombing of Dresden. Once I heard that I felt even more sorry I hadn't defended them when the good boys were about to throw bricks because karma had gotten Heinz and Hans a motorcycle. But I still, dutifully, hated all Germans.

"Roshi doesn't hate foreigners," I said. "I heard him deliver a *teisho* on the subject, a Sunday morning lecture in the big dharma hall, with the percussion orchestra going, with all the lay supporters of the temple present, a big gala occasion. The monks were dressed up in their Sunday robes, and I wore a tie and a jacket. The monks had been laughing at me, saying that a clumsy foreigner who pisses like a horse cannot realize his true nature. Roshi told them off about that. Everybody has the Buddha nature. He told them that Joshu didn't always say Mu. He sometimes said U. 'U' means everything, everybody, even foreigners who piss like horses."

"You don't speak Japanese too good," Trevor said. "You're sure Roshi said that?"

I told him Roshi had appointed Han-san as an instant translator, Roshi spoke slowly, Han-san whispered the translation into my ears. It was important that I got what Roshi was saying.

Adam also thought that Roshi didn't hate foreigners. He didn't think Roshi would hate anyone. "He can't. I think he is beyond any value system."

Trevor, Adam, and I eventually came up with a theory that suited us better. We were being discriminated against by Roshi, sure, but for excellent reasons. We were superior students, more idealistically motivated than the career-minded monks who only put up with the austerities and stress of their three-year stint in the sodo to become luxurious priests in comfortable temples later. Trevor and Adam as students of the humanities, specializing in Japanese religion for now, and I, trying to find a cure for an affliction that I insisted on defining as "philosophical curiosity," were serious and intelligent students enquiring into the mystery of the universe. For monks who merely wanted to be priests in nice temples, Roshi used a kindergarten method of staggered goals that could be easily reached. However, Roshi was guiding *us* in a difficult but, in the end, definitely more rewarding way by keeping us on the Mu, the number one koan, rather than have us fritter our energy away on the little koans and a bunch of cut-up poems. We, future Maitreyas, were climbing Mount Sumeru straight up, with some occasional dangling from cliffs, while the monks followed the endlessly winding, far easier path.

That was nice. We were all happy. We all got through the tough meditation week. We would also be getting through our lives. Forty years later I went to a memorial after Trevor's death. He had become a Buddhist and had a successful university career. The Beatles sang "Yellow Submarine" as we stood in line to burn incense. His photograph on a red lacquered table was framed by candles and two bottles of Old Turkey, his favorite beverage, especially in later years. Adam, also a practicing Buddhist now, is teaching, writing, and translating. I read his writing when I need to be reminded of the time that I was concerned with looking into my own nature. I never found my true nature. Sensei, much later, toward the end of the trying years when I was his student, shed some light on the subject by giving me the Master Toso (known in China as Tou-shuai, 1044–1091) "three barrier" koan to work on.

You beat the grass and probe the Principle
only to see into your nature,
Right now where is your nature?

It seems some koans can be answered only in anger. Having to memorize the many solemn words of this little story and carry them around between drafty buildings during blizzards and rainstorms began to bore me. "Beating the grass," we (Sensei and I during many sanzen sessions) had established by then, meant *getting rid of ignorance.* "Probing the Principle" would be *to be enlightened by Buddha's teaching.* The matter of "my nature" remained for many months. What could it mean? Did it exist? If it did, what on Earth would I do with my "own nature"? Frame it, hang it on the wall? Burn incense to the thing? What is so important about my nature? Finally some truth dawned. Whoever looks for his own nature is lost from the start. I can find something temporary, my personality, but who, including myself, cares about that? Mostly the personality is boring and irritating. As long as it is used as a polite mask, expressing a little loving-kindness in daily dealings, as long as it pays bills, does the regular routine in a pleasing manner, the personality will serve until the day the body, another not too important and temporary manifestation, falters and is no more. I'm not my mask. Surely I'm not my body either. The body is a useful instrument, has to be washed and shaved, fed, treated kindly, but we don't have to get ridiculous here. It doesn't really matter that much. Do we care about the body's longevity, the personality's eternity? Do we care to have our minds repeating familiar thought patterns? Who is the Who who cares?

There is the story about the monk with the troubled mind who goes to the master to quiet the damn thing. "Can you do that, sir?" "Let's see, my friend, bring me your mind so I can examine it." "I can't find my mind, sir." "There you are, I have quieted it down for you." "The monk's mind is no longer troubled."

But all this is a play with words. Minds are never untroubled. It's the mind's business to be always busy, always troubled about something. *If it isn't one damned thing, it's another.* The mind is just an instrument, like a computer, to analyze daily troubles, order them, find a solution. Once that is done, take a nap and shut it down for a while. Put it in sleep mode. I'm not my computer, my mind, my body. What's beyond? Nothing. Mu. But *Mu* is a word used to express the inexpressible. So, pushed to the extreme, I told Sensei to forget the whole thing. And to forget me too. There is no me. No me-nature, no real-nature, no true-nature, no nothing. I looked around the sanzen room. "I can beat the grass here forever and probe the principle forever, and I'll never see my nature. Why should I anyway? Who cares?"

"Right," he said, "so your nature isn't there. I knew that." His smile was tired. It was 4 A.M.; I knew he had been to a party the night before. He stretched and yawned. "Okay. Next move. Let me tell you about it tomorrow, yes? Your next move has to do with death, one of your favorite subjects." He gestured defensively. "Don't look so upset. So you looked for something that wasn't there. It's human nature, you know." He laughed. He wanted me to laugh too.

MICHAEL VENTURA

Fifty-Two
from The Sun

Age. For most of human history, to be old has been a mark of honor. Today it's a source of fear, even shame. Yet my fiftieth birthday was strangely joyous. It began as my days usually begin: I walked to the corner cafe, drank my coffee, read my *New York Times,* watched the world go by for a while. (Tough life, right?) Usually, after this languid beginning, I do what writers call "work": a kind of restless hunting, tracking a strange beast in the jungle of oneself. In my case, this looks like hours of pacing up and down, smoking lots of cigarettes, and drinking many cups of strong tea while staring out the window. (When the beast is finally found, the writer-hunter must then refrain from killing it; rather, you sit very still and let the creature devour you.)

But on my fiftieth birthday I gave myself the day off (*very* tough life), and I walked. And walked, and walked. I set myself the walking task of remembering every birthday as far back as I could. I focused my thoughts until I could recall at least one specific thing about each: a friend, a song, something said or left unsaid. The quiet girl who sat at the next desk in fifth grade. The fight with Ginger on the way to the Springsteen concert. Me alone in the Mojave reading the poems of George Seferis. Chris in a witch's wig. Mama pretending she wasn't ill when the heat got shut off on Decatur Street. Mama, when I was seven, screaming, "Your birthday is a day like any other!" Our senior class Halloween party for the little kids, where a dark-eyed, scared-eyed, tiny girl came straight up to me and took my hand and wouldn't let it go for the whole party.

I wouldn't have imagined it possible, but I "saw" something of every birthday all the way back to age five. Once a specific bit of memory was retrieved, it became easier to see who I had been that year. In this way I met long-gone Michaels I'd forgotten—it was painful how many, and why I'd needed to forget them. I was embarrassed by some, ashamed of others; a few I even feared. But some were still my pals, and of three or four I was very proud. They walked beside me, that gang of Michaels, many of them strangers to one another, but walking together, for this one day, with a grateful feeling of companionship.

When I told this to a friend, she said I was forgiving myself, but I don't think so. I don't think we have the right to forgive ourselves. Forgiveness can come only from those we've sinned against, if they find it in their hearts, and perhaps from God, if God is interested. Rather, that walk was a look into my own eyes—the eyes of the many I'd been and the one I was. I suspect that looking into your own eyes, or another's, is a tougher task than forgiving: looking, seeing, and living with—or choosing to live without—what you see.

When that walk was over, I recalled something my brother Aldo had once said to me: "Unless you practice seeing yourself, you become invisible to yourself." I felt less invisible to myself that day. Lighter and darker, both. It was a good way to pass my half-century mark.

But . . . well, sometimes you try to see yourself and you see someone else, someone you didn't expect at all. He is you and not-you—or perhaps a you who has always been waiting within. This was the lesson (learned not for the first time, and probably not the last) of my most recent birthday, my fifty-second.

On this day, too, I planned nothing. I've learned to leave birthdays unplanned, or almost so, to let the day unfold on its own, because a birthday is a teaching day; it has something to reveal. Too many plans constrict its ability to speak. Left to itself, any day will, at some unexpected moment, find its voice and deliver its message. This is especially true of birthdays, for, as Thomas Hardy once observed, your birthday exists in relation to another day, a day that is impossible to know: we pass silently, every year, over the anniversary of our death.

At forty, you may have half your life in front of you; at fifty-two, it's not likely. In your thirties you may worry about losing your looks; in your fifties you worry about losing your capacities. At thirty you have maybe thirty-five years before serious deterioration sets in. At fifty-two, you have . . . fifteen years left of reasonably adequate strength? Less? Ten, *maybe?* If your bad habits don't get you first?

Every age has its wisdom (youth knows truths that middle age can no longer bear), but one difference between being young and no-longer-young is: the young don't *know* they are going to die, not really; the no-longer-young know. We know, consciously or not, that one day of the year is the anniversary (the counting-backward anniversary, if you like) of our death. So we walk more softly through our days, or more bitterly, or even more recklessly, depending on our natures; but our walk does alter, because, as James Baldwin wrote, "there will come a day you won't remember"—the day you die.

There is an Old One inside that helps with this. One of the tragedies of America today is that it ignores and shames this Old One.

It's become a cliché that inside everyone there's an "inner child." Pop culture is an enormous, omnipresent machine designed to tantalize and trick this Young One within. The Young One seems the only part of you that our commercial culture takes seriously. Your Young One is seduced into consuming like an adult while remaining too young to think like one. Your Young One is flattered into thinking it's your true self, the one you must always look like, the one you must never leave behind. This gives the Young One burdens and responsibilities beyond its capacities—making your Young One all the more insecure, all the more vulnerable, and thus all the more susceptible to the lies it is being sold. And selling *is* the object of this delusion. As we age, we're frightened into buying all manner of chemicals, operations, and concoctions to retain some ghost of the Young One. Few see that what they're really doing is devoting lots of time and money to being afraid, or that this only feeds their fear and makes it stronger.

The most insidious result of our buying into this cult of the Young One is that we insult and shame the Old One.

The Old One has been in us from the beginning, just like the Young One. You can see its expression sometimes even in the face of an infant. Or in your own face in a childhood photograph. Or in the unexpected wisdom of a grade school or high school kid—something utterly true and perceptive, completely beyond their experience, yet theirs nonetheless. It's the Old One talking. The Old One is in us, waiting to take over from the Young One when it is time.

When adults of other eras taught their young to "respect your elders," they were also respecting the Old One who lived within each young person—strengthening the Old One, giving the Old One a source of pride, so that it would be up to the task when it was needed. But our culture insults and shames the Old One at every turn—and sells the idea that, in order to be accepted, we too must insult and shame our Old One by trying to stay young. After fifty years or more of insult and shame, our Old One is weak and frightened and riven with self-doubt. It's no wonder we are afraid of aging, for how can such an Old One come forth in us and be strong when its time comes?

So we are left with only the Young One with which to face infirmity and death. But the Young One is unprepared for this, for the Young One is incapable of believing in death. You might say that its *job* is not to believe in death, not to value, much less respect, death. That's part of the Young One's beauty. With its audacity, the Young One gives us great strength, at the proper time. But that time passes. And after it passes, only the Old One can give us the strength we need. But it's difficult to be strong after a half century of ceaseless shaming.

When I turned fifty-two, my Old One came to me. Not-yet-me, but me, my Old One counseled me not to be repelled by the changes in my face and body, by the graying and loss of my hair. He bade me to respect him, feed him, sing to him, speak to him, listen to him, walk with him; to cease shaming him, to keep others from shaming him, and to comfort the shamed parts of him; to make a place for him to occupy, so he can do his job, when it's time. For time doesn't kid around. It will come soon enough, the day when I'll awake and be very lonely and frightened if the Old One isn't there or isn't able.

PAUL J. WILLIS

The Wardrobe Wars
from Books & Culture

In my freshman year at Wheaton College, back in the early seventies, the Wade Collection in Blanchard Hall acquired some new closet space—a wardrobe, to be exact. This wasn't a wardrobe that anyone actually used. It was just to look at, or perhaps to admire, or maybe even to worship. One student editorial in the campus paper suggested we cut slivers from the back of it and sell them as relics.

For this, of course, was not just any wardrobe, but one that had once belonged to C. S. Lewis, the unofficial patron saint of Wheaton College. And a beautiful piece of dark oak furniture it was—painstakingly handmade and elaborately handcarved by C. S. Lewis's grandfather and brought by Lewis from his boyhood home in Belfast to the Kilns, the house he shared with his brother, Warren, outside of Oxford. The college bought it at auction just after Warren died.

Other items of Lewis furniture from the Kilns were purchased by the college as well, including the obvious choice of a desk. But the wardrobe was particularly important because of its role in the first of the Chronicles of Narnia, *The Lion, the Witch and the Wardrobe.* The wardrobe in the story is the threshold to fantasy; in the Wade Collection it became a tangible symbol of Lewis's powers as a writer, a sacrament of the literary imagination. It was the closest *thing* we had to Narnia.

The problem with literary relics, however, is that some Chaucerian Pardoner will always claim to have better ones. When I began teaching in the late eighties at Westmont College in Santa Barbara, I was surprised to see a somewhat plain but rather old wardrobe in the English department across from our secretary's desk and not far from an equally old fireplace. On top of it lay a huge stuffed lion, which should have been my clue. This was the wardrobe, I was told. *The* wardrobe. (Surprising, isn't it, how definite that definite article sometimes becomes?) It had been obtained from the Kilns in 1975.

"But I thought the wardrobe was at Wheaton," I told my new colleagues.

"No way," they told me. "Wheaton's wardrobe is not even close to the one described in the novel."

Then I was duly chaptered and versed by references to the sacred text. What the Pevensie children find in the empty room of the old Professor's country house is "one big wardrobe, the sort that has a looking glass in the door." I had to admit that the wardrobe before me was larger than the one I remembered from my undergraduate days and that its door—its one door—was indeed covered with a looking glass. The Wheaton wardrobe, I was reminded, sadly lacked a looking glass on either of its two doors.

Once Lucy is left behind in the room, "she thought it would be worth while trying the door of the wardrobe, even though she felt almost sure that it would be locked." And sure enough, the Westmont wardrobe had a keyhole—as did the Wheaton wardrobe, if memory served me correctly. Inside the unlocked wardrobe, Lucy finds "a second row of coats hanging up behind the first one." This second row of coats is hanging on "hooks" or "pegs," and my colleagues opened the looking-glass door to point these out to me, hidden behind a first row of fur coats on hangers. The Wheaton wardrobe, I was told, might have hooks in the back as well (or were they pegs?), but did not have a row of hangers in front of them.

With the door thrown open, I was shown how easily Lucy could have "stepped into the wardrobe"—the threshold was just a foot off the floor. The Wheaton wardrobe, I was reminded, was more like a high-waisted cabinet. Lucy could only have *climbed* into it at best. Finally, my colleagues reminded me that the wardrobe in question had to be "a perfectly ordinary wardrobe," just like the one in the book. Did our wardrobe have any decorative carving? It did not. Wheaton had an ornate family heirloom, but it did not have the real thing.

Wardrobe closed. Case dismissed.

Has my alma mater been impressed by this impeccable brand of literary fundamentalism? Apparently not. According to one Wheaton brochure, theirs is the "wardrobe from which Lewis drew inspiration for *The Lion, the Witch and the Wardrobe.*" And on the back of a postcard of the Wheaton wardrobe itself, we are likewise told that "according to Lewis's brother Warren, it was the inspiration for the wardrobe" in the celebrated novel. Old claims never die. They just grow more specific with time.

I was back at Wheaton for a conference just a couple of years ago. During a period of announcements, a curator from the Wade Collection invited the conference participants to visit the collection and see the many books and papers that had belonged to Lewis and his associates. At the end of her announcement, she told us, "We also have the wardrobe that served as the original for the one in the Narnia Chronicles."

There it was, that definite article again. In a remarkable display of maturity I put up my hand and said, "Excuse me, but *the* wardrobe is at Westmont College in Santa Barbara."

The woman gave me a long, hard look of the "we are not

amused" variety. That was all. I wasn't able to find her after the session was over to clear things up.

Not that we could have, really. Of course, if pressed, I suspect we would both admit the wardrobe we are really concerned with exists only within the covers of a book, and that not even this wardrobe is so important as the story of which it is a part, and that the story is not so important as the sense of infinite longing that it stirs within our souls, and that this longing is not so important as the One—more real than Aslan himself—to whom it directs us. But that would be asking too much of either the curator or myself. To worship at our respective wardrobes, whether they be in Jerusalem or Samaria, is indeed to live in the shadowlands. And that is where we like it.

Lewis himself would doubtless say that the physical wardrobes in our possession are but copies of a faint copy. He might even claim, to our horror, that no single wardrobe inspired the one found in his book. Then he might add under his breath, like the Professor in *The Last Battle* who has passed on to the next life, "It's all in Plato, all in Plato: bless me, what *do* they teach them at these schools!"

The reason that the Westmont wardrobe remained at the Kilns after the auction of other furniture was that it could not fit out the doorway of Joy Davidman's bedroom. The hall or door had been made smaller in the forties—and remember, it is a *large* wardrobe. The new owner of the house apparently cared little for Lewis's furniture and was prepared to destroy the wardrobe to make room for an American-style built-in closet. Walter Hooper, who has long served as Lewis's literary executor, reportedly thought it a great pity that the last remaining piece of furniture from C. S. Lewis's house should in all likelihood end up as firewood. That is when a group of Westmont students and faculty bought the wardrobe for next to nothing, had it dismantled, shipped it in pieces to Santa Barbara, and reassembled it carefully near the fireplace in Reynolds Hall.

But I have a little fantasy, thanks perhaps to Walter Hooper, about our wardrobe's proper end. Late some rainy California winter evening, long after my colleagues have returned to their homes and the students have slogged back up the hill to the residence halls, I will let myself back into the building, lock the doors, raise an axe high over my head, and with dolorous strokes split the wardrobe into kindling. Then I will stack the broken wood high in the old fireplace and start myself a cheerful blaze. By the light of this fire I will settle into a wingback chair, open a tattered book that was the first book to open me, and read far into the night.

LARRY WOIWODE

A Fifty-Year Walk
from Books & Culture

When I was twelve and what happens to boys hadn't happened to me yet, I loved to walk alone. I would walk five miles down a railroad track to my grandparents' place or walk seven miles in the opposite direction to a lake I liked to look at, after I had walked to the far corners of our town a half-dozen times that day. It wasn't beyond me to walk twenty miles without even stopping to think about it, as I haven't, really, until now.

The places I most liked to walk were outside any sign of habitation—in the carved gap of a railroad line or along a dirt road that led through pastures or cornfields to a woods. When I walked I thought of others who had walked this way before, and the only ones I had heard of who had walked as much as I seemed to walk were the apostles of Jesus Christ (along with Jesus, of course), and a U.S. president who once lived in the area of Illinois where my family was living—Abraham Lincoln.

The place I liked above all to walk was to a woods halfway between my grandparents and the lake I liked, the straight north of those two points, or so it seemed to me then, though its actual direction was west. I strolled toward it along the edge of a road that was such pure sand it was as hard to walk as the sand of an unpacked beach. All along the route hedge apples lay in the sand like limes so bloated that the pebbling of their peels resembled worms locked in molten swirls. You didn't want to think what the thing was up to. The hedge apples struck the sand like shot puts, and if I kicked one it was almost as heavy and left a gooey sap on my bare toes. Hedgerows crowded the road, growing wild in this place as deserted and hot as the Sahara—the perimeter of a state forest I was headed toward.

Once I had sized up my route for the next mile or so, or to the next hill or curve, I never looked ahead of my feet as I walked. I don't know why. What flowed past or flew in from the side or swung up to encounter me was more of a surprise that way, I suspect. I partly wanted to be surprised, or safely scared, as boys that age do—a natural scare that never approached the terror I lived with. My mother was dead and had died away from home of a disease I had never been able to fathom or my father had never been able to explain, so I had come to feel that my worst thoughts about her had caused her death.

The latticework of shadow from the hedge-apple rows thickened to trunks and overarching shadows of trees—tall elms still free from the Dutch elm blight—maples, burr oaks all gnarled, horse chestnut, and a dozen other varieties our science teacher had pointed out on a field trip when I was so overwhelmed by the trees themselves I couldn't take in their names.

But I knew them as well as aunts and uncles from my weekly walks through this state forest that was also becoming a wildlife sanctuary. I felt so much at home I sang as I sang nowhere else, sometimes mere notes that I felt began to reach the tones and patterns of plainsong—this I loved, mixed with incense, as much as anything about the church I attended each week.

"Oh, beautiful trees!" I sang. "Oh, sky above me! Oh, earth beneath my feet!" It was really a shout, blasts of assurance, the same song I sang each time I walked, as if to announce my presence to the elements I addressed—the sky and earth that had seemed to govern my life from its beginning. Then these trees.

I was never afraid or lost my way no matter how many and how varied the routes I took (besides not looking ahead), and I never felt the sense of the absence of my mother that I felt everywhere else. She was born on the plains, far from actual woods, where an individual tree offered shade but too many got in your way and were a bother or threat. I had walked with her in the spaces of the plains and at the edges of woods, the blue-green conifers of Minnesota mostly, and the movement and placement of her limbs as she walked communicated to me a sense of this. But people were made to talk, unlike the spaces of earth (both empty and filled up) that seemed to want so much to talk they trembled with an omniscience that caused me to listen as I never did with people, not even her.

Now as I sang and walked, matching the words to my right-left pace, I saw rough trunks crowd close, their shadows lying on leaves and needles they had shed, all of this closeness intertwining in a way that caused the light I saw striking my feet to take on substance. The chill of a presence slid over me as if I were shedding leaves myself, and I stopped and looked up.

The patterns of the scribbled multitude of twigs and the matching gaps of designated light matching the movement of the limbs were as much a song or shout as what I sang. This was the earth, these its trees in their multitude of beauty, twigs to branches to trunks, the sky and space brimming with angels and voices that would soon break into appearance or speech. I felt no terror, gripped by a presence of greater substance than my mother's hand, and tears of laughter leaped out like the appearances and voices that seemed so imminent.

One presence was here, I saw, as I turned with my face raised, in the trees and sky and the earth that supported me as I turned. This presence had put all this in place to teach me about myself and its own qualities and makeup: *God.* I had been instructed to love Him, but the words of English I knew couldn't approach the language pouring from everything around with a familiarity that aroused in me a wordless love that for the life of me I couldn't define. I was given a glimpse of it when I came to read, *The Heavens declare the glory of God. . . . Day unto day utters speech. . . . There is no speech or language where their voice is not heard. . . . For since the creation of the world His invisible attributes are clearly seen, being understood by the things that are made. . . . For by Him all things were created that are in heaven and that are on earth, visible and invisible, whether thrones or principalities or powers. All things were created through Him and for Him. And He is before all things, and in Him all things consist.*

Here were two languages put partly into English, and what they stated in the language I partly knew was so unimaginable— especially that last phrase—that I'm jolted from the trees and left flat-footed in the present. As I studied the statement, I found it has been so seldom touched upon by any portion of official Christendom you would think it doesn't exist. And the more I studied it and turned it every which way, it still persisted in saying, *in Him all things consist.* How could I reconcile this with my present-day understanding of nature, pragmatic and tone deaf— my hard-heartedness toward grass and trees and birds and fish and beasts and bracken and oceans and the stormy wind that He says fulfills His word? Lopped off from that boy who hadn't learned to reason and didn't pay any more attention to his body and its developments (or so far, anyway) than the developed creation around him, I seem farther from the truth of the actual words of that statement than those who worshiped trees and imaginary or real spirits trapped inside them.

And those who practiced that missed the truth that this statement, and all the others before it, also teach: it's more than trees or the spirits trapped in them, when you understand that they are communications of Christ.

Carefully and with the greatest accuracy I may write a description of my favorite six-foot patch of nature or, if my spirit is feeling expansive, my favorite ten acres, and if anyone who reads it afterward doesn't sense in the description some hidden attributes of God that we are told exist but try to deny because they do not fit with the rationalism that enlightened thinking (rather than the language of God) has brought to us, then our description is a failure in His face.

Language was given to return to Him the sort of language He proclaims to us, when we normally hear only if we're surrounded by stereo equipment.

On some days, if I lie for hours on the ground or crawl on my belly through grass or weeds or walk into a forest where I might get lost and lie down and take a nap and then wake—on those days I sense voices clamoring from all sides as they did when I went walking in the woods. Do you ever roll in new-mown grass and feel the reek of its greenness fill your nostrils until it seems your nose will bleed and then realize that the reeking is the blood of grass, or something more astonishing than your grip on language has been able to grasp?

There are times when, with a warning in my legs of a spongy weakness, the earth is revealed as molecular—able to give way at any second—and every gesture and word formed and even every thought is being weighed and measured (right foot, left foot) on shifting scales that are accurate to every millimeter of infinity. The giving earth itself is His handiwork, and my treading on it is communicated through a network so complex that even our mightiest computers can't begin to estimate its effect. I sense this and tend to rest on its evidence even when it's unseen.

This is faith.
In whom do I have faith?
In God.
Where is God?
Everywhere.

That's what I learned in the English language.
Then why don't I bump into Him or step on Him?
I do, in a sense, but wouldn't know it if He appeared in front of me, since I so seldom acknowledge that.

If God is everywhere, it's as Spirit that He is. This is the age of the Spirit He has given the world through His Son, and even though the world came into being for that purpose, the world does not know Him or recognize Him or receive Him or the message that the handiwork of His world continues to communicate in every detail we take in.

A glimpse of this was given to a poet who had suffered the rigors of the Gulag and was trying to read an anthology of modern English poetry with his faulty command of the language. He says,

> I remember sitting there in the small wooden shack, peering through the square, porthole-size window at the wet, muddy, dirt road with a few stray chickens on it, half believing what I'd just read, half wondering whether my grasp of English wasn't playing tricks on me. I had there a veritable boulder of an English-Russian dictionary, and I went through its pages time and again, checking every word, every allusion, hoping that they might spare me the meaning that stared at me from the page. I guess I was simply refusing to believe that way back in 1939 an English poet had said, "Time . . . worships language," and yet the world around was still what it was.

This is Joseph Brodsky, the Nobel laureate, and he wanted to make clear the effect on him of that distilled statement from W. H. Auden's "In Memory of W. B. Yeats"—time worships language. Brodsky abhorred artifice and sham and was so attuned to language, and especially the language of the Bible, that he saw Auden's statement as so revolutionary it should have altered the known world. Time is the lesser compatriot to language, and so time, whom many of us personify and revere as a god, bows to language. With language people build adornments that will last while time merely passes away—just as God, through a poured-out language, the breath of His mouth, He says, formed worlds that endure and will last for eternity. A Russian poet grasped this on first sight under straitened conditions, but it flies past most of us—with the thrumming beat and glide of a flicker, I hope; the bird, I mean, with its yellow-gold ribs and that flash of red you can't miss.

When I remember how I drew in as if in gulps the words of Brodsky as he explained the struggle he underwent toward his transformation, I can see my feet moving through the woods and hear the words of the song I shout. The words were given to me, and just as Brodsky, arriving by the labored steps of an unfamiliar language to the understanding that transformed him, could not believe the world had remained the same, so I once suffered in a smaller sense. When I set down "I feel a pressure behind and turn and there are the cottonwoods and willows at the far end of the street, along the edge of the lake, flying the maidenhair faces of their leaves into the wind, and beyond their crowns of trembling insubstantiality, across the lake dotted with cottonwood pollen, the blue and azure plain abuts against the horizon at infinity"— when I set that down, as it arrived on its own, I knew I would never be the same. It was a period when the balancing scales beneath me were jiggling so much I was sure they would give way, and my search became a desire to rest, as if on a tree, on Him.

But I forget and become deadened, as I think I've said, and walk around whispering, *Sure, God's everywhere, that's why my life's so wonderful*—this in a detached and abstract cynicism so bitter it could burn holes in the air. When I reached a moment like that once again, a year ago, my wife said, "Will you pray, please?" *Sure,* I thought, *sure, I'll pray,* and lit into a prayer with such anger a hole indeed appeared to burn open to the presence I'd forgotten or abandoned, and I felt the ladder that Jacob had dreamed, with angels ascending and descending on it, appear. The pure power of the Spirit poured down on me with such force that prayers for my wife and children, who had gathered, were pressed from me as prayer had never been pressed before in fifty years, and when I looked up I felt I was seeing each of my family for the first time, transformed.

They were clearly in Him, as I was, or more than I. They had waited for this confirmation, it seemed, and I had been too cautious and rational and bitter (if I could have explained my state in words) to give in to that presence mightier than Time.

I went to bed. It was all I could do. But in bed I couldn't sleep. The pressure that had once caused me to turn in recognition of a horizon exerted a fraction of its real weight, as I sensed, and I couldn't move. I lay underneath it—a molecular current containing, yet revivifying me—and every petty act of mine was an electron above an abyss in the magnificence of the current that kept flowing through and out of me. I couldn't move for hours. Everyone I had hated or could not forgive appeared over the night, not so I could see them, but I sensed the presence of each one and knew who it was and was astonished and grieved at the smallness of my hate in the weighty glory of the forgiveness I was receiving. Tears sprang from my eyes as they had in the woods, and I was lodged so close to joy I felt that if this was the end, so be it. And it was the end in one way, perhaps (you will find me as unforgiving and petty as always, I suspect, the next time we meet), because I understood I was being called to rise up and walk.

I couldn't move but had to, and once I was out of bed and made it from the room, barely (never waking my wife; she never woke this whole night), I slowly ground around the perimeter of two small rooms and a hall, my pacing grounds, and was given a partial sense of bearing in a body the weight of glory for those steps, all I could bear. I realized I had been prepared for this by that sense of pressure, the turn to a new horizon, but even more by those walks in the woods where I watched my feet lit by the sun as I listened to a language leaping past time and entering me in a beginning I couldn't begin to explain, or wouldn't have been able to, until I sat down and reentered that fifty-year-old walk.

Biographical Notes

VIRGINIA HAMILTON ADAIR was born in New York City in 1913 and got her college education at Mount Holyoke and Radcliffe. Married to the distinguished historian Douglass Adair, she moved with him and their three children to Claremont in 1955. In 1994, her friend Robert Mezey persuaded her to select the best poems from all that she had written in the last seventy years and try to publish a first book. This book, *Ants on the Melon,* was published two years later and has sold many thousands of copies.

MAX APPLE's most recent books are *Roommates* (1994) and *I Love Gootie* (1998). He teaches at Rice University.

MARVIN BARRETT has been a member of the editorial staffs of *Time, Newsweek, Show, Atlas,* and *Parabola* and of the faculty of the Columbia Graduate School of Journalism from 1968 to 1984. His fifteen books include *The Years Between, The End of the Party,* the award-winning *Moments of Truth?, Spare Days,* and *Second Chance: A Life After Death.* He is married to the writer Mary Ellin Barrett and lives in New York City. They have four children and five grandchildren.

WENDELL BERRY is the author of more than thirty books of poetry, essays, and fiction, including *Entries, Another Turn of the Crank,* and *A World Lost.* He lives in Henry County, Kentucky, with his wife.

S. PAUL BURHOLT works as a psychotherapist in southeastern Vermont and is a frequent contributor to *Parabola* magazine. He has been a lifelong student of Christian spiritual theology, especially the writings of the Greek Fathers. He and his wife, Gabrielle, are parishioners at the Orthodox church in Claremont, New Hampshire.

DOUGLAS BURTON-CHRISTIE teaches in the Theological Studies Department at Loyola Marymount University. He is the author of *The Word in the Desert: Scripture and the Quest for Holiness in Early Christian Monasticism* and is currently at work on a book about nature, spirit, and the contemporary poetic imagination. He lives in Los Angeles with his wife and daughter.

LÉONIE CALDECOTT has written for a broad spectrum of publications in Europe and North America, including the *Guardian, Sunday Times, Observer, Good Housekeeping, Resurgence,* the *Village Voice,* and the *New York Times Book Review.* She has also written for many religious publications, including *Catholic World*

Report, National Catholic Register, The Universe, Adoremus, The Chesterton Review, Communio, and *Inside the Vatican.* She is a contributor and guest editor for *The Chesterton Review* and a consulting editor for *Communio.* A recipient of the Catherine Pakenham Award for young female journalists, she lives in Oxford, England, with her husband and three daughters.

TRACY COCHRAN is coauthor of *Transformations: Awakening to the Sacred in Ourselves* and a contributing editor to *Tricycle* and *New Age Journal.* Her work appears regularly in *Tricycle, Parabola,* and *Publishers Weekly.* She lives with her husband and daughter in the New York City area.

ROBERT CORDING teaches English and creative writing at Holy Cross College, where he is professor of English and poet-in-residence. He has published three collections of poems: *Life-list,* which won the Ohio State University Press/Journal award in 1987, *What Binds Us to This World,* and *Heavy Grace.* He has received fellowships from the National Endowment for the Arts, the Connecticut Commission of the Arts, and Bread Loaf. His poems have appeared in *The Nation, Poetry, DoubleTake, The New Yorker,* and elsewhere. He lives in Woodstock, Connecticut, with his wife and three children.

ANNIE DILLARD is the author of many books, including *Pilgrim at Tinker Creek, Holy the Firm, Teaching a Stone to Talk, The Living, An American Childhood,* and her latest, *For the Time Being.*

BRIAN DOYLE is the editor of *Portland Magazine* at the University of Portland, in Oregon. He is the author of *Credo,* a collection of essays, and coauthor, with his father, Jim Doyle, of *Two Voices,* a collection of their essays. Brian's essay "Altar Boy" appears in *The Best American Essays 1998.*

ANDRE DUBUS III is the author of a collection of short fiction, *The Cage Keeper and Other Stories,* and the novels *Bluesman* and *House of Sand and Fog.* His stories and essays have appeared in *Playboy, Yankee, Hope,* and various literary quarterlies. He has been the recipient of a Bread Loaf Scholarship and a St. Botolph Club Foundation Grant, and his work has been included in *The Best American Essays 1994.* He has won the National Magazine Award for Fiction and the Pushcart Prize and was a 1994 Finalist for the Prix de Rome Fellowship from the American Academy of Arts and Letters. He teaches writing at Tufts University and in Emerson College's Master of Fine Arts in Writing program. He lives in Newburyport, Massachusetts, with his wife, dancer/choreographer Fontaine Dollas, and their three children.

ALMA ROBERTS GIORDAN's essays and poems have appeared frequently for over fifty years in *America, The Christian Science Monitor, The New York Times,*

Catholic Digest, Saturday Review, Yankee, The Hartford Courant, and elsewhere. Her collection of published poems, *Torch Bearer,* was published in 1972. She is a frequent contributor to the weekly newspaper *The Litchfield County Times* and for some fifteen years collaborated with her late artist-husband, Robert, on a page called "The Last Word" in the Sunday Magazine of the Waterbury, Connecticut, *Sunday Republican.*

ROSHI BERNIE GLASSMAN is cofounder, along with his wife, Jishu Holmes, of the Zen Peacemaker Order. He is the abbot of the Zen Community of New York and the Zen Center of Los Angeles and is the author of *Bearing Witness.*

MARY GORDON is the author of the novels *Spending, The Company of Women, The Rest of Life,* and *The Other Side,* as well as a critically acclaimed memoir, *The Shadow Man.* Winner of the Lila Acheson Wallace Reader's Digest Award, a Guggenheim Fellowship, and the 1996 O. Henry Prize for best short story, she teaches at Barnard College and lives in New York City.

RON HANSEN's books include *Hitler's Niece, Desperadoes, The Assassination of Jesse James by the Coward Robert Ford,* and the short story collection *Nebraska,* for which he received an Award in Literature from the American Academy and Institute of Arts and Letters. He currently teaches at the University of California, Santa Cruz.

SEAMUS HEANEY's many books include *Opened Ground: Selected Poems, 1966–1996* (1998), *The Spirit Level* (1996), and *The Redress of Poetry* (1995). He received the 1995 Nobel Prize in Literature.

EDWARD HIRSCH has published five books of poems, most recently *On Love* (1998) and *Earthly Measures* (1994). He has two new books of prose, *Responsive Reading* (1999) and *How to Read a Poem and Fall in Love with Poetry* (1999).

PICO IYER is a longtime essayist for *Time* and the author of several books, including *Video Night in Kathmandu, The Lady and the Monk,* and *Cuba and the Night* (a novel). Born to Indian parents in England, and growing up in California, he has been a traveler all his life and now divides his time as much as possible between Big Sur, California, and suburban Japan. His book about such issues, *The Global Soul,* comes out in early 2000.

TOM JUNOD grew up Catholic, but after meeting Mister Rogers he has been flirting—if only in his mind—with Presbyterianism. Presently a writer for *Esquire,* he has also worked for *Sports Illustrated, Life,* and *GQ.* He has been a finalist for the National Magazine Award seven times, and he won the award for feature writing in 1995 and 1996. He lives outside of Atlanta, Georgia, with his wife, Janet, and two dogs, Hawk and Marco.

Philip Levine lives in Fresno, California, for half the year and Brooklyn, New York, for the other half. He teaches poetry writing each fall at New York University. His new book of poems is *The Mercy*. His previous book, *The Simple Truth*, won the Pulitzer Prize in 1995.

Barry Lopez is the author of numerous works, including *About This Life, Arctic Dreams, Of Wolves and Men, Field Notes,* and *Winter Count*. His work appears regularly in *Harper's Magazine,* where he is a contributing editor, as well as in *The Paris Review, Orion,* and *The Georgia Review*. The recipient of numerous literary awards, including the National Book Award for nonfiction, he lives in western Oregon.

Anita Mathias has published in *The Washington Post, The Virginia Quarterly Review, The London Magazine, New Letters, America,* and *The Journal*. She is the recipient of a 1998 National Endowment for the Arts fellowship in nonfiction, an individual artist fellowship from the Minnesota State Arts Board, and a literary travel grant from the Jerome Foundation. She lives in Williamsburg, Virginia, with her husband and her young daughters, Zoe and Irene.

Walt McDonald is director of creative writing at Texas Tech University. He was an Air Force pilot and has published sixteen collections of poetry and a book of fiction, including *Blessings the Body Gave, Counting Survivors, Night Landings, After the Noise of Saigon,* and *The Flying Dutchman*. Three other books won Western Heritage Awards from the National Cowboy Hall of Fame. He has published more than 1,700 poems in journals including *APR, The American Scholar, Atlantic Monthly, First Things, The Georgia Review, The Kenyon Review, The Nation, The New York Review of Books, The Paris Review, Poetry, The Sewanee Review,* and *The Southern Review*.

Thomas Moore is the author of the best-selling *Care of the Soul, SoulMates, The Re-enchantment of Everyday Life, The Soul of Sex, On the Monk Who Lives in Daily Life,* and many other books. He has also produced several audiotapes, videotapes, and the compact discs *Music for the Soul* and *The Soul of Christmas*. He lives in New England with his wife, Joan Hanley, his daughter, Siobhan, and his stepson, Abraham.

Kathleen Norris's many books include *Amazing Grace: A Vocabulary of Faith* (1998), *The Cloister Walk* (1996), and *Dakota: A Spiritual Geography* (1993).

Louise Rafkin is a writer and housecleaner. She is the author, most recently, of *Other People's Dirt: A Housecleaner's Adventures from Cape Cod to Kyoto*.

Pattiann Rogers's seven books of poetry include *Eating Bread and Honey* (1997) and *Firekeeper: New and Selected Poems* (1994). She is one of five finalists for the Lenore Marshall Award of the Academy of American Poets. She has received two NEA grants, a Guggenheim Fellowship, and a Poetry Fellowship from the Lannan Foundation. Her *Collected Poems* will be published in 2001.

JONATHAN ROSEN is the cultural editor of the *Forward* and the creator of the newspaper's Arts and Letters Section. His essays have appeared in *The New York Times Magazine, The New York Times Book Review,* and *Vanity Fair,* among other publications. He is the author of the critically acclaimed novel *Eve's Apple.*

DAVID ROTHENBERG is a musician and philosopher. He is the author of *Hand's End: Technology and the Limits of Nature* and *Is It Painful to Think? Conversations with Arne Naess* and is the editor of numerous anthologies. His latest compact disc is *Before the War.* "The Necessary Note" is an excerpt from his forthcoming book on improvisation and nature, *Sudden Music.*

LUCI SHAW is a poet, essayist, and teacher. She is author of a number of prose books and seven volumes of poetry, the most recent being *Writing the River,* and she has edited three poetry anthologies. Writer-in-residence at Regent College, Vancouver, Canada, she lives in Bellingham, Washington.

ELIEZER SHORE writes on topics of Jewish spirituality. He teaches in a yeshiva for Talmud studies in Jerusalem and publishes *Bas Ayin,* a journal of contemporary Hasidic thought. He is also a storyteller of original and classic Jewish tales.

LOUIS SIMPSON's *Modern Poets of France: A Bilingual Anthology* recently won the Harold Morton Landon Translation Award given by the Academy of American Poets. Other recent publications are a memoir, *The King My Father's Wreck,* a collection of poems, *There You Are,* a selection of his poems translated in French, *Nombres et poussiere,* and a selection of his poems translated in Swedish, *Kaviar pa begravninge.* He lives in Stony Brook, New York.

JACK STEWART's work has appeared in many journals and anthologies, including *Poetry, The Gettysburg Review, The Antioch Review, The Southern Humanities Review,* and others. He has been nominated for the Pushcart Prize several times. He was a Brittain Fellow at the Georgia Institute of Technology, and he currently teaches at the Montgomery Academy. He lives with his wife and daughter in Montgomery, Alabama.

BARBARA BROWN TAYLOR is an Episcopal priest in the Diocese of Atlanta and is Butman Professor of Religion and Philosophy at Piedmont College in Demorest, Georgia. She is the author of seven books, including *When God Is Silent* and *God in Pain: Teaching Sermons on Suffering.*

PTOLEMY TOMPKINS is the author of *This Tree Grows Out of Hell* and *Paradise Fever. The Book of Answers,* of which "Lao Tzu's Water, Chuang Tzu's Mud" is the first chapter, will be published in 2001. He lives in New York City.

JANWILLEM VAN DE WETERING was born in the Netherlands and worked, studied, and traveled in Europe, Australia, South America, and Africa until he settled in 1975 on the coast of Maine. He reported on his Zen practice in *The Empty Mirror, A Glimpse of Nothingness,* and his final Buddhist autobiographical essay, *Afterzen,* from which "Seeing into Your Nature and Other Pastimes" is taken. His service with the Amsterdam police inspired the ongoing "Dutch cops" series, the latest of which is *The Perfidious Parrot.*

MICHAEL VENTURA is a novelist and essayist. His present work-in-progress is *The Las Vegas Trilogy.*

PAUL J. WILLIS is the author of two novels, *No Clock in the Forest* and *The Stolen River,* and a poetry chapbook, *Poison Oak.* His poems have appeared in *Poetry, Wilderness,* and *The Best American Poetry 1996.* He is a professor of English at Westmont College in Santa Barbara, California, where he lives with his wife and two children.

LARRY WOIWODE is the author of five novels, including *Indian Affairs* and *Beyond the Bedroom Wall.* He has written for *The New Yorker* and *Books & Culture,* among others, and published a commentary on the Acts of the Apostles in 1993. He is poet laureate of North Dakota, and his work in the short story brought him the Medal of Merit from the American Academy of Arts and Letters in 1995.

PHILIP ZALESKI is the editor of the Best Spiritual Writing series. His books include *The Recollected Heart, Gifts of the Spirit* (with Paul Kaufman), and a forthcoming anthology of writings about heaven. He is a senior editor of *Parabola,* and his writings appear frequently in *The New York Times, First Things, Reader's Digest,* and elsewhere. He teaches religion at Smith College and lives in western Massachusetts with his wife, Carol, and his sons, John and Andy.

Notable Spiritual Writing of 1998

Rob Baker
"Oracles Within," *Gnosis,* Winter.

Joyce Bennett
"Courtesy," *Chronicles,* January.

Susan Bergman
"Seeing Signs and Wonders," *Christian Century,* August 26–September 2.

David Biro
"Silent Bond," *The New York Times Magazine,* October 11.

Roberta C. Bondi
"Your Kingdom Come, Your Will Be Done," *Weavings,* March/April.

Stratford Caldecott
"The Return of the King," *The Chesterton Review,* February/May.

Eido Francis Carney
"Zen and the Art of Begging," *Tricycle,* Fall.

Catherine Caufield
"Selling a Piece of Your Mother," *Whole Earth,* Fall.

Sienna Craig
"Riding in the Rain Shadow," *Tricycle,* Summer.

E. Wade Davis
"Richard Evans Schultes and the Amazon," *Lapis,* Six.

Austin Doran
"The Listening Heart," *Spiritual Life,* Fall.

David James Duncan
"Gladly," *Portland,* Autumn.

Gretel Ehrlich
"Cowboy Sage," *Shambhala Sun,* July.

Joseph Epstein
"Bigger Than Life," *Notre Dame,* Spring.

NORA GALLAGHER
"Things Seen and Unseen," *DoubleTake,* Fall.

HOLLY HAMMOND
"Travels in Taoist China," *Yoga Journal,* February.

KABIR HELMINSKI
"I Will Make Myself Mad," *Parabola,* Summer.

GRAY HENRY
"The Blessed State," *Parabola,* Fall.

LAURA HERBST
"Warja's Feast," *The Sun,* August.

ROGER HOUSDEN
"Sahara: The Fruitful Void," *New Age Journal,* March/April.

LIN JENSEN
"The Least I Can Do," *The Quest,* Spring.

FENTON JOHNSON
"Beyond Belief," *Harper's Magazine,* September.

DIANE KOMP
"The Anatomy of a Lie," *Books & Culture,* September/October.

MARTIN LINGS
"Frithjof Schuon: An Autobiographical Approach," *Sophia,* Winter.

Michael R. Linton
"Music for the End of Time," *First Things,* November.

MICHAEL LOWENTHAL
"Nowhere Man," *The New York Times Magazine,* March 1.

STEPHEN J. LYONS
"What's for Lunch?" *The Sun,* February.

WILDRED M. McCLAY
"Mr. Emerson's Tombstone," *First Things,* May.

MARY McCUE
"The Red-Haired Angel," *Common Boundary,* July/August.

GILBERT MEILAENDER
"The Everyday C. S. Lewis," *First Things,* August/September.

SY MONTGOMERY
"The Search for the Pink Dolphins," *New Age Journal,* November/December.

VIRGINIA STEM OWENS
"Karla Faye's Final Stop," *Christianity Today,* July 13.

CORNELIUS PLANTINGA, JR.
"Pray the Lord My Mind to Keep," *Christianity Today,* August 10.

HELEN PREJEAN
"A Way Out of No Way," *America,* August 29.

HANK ROSENFELD
"Somewhere over the Rainbow Way Up High," *Shambhala Sun,* November.

DAVID ROSKIES
"A Revolution Set in Stone," *Pakn Treger,* Spring.

SCOTT RUSSELL SANDERS
"Staying True," *Hope,* November/December.

TIM STAFFORD
"God Is in the Blueprints," *Christianity Today,* September 7.

ALEXANDER STILLE
"The Ganges Next Life," *The New Yorker,* January 19.

ERIK FRASER STORLIE
"Zen on Ice," *The Quest,* Winter.

MARY SWANDER
"The Fifth Chair," *Image,* Winter.

J. L. WALKER
"Building the Buddha-field," *Parabola,* Spring.

BARBARA WATSON
"Does God Come to Seclusion Rooms?" *Spiritual Life,* Spring.

NANCY WESTERFIELD
"Among the Monks," *Commonweal,* March 13.

ART WINTER,
"Great Gardener," *Praying,* October 15.

JOHN WOMACK, JR.
"A Bishop's Conversion," *DoubleTake,* Winter.

Reader's Directory

For more information about or subscriptions to the twenty-five periodicals represented in *The Best Spiritual Writing 1999,* please contact:

America
106 West 56th Street
New York, NY 10019

The American Scholar
Phi Beta Kappa Society
1785 Massachusetts Avenue, N.W., 4th Floor
Washington, DC 20036

Bas Ayin
14 Hutchinson Court
Great Neck, NY 11023

Books & Culture
465 Gundersen Drive
Carol Stream, IL 60188

Christianity Today
465 Gundersen Drive
Carol Stream, IL 60188

Chronicles
The Rockford Institute
928 North Main Street
Rockford, IL 61103

DoubleTake
The Center for Documentary Studies at Duke University
1317 West Pettigrew Street
Durham, NC 27705

Esquire
386 Park Avenue South
New York, NY 10016

First Things
The Institute on Religion and Public Life
156 Fifth Avenue, Suite 400
New York, NY 10010

Harper's Magazine
666 Broadway
New York, NY 10012

Hope
P.O. Box 160
Brooklin, ME 04616

Image
P.O. Box 674
Kennet Square, PA 19348

The New Yorker
20 West 43rd Street
New York, NY 10036

Northeast Magazine
285 Broad Street
Hartford, CT 06115

Notre Dame Magazine
583 Grace Hall
Notre Dame, IN 46556-5612

Orion
Orion Society
195 Main Street
Great Barrington, MA 01230

Pakn Treger
The National Jewish Book Center
Harry and Jeanette Weinberg Building
1021 West Street
Amherst, MA 01002-3375

Parabola
656 Broadway
New York, NY 10012

Poetry
60 West Walton Street
Chicago, IL 60610

Shambhala Sun
1585 Barrington Street, Suite 300
Halifax, Nova Scotia, Canada B3J1Z8

The Sun
107 North Roberson Street
Chapel Hill, NC 27516

Tikkun
26 Fell Street
San Francisco, CA 94102

Tricycle
92 Vandam Street
New York, NY 10013

Weavings
1908 Grand Avenue
P.O. Box 189
Nashville, TN 37202-0189

Wild Earth
P.O. Box 455
Richmond, VT 05477

Credits